Praise for *Godly Republic*

"Having excelled at opening government's doors to a greater role for faith-based social work, John DiIulio in *Godly Republic* makes clear that the pedigree for such openness lies deep in our founding principles. Like it or not, America has entered a wide-ranging debate about religion's place in our civil life. *Godly Republic* supplies an indispensable framework for this debate."

JEFFREY BELL, author of *Populism and Elitism*

"John DiIulio is likely the only person writing today who combines stellar academic credentials and firsthand experience in the corridors of political power and on the streets with faith-based and community organizations. Often compelling, at times challenging, but always thought-provoking, *Godly Republic* offers sharp insights and insider stories to provide a much-needed corrective to many myths about religion and government in America."

AMY E. BLACK, Wheaton College, co-author of *Of Little Faith*

"John DiIulio has done more than anyone in America to unleash the power and capacity of sacred places to serve the poor and needy. In *Godly Republic,* he lays a foundation for splitting the atom of faith-based civic power. This sage and saint of the compassion agenda might just pull it off—and bring our country around a faith-based agenda that could ignite millions of Americans in service to the nation."

JOHN M. BRIDGELAND, former director, White House Domestic Policy Council and USA Freedom Corps

"John DiIulio rejects the kind of Evangelical triumphalism that declares America to be a Christian nation, even as he turns from that secularity which leaves no room for religion in the public sector. Writing in a lucid style, he shows how religion and government can maintain a legal relationship that addresses some of the greatest social needs of our time."

REVEREND TONY CAMPOLO, professor emeritus, Eastern University

"At a time when we struggle with the role and status of religious faith in the public square, John DiIulio, in his usual urbane and scholarly manner, clarifies the misconceptions of the liberal left and religious right. Thank you, John, for providing us the Good News that faith and religion have always been part of the public square."

REVEREND LUIS CORTÉS, JR., president, Esperanza USA, America's largest Latino faith-based organization

"This is a very impressive book, exactly what one would expect from a political scientist as able as John DiIulio. He takes seriously the flawed arguments and popular myths promoted by extremists on the political right and left, and he writes calmly about issues that many are shouting about. He is a scholar and experienced practitioner who cares passionately about his subject. How we resolve these constitutional disputes will affect our public policies for years to come, and DiIulio wants to make sure we get our historical, and contemporary, facts right. People on all sides need to attend to his arguments, because the potential welfare of millions of lives is at stake."

MICHAEL CROMARTIE, vice president, Ethics and Public Policy Center

"Take a brilliant analytical mind, add in a huge heart, a passion for justice and a deep religious faith, combine all that with a lively facility of expression, and you have John DiIulio. This is a book so many have been waiting for, the tough-minded reflections of a man who went into the White House trenches to pursue his carefully thought-through dreams of how compassion might be realized through social policy. By offering an honest, searching and deeply intelligent explanation for why things did not quite work out as he planned, DiIulio offers hope that we can get things right the next time around. And he makes clear how urgent it is that we try. DiIulio is a national treasure."

E. J. DIONNE *The Washington Post* syndicated columnist and author of *Why Americans Hate Politics*

"This wise and engaging book accomplishes an awesome feat—it is both important and a pleasure to read."

JANE EISNER, vice president, National Constitution Center, and former editorial-page editor of The Philadelphia Inquirer

"John DiIulio presents a succinct and authoritative statement on what the Founding Fathers actually intended as operating principles for a healthy democratic society. . . . A scholar and a man of deep religious faith, he brings to this book firsthand experience. . . . *Godly Republic* will be of enormous value to leaders in political, academic, and religious circles as well as citizens in all walks of life."

GEORGE GALLUP, JR., pollster and founding chairman, George H. Gallup Institute

"John DiIulio's *Godly Republic: A Centrist Blueprint for America's Faith-Based Future* is a splendid book. It is a much needed book. It is a book that will raise eyebrows and raise hackles—at both edges of the political spectrum. It will also raise the consciousness of readers who are willing to consider dispassionately the careful, thoughtful, and quite penetrating argument Professor DiIulio makes for a *via media* on the question of public aid to religiously based providers of social services to our fellow citizens who are in need. I hope and—dare I say it?—pray that there will be many such readers."

ROBERT P. GEORGE, Princeton University

"With his trademark combination of candor and intellectual rigor—and a powerful gift for weaving a story—John DiIulio seeks a middle ground in today's increasingly rancorous church-state debates. . . . With him, we travel back to the start of our 'Godly Republic' and into the minds of our nation's framers; peer into the most private rooms of the White House, where he served as a top aide; and glimpse what the future can hold in a nation that both respects religious pluralism and allows faith-based institutions to help the most disadvantaged among us."

GIGI GEORGES, former state director, office of New York senator Hillary Rodham Clinton, and partner, The Glover Park Group

"John DiIulio has done his country another important service. *Godly Republic* makes a compelling case that respect for religious influence and genuine pluralism go hand in hand in American history. John is a voice of reason and civility in a debate that needs more of both."

MICHAEL GERSON, senior fellow at the Council on Foreign Relations and former chief speechwriter for President George W. Bush

"No one in the country better understands the connection between policy and on-the-street results than John DiIulio. In *Godly Republic* he combines his experiences, from urban neighborhoods to the White House, to convincingly show how faith can be a unifying force for citizens and their communities all across the country."

STEPHEN GOLDSMITH, chairman, Corporation for National Service, and former mayor of Indianapolis

"John DiIulio has made a brilliant contribution to the ongoing debate on the place of religion in the public square. Through good, sound research and reader-friendly language, he has presented our nation with a unique and valuable book that should bring much clarity to the issue of the separation of church and state. . . . It should be read by every elected official, policy maker and religious leader."

> REVEREND DR. W. WILSON GOODE, SR., director, Amachi Mentoring Program, and former mayor of Philadelphia

"God and America, what could be more important? And no one is better qualified to explore one of the most important issues of our time than John DiIulio. In a book that weaves a seamless web between superb social science and his own experiences in government, DiIulio has written a must-read for any serious citizen—religious or not."

> ELAINE KAMARCK, public policy lecturer, Harvard University, and former senior advisor to Vice President Al Gore

"*Godly Republic* is lively, stimulating, and thought provoking—just what we have all come to expect from John DiIulio, one of America's leading political thinkers."

> WILLIAM KRISTOL, editor of *The Weekly Standard*

"John DiIulio's renowned leadership in the faith-based initiatives debate is here complemented by his keen scholarship. James Madison's erudition shines in glory as DiIulio explains how the framers of the Constitution balanced John Witherspoon's orthodox Christianity and Thomas Jefferson's deistic perspective, thereby creating the 'Godly Republic.' This is a must-read for friend and foe alike of the faith-based movements that will impact American government for generations to come."

> REVEREND PETER LILLBACK, president, Providence Forum and Westminster Theological Seminary

"In the midst of the myth, mystery, and misunderstanding surrounding the separation of church and state, John DiIulio's book offer challenging insights. Whatever your politics, position, or perspective, *Godly Republic* is a must read."

> REVEREND DR. HERBERT HOOVER LUSK III, Greater Exodus Baptist Church

"In *Godly Republic,* John DiIulio gives us a timely book for the elevation of our public policy and public discourse. It is a terrific read that reminds us that tolerance is both a religious and an American virtue."

MARTIN O'MALLEY, governor of Maryland and former mayor of Baltimore

"A must-read gem written by a rarity: a respected and courageous former public servant who is also one of America's most influential academics on the intersection of religion, politics and social policy. His brilliance and decency shine through on every page."

RABBI DAVID SAPERSTEIN, director, Religious Action Center of Reform Judaism

"DiIulio's manuscript punctures myths that have surrounded our understanding of constitutional history, law, and religion, the public administration of social services programs, the nature of religious service organizations, and the politics surrounding faith-based programs. His style is casual, breezy, often funny, and filled with autobiographical detail. Only DiIulio, who is not only a streetwise activist for the poor but also a prominent social scientist and political figure, could have written this important book."

STEVEN SHIFFRIN, professor, Cornell Law School

"John DiIulio is a person of faith, learning, and wisdom. He brings his passion for truth and history to his examination of the right relationship between religion and government, faith and politics. This illuminating book is a must-read for all who seek insight and guidance on these difficult questions."

KATHLEEN KENNEDY TOWNSEND, former lieutenant governor of Maryland, adjunct professor at Georgetown University, and author of *Failing the Faithful*

"In the White House and in his scholarship and civic service, John DiIulio has explored the theory and practice of allowing faith to inform government action. The unending—indeed, unendable—debate on the proper relationship between religion and government will be livelier and more civil because of this book."

GEORGE WILL, *ABC News* and syndicated columnist

Godly Republic

THE AARON WILDAVSKY FORUM
FOR PUBLIC POLICY

Edited by Lee Friedman

This series is to sustain the intellectual excitement that Aaron Wildavsky created for scholars of public policy everywhere. The ideas in each volume are initially presented and discussed at a public lecture and forum held at the University of California.

Godly Republic

A CENTRIST BLUEPRINT FOR AMERICA'S FAITH-BASED FUTURE

John J. DiIulio, Jr.

UNIVERSITY OF CALIFORNIA PRESS
Berkeley   Los Angeles   London

University of California Press, one of the most distinguished university presses in the United States, enriches lives around the world by advancing scholarship in the humanities, social sciences, and natural sciences. Its activities are supported by the UC Press Foundation and by philanthropic contributions from individuals and institutions. For more information, visit www.ucpress.edu.

A Caravan Book
For more information, visit www.caravanbooks.org.

University of California Press
Berkeley and Los Angeles, California

University of California Press, Ltd.
London, England

© 2007 by The Regents of the University of California

Library of Congress Cataloging-in-Publication Data
DiIulio, John J.
    Godly republic : a centrist blueprint for America's faith-based future / John J. DiIulio, Jr.
        p.   cm. – (The Aaron Wildavsky forum for public policy ; 5)
    Includes bibliographical references and index.
    ISBN: 978-0-520-25414-5 (cloth : alk. paper)
    1. Christianity and politics—United States.   2. Religion and politics—United States.   3. United States—Church history.   I. Title.
BR516.D55   2007
322'.10973—dc22   2007011434

Manufactured in the United States of America
17   16   15   14   13   12   11   10   09   08
10   9   8   7   6   5   4   3   2   1
The paper used in this publication meets the minimum requirements of ANSI/NISO Z39.48–1992 (R 1997) (*Permanence of Paper*).

In memory of

Dr. David B. Larson
(March 13, 1947–March 5, 2002)
"Faith Factor" Evangelist
Model Family Man
Soul of Humility

Contents

Acknowledgments

I remember when "faith-based" drew only blank stares. I remember being told by many, including many I respected (and still do), to forget it. Bless those associated, now or formerly, with the Brookings Institution, the Manhattan Institute, Public/Private Ventures, the Gesu School, the Pew Forum on Religion and Public Life, Princeton University, and the University of Pennsylvania (especially my successive "Penn seminarians") and bless those leaders and volunteers associated with community-serving religious organizations too numerous to mention; all helped to stimulate or support me in this and related quasi-academic work (and civic good works). Special thanks to Lee Friedman and others with the Aaron Wildavsky Forum at the University of California at Berkeley for encouraging me to finally write this up, and to my editor, Naomi Schneider, as well as Kathleen MacDougall and others at the University of California Press for shepherding it into print. Special thanks as well to Stephen Shiffrin, Robert George, Joseph Tierney, Pam Lunardi, Jane Eisner, and Mark Alan Hughes, each of whom read and commented on all or parts of the first complete draft. I remain grateful to the many policymakers—federal, state, and local, Democratic and Republican, elected and appointed, past and present, left, right, and center—who, over the years, have listened to me on the subject (agree or not, act accordingly or not) and from whom I have learned, most especially President George W. Bush, Senator Hillary Rodham Clinton, Senator Joseph Lieberman, Senator Rick Santorum, Representative Tony Hall, Mayor Stephen Goldsmith,

Mayor Martin O'Malley, Mayor Marc Morial, and Mayor John Street. Finally, God bless those who faithfully served with me during my time in the White House, including John Bridgeland, Michael Gerson, Pete Wehner, Don Eberly, Don Willett, David Kuo, the Reverend Mark Scott, Lisa Trevino-Cummins, Stanley Carlson-Ties, Michelle Tennery, Catherine Ryun, and many "faith center" leaders, staff interns, and volunteers. As Aaron Wildavsky often preached, a civic-minded, policy-oriented scholar should be all about "speaking truth to power." I acknowledge that, on this topic and others, I have always tried, but often failed, to do just that. Whether in recounting White House days or regarding other matters covered in this book, any failures, and all mundane mistakes, are all mine.

Introduction

"DO YOU KNOW IF YOU ARE GOING TO HEAVEN?"

It was not a question that I would have expected to be asked at a White House reception while standing just a few paces away from the president of the United States. My inquisitor, a television evangelist, was at the White House for a ceremonial meeting with religious clergy. I was there as an Assistant to the President and first director of the White House Office of Faith-Based and Community Initiatives.

I knew what he wanted to hear. Had he asked me as one private citizen to another, I might have humored him. I started to do just that. But then I caught myself. He was not asking me, the private citizen. He was asking me, the nation's first "faith czar." A visible government official. A top presidential appointee. Someone responsible for assisting President George W. Bush in faithfully upholding the Constitution, faithfully executing democratically enacted public laws, and faithfully acting in the public interest without regard to religious identities (and all contrary political purposes be damned). So I paused. Over my left shoulder I could hear the president greeting the guests who were still in the reception line. In my peripheral vision I could see his hearty handshakes, mini-hugs, and pats on the back.

I refocused on my questioner's face. As I tried not to stare, my mind started to race. Earlier that day I had heard rumors that groups dedicated to the extreme separation of church and state (no "under God" in the Pledge of Allegiance, no "In God We Trust" on U.S. currency, and the like) were planning to sue me, my office, and God only knew who else over federal funding for religious organizations. Since the 1940s ideologically liberal activists who wanted to remove every last trace of religion from the public square had promoted the historically specious notion that America was founded, and should function today, as a strictly secular state.

These orthodox secularists, as I had taken to terming them, had won several big legal and legislative battles but had lost every major war. Since 1980 they had lost in the U.S. Supreme Court far more often than not. By 1990, even as church attendance rates dropped, they had lost decisively in the stubbornly faith-friendly court of American public opinion. By 2000 the orthodox secular groups had also lost in the workaday realms of public administration and street-level social service delivery. With government financial support and technical assistance, national religious charities as well as local churches, synagogues, mosques, and other faith-based nonprofit organizations now supplied myriad social services, including food pantries, low-income housing, welfare-to-work programs, health screening, computer training, drug and alcohol prevention, day care centers, anti–gang violence programs, and scores of other programs. Even with no public funding or philanthropic support, in cities from coast to coast volunteer-driven grassroots religious groups or "blessing station" ministries provided over two hundred discrete types of social services to people in need.

To the chagrin of secular state evangelists, such community-serving faith-based initiatives had won broadly bipartisan support. For instance, in 1996 John Ashcroft, Missouri's Republican senator, spearheaded a push for legislation that would prohibit grant-making federal government agencies from discriminating on the basis of religion against otherwise qualified faith-based organizations that served people in need. This legislation passed as a provision of the 1996 federal welfare reform law (officially, Section 104 of the Personal Responsibility and Work Opportunity Reconciliation Act of 1996). President Bill Clinton signed this provision into law. Between 1998 and 2000 President Clinton put three more such laws on the federal books.

I was delighted and gratified by these Clinton-era so-called charitable choice laws. In the mid-1990s I had personally shared "faith factor" empirical research findings and related policy ideas with Ashcroft, many other congressional leaders in both parties, top Clinton administration officials, and many other elected leaders, public administrators, journalists, and policy wonks—left, right, and center. Ashcroft, who later became Bush's first attorney general, was a staunch and often controversial religious conservative. He hailed from the charismatic Pentecostal tradition (in his case, the Assemblies of God church). His Senate day often began with an open-to-all prayer meeting.

But Ashcroft strongly agreed (in fact, he insisted) that the 1996 provision, and all related public laws and programs, should respect settled constitutional limits on church-state collaboration. Thus, the 1996 charitable choice provision's black-letter language contained this explicit prohibition:

> No public funds provided directly to institutions or organizations to provide services or administer programs . . . shall be used for sectarian worship, instruction, or proselytization.

Here and there in the 1990s, sacred places that served civic purposes made for strange but wonderful Washington political bedfellows. In addition to Ashcroft and many other right-wing Republicans, several liberal Democrats were big advocates of faith-based and community initiatives. One was Andrew Cuomo, son of former New York governor Mario Cuomo and Clinton's secretary of the Department of Housing and Urban Development (HUD). At HUD, Cuomo established the first "faith center" in the federal bureaucracy. His faith-friendly efforts and those begun by other Clinton administration officials were backed enthusiastically by then–first lady Hillary Rodham Clinton.

During the 2000 presidential campaign, both Bush and Vice President Al Gore underscored this consensus. The national government, they agreed, could and should do even more to help religious organizations help people in need, most especially in low-income urban communities. Each candidate vowed respect for religious pluralism. Each reiterated settled constitutional limits on church-state collaboration. And each promised not to play partisan political games with faith-based and community initiatives.

That day in the White House, I knew that my questioner loathed the idea that America was, is, or ought to become a secular state. But I also knew that he loved the equally specious notion that America was founded as a Christian nation.

In 1962 the U.S. Supreme Court declared state-sponsored prayer in public schools unconstitutional. Thereafter, religious conservatives, led by theologically orthodox, politically conservative Protestant preachers, crusaded against "Godless schools." In the ensuing decades, advocacy for new issues, such as abortion and gay rights, and old ones, such as the teaching of evolution, gained adherents and reached larger audiences. So did the demographic boom among tradition-minded Protestants. Today, about a third of Americans are affiliated with evangelical Protestant churches. Two-fifths consider themselves to be born-again Christians (that is, they accept the authority of the Bible, believe in salvation through a personal relationship with Jesus Christ, and feel called to share the "Good News" of Jesus Christ with others).

By no means are all evangelical Christian leaders—or followers—theologically orthodox and politically conservative. Regardless, most rank-and-file Evangelicals resonate deeply to the idea that the civic state of the union depends critically on the religious state of the union. They figure prominently among so-called moral-values voters who think that the country would be better off if it reclaimed the definitively Christian vision that supposedly animated the founding fathers and infused the Constitution.

Then as now, my view was that while the extreme secular state minions were just dead wrong the Christian nation legions, led by clergymen like my questioner, were insidiously half-right.

It is undeniably true that the American Revolution's leaders and the Constitution's framers were, almost to a man, committed Christians. Take the Reverend John Witherspoon, who signed both the Declaration of Independence and the Constitution. Or take Witherspoon's prize Princeton University (then College of New Jersey) pupil, James Madison. Madison was the Constitution's chief intellectual architect and chief negotiator when it came to drafting and ratifying the Bill of Rights (the first ten amendments to the Constitution).

Witherspoon, Madison, and most others among the early republic's key leaders did not lead by leaving their most cherished Christian convictions outside Philadelphia's meeting rooms, their states' ratifying conventions, or the first Congress. Nor were they shy about Christian prayer on the battlefields or in the first presidential mansion. Many a secular state mythologist has misrepresented George Washington (no less) and other founding fathers as European Enlightenment-minded, Great Awakening-be-damned Deists who conceded that some God probably existed but doubted or denied that this semi-Supreme, or Supreme, Being had revealed any particular religion as true.

By every valid historical source and measure, however, Washington and most other patriotic leaders and framers were indisputably Bible-believing Protestants. They made frequent and explicit reference to their Reformed Christian beliefs. And they did so not just in private or during Sunday services at Philadelphia's Christ's Church, but in public as citizens and statesmen.

Certainly several among the most prominent leaders who formed the nation were pretty much Deists (such as Thomas Jefferson, the Declaration's chief author and, together with Witherspoon, Madison's other chief mentor) or agnostics (most notably Benjamin Franklin, who mentored and influenced nearly everyone). But even these founders were unfailingly faith-friendly. Whenever they expressed any religious preference, they almost always favored Christian beliefs and tenets. For example, President Jefferson's much-misunderstood "wall of separation" metaphor is overshadowed by the book entitled *The Life and Morals of Jesus of Nazareth* that he drafted and had distributed at public expense to certain Indian tribes; and Franklin called for prayer at the Constitutional Convention and insisted that public schools teach that the Bible's God is real.

All true, but Christian nation–mongers ignore an inconvenient historical truth: while almost all of the founding fathers were either committed Christians or favored Christianity, the selfsame early leaders themselves plainly and persistently rejected as pernicious (or worse) the idea that the new nation should favor Christians or any other religious group. Although most were truly Bible-believing Protestants, they repeatedly and explicitly rejected the idea that the new nation should privilege Protestants or any other particular religious group.

Constitutionally, the American republic founded by Witherspoon, Madison, Washington, Jefferson, Franklin, and others was to be neither a Christian nation nor a secular state. Rather, they hoped and prayed that the new nation would be a godly republic in which a "multiplicity of sects" would thrive. The phrase is from one of Presbyterian-bred Madison's essays defending the proposed Constitution against its critics (Federalist Papers No. 51).

In their godly republic, political institutions would frankly presuppose a Supreme Being, and not just any Supreme Being—the God of Abraham mainly, but not exclusively, as that God was understood by most Anglo-American Protestants. But the right to hold federal office and enjoy the full rights of citizenship would not require any American to profess any particular religious beliefs or tenets. In their godly republic, everyone from Anglicans to atheists would, could, and should become American citizens or statesmen. Methodists, Muslims, and Mormons were welcomed, and so were Quakers, Catholics, Jews, and nonbelievers.

The Christian nation zealots' civic patron saints are to be found among the so-called Anti-Federalists, who bitterly opposed the Constitution's ratification. These Anti-Federalists trashed the Constitution because they despised the framers' religious pluralism. Essentially, they wanted Protestants to have and to forever hold a privileged place in the new nation. To them, the constitutional provision forbidding religious qualifications for federal officeholding was not only bad policy but a virtual blasphemy. They saw it as akin to erasing the Bible passage (Leviticus 25:10) that graced the Liberty Bell: "Proclaim liberty throughout the land unto all the inhabitants thereof."

Thus the Anti-Federalists, who can be counted as being among the first Christian nation enthusiasts (or at least those who were not from the South), would be glad to know that Abraham Lincoln, the only president to serve during a civil war, spoke about "this nation, under God" in an address that is still memorized by schoolchildren (the Gettysburg Address) and memorialized in marble (on the Lincoln Memorial). They would also be glad to know that the only non-elected president in the nation's history, Gerald Ford, when pardoning the only president ever forced to resign the office, Richard Nixon, justified his decision not with a secular legal brief but by a public speech punctuated by references to God:

> I have promised to uphold the Constitution, to do what is right as God gives me to see the right. . . . The Constitution is the supreme law of our land. . . . Only the laws of God, which govern our consciences, are superior to it. As we are a nation under God, so I am sworn to uphold our laws with the help of God. . . . I, not as President but as a humble servant of God, will receive justice without mercy if I fail to show mercy.[1]

But these same Anti-Federalists would not be happy to hear that Roman Catholics are the single largest religious group (29 percent) in the 110th Congress that assembled in 2007 or that the Congress included over three dozen Jews, a dozen Mormons, the first Buddhists ever elected to Congress (Representatives Mazie Hirono of Hawaii and Hank Johnson of Georgia), the first Muslim ever elected to Congress (Representative Keith Ellison of Minnesota, a former Catholic, who sparked a controversy by asking to use a Koran in his private swearing-in ceremony), and six members professing no religious faith.

And they would surely be perplexed or even apoplectic about how the U.S. Department of Veterans Affairs authorizes thirty-nine different kinds of religious plaques—not just Protestant crosses or the Catholic crucifix, but also the Jewish Star of David, the Muslim crescent, the Buddhist wheel, the Mormon angel, and even the atomic whirl for atheists and the pentacle for Wiccans—for use at national veterans' cemeteries.

SAVED IN SOUTH JERSEY

Impatience began to register on my questioner's face as he prodded me for what he called "the right answer." As my British friends would say, I suddenly felt "slightly put out." I had begun my day being bashed and threatened with legal action by orthodox secularists; now I was being called to account by an orthodox sectarian. And he was hardly the only one in the room.

The event's guest list had been handled by the West Wing's political affairs and public liaison staff. During the ceremony preceding the reception, I had noticed that few African American, Latino, and Catholic religious leaders were in the crowd. I motioned to a White House public liaison officer. He seemed to know my concern even before I voiced it. "I know," he whispered, "but the seats closest" to the president's podium had been reserved for the "big supporters." "Not just those seats," I complained.

As the president entered and began to make his way to the podium, the Reverend Mark Scott and Lisa Trevino-Cummins kept a close eye on what I did next. They were, respectively, my associate directors for outreach to African American clergy and to Latino faith-based leaders. They were also the only two people I had gotten to hire to that point. Scott was an African American (Church of God in Christ) Pentecostal who had done incredible community service work in Boston and nationally. Trevino-Cummins, a Latina, was a former corporate executive who had expertly advised banks and foundations on faith-based economic development projects and the like. My office's deputy director, Don Eberly, was justly famous for his pioneering research and other work promoting pro-fatherhood policies. Our chief legal counsel, Don Willett, was a bright and warm-hearted Bush loyalist from Texas.

"The Dons," as I affectionately baptized the Eberly-Willet duo, had worked on the president's campaign and also on his post–Florida controversy transition team. I was senior staff, an Assistant to the President. That meant that I was equal in rank to such top aides as Karl Rove, Karen Hughes, and Condoleezza Rice and had a seat at just about any meeting I chose to attend, including the daily senior staff morning meeting in the Roosevelt Room. I was generally well-liked, including by the president himself. He persistently prodded me, "Big John," to "get on [his] dance card" (that is, get on the Oval Office schedule to brief him personally rather than through White House Chief of Staff Andrew Card or others).

Still, I was the consummate West Wing inside-outsider. I was "the Philly Democrat" who had advised both Bush and Gore during the campaign; "the Ivy intellectual" who had publicly criticized the Supreme

Court decision that gave Bush the White House; the "God guy" who had a Catholic-bred "pro-poor" civic mission that conflicted with partisan politics as usual; and the top aide who publicly announced in January 2001 just how soon he would leave the White House—namely, in six months— in order to resume local community-based work, academic research, and undergraduate teaching (I left after eight months).

"I checked with the Dons," the public liaison officer added in self-defense as he walked back to his seat. I rose from my chair to walk out of the room, but Trevino-Cummins had read my mind. She discreetly but firmly grabbed me by my right jacket sleeve. "Don't," she said with an understanding smile: "They just weren't thinking." Scott seconded her no-commotion motion. "Let it go, Brother John," he said with a knowing chuckle: "It won't get nobody paid."

The "big supporters." The words simmered in my ears. As the ceremony commenced and the president prayed, I mediated on the fact that the first church to endorse his original faith-based and community initiatives plan was none other than Scott's Church of God in Christ (better known as COGIC). The first national network of religious organizations to do so was led by urban Latino clergy connected to Trevino-Cummins. The first major religious representatives to visit with the president at the White House were my own cadres of Catholic bishops and lay leaders.

Still, I was far from unsympathetic to my questioner's theological perspective. In the preceding half-decade, many in the evangelical Christian press had echoed my ideas about faith-based and community initiatives and embraced me as a "pro-life, pro-family, pro-poor Democrat" or "born-again Catholic." I had served on the boards of major evangelical Christian nonprofit organizations. With gusto, I had publicly beaten back assorted challenges from secular state bullies.

Just the same, before I had completed my first week in the White House, a small but vocal cadre of evangelical Christian leaders had called for my resignation. They began casting verbal stones my way as soon as I publicly and privately cast out their proposals for new laws or executive orders that plainly violated the Constitution and would only serve to sow misunderstanding and undermine support for all, including the urban ministries, that served poor people in need without regard to religion.

I was not simply saying and doing what I believed to be right but also what the president had plainly and sincerely stated, both in public and in private, that I was supposed to do. In 1999 and 2000 Bush's words about faith-based initiatives had repeatedly emphasized that while "government cannot be replaced" by diverse religious charities and faith-based groups, "it should welcome them as partners, not resent them as rivals." His plan, he frequently proclaimed, was to include "Methodists, Muslims, and Mormons, or good people of no faith at all."

As Bush liked to say, "job one" was to measurably and cost-effectively help all people in need without regard to religion. To that civic end, grassroots religious groups had to be free to seek public-private partnerships, including federal funding and technical assistance, on exactly the same basis as all other nonprofit organizations, religious and secular, national and local. Each time I used core mission phrases like "We aim to truly help all the 'least of these' by leveling, not tilting, the federal playing field," Bush would voice strong approval: "You got it, Big John."

Fidelity to the president's politically centrist "compassion" vision precluded any push to permit tax-supported proselytizing or legalize religious discrimination against program beneficiaries. It also precluded any proposal to radically revamp decades-old federal civil rights laws that governed religious hiring rights. Those federal laws, as the president had agreed on several occasions, had struck a proper balance. With respect to using private funds in hiring people to conduct worship services, the rights of religious organizations were absolute. But with respect to using public funds in hiring people to deliver social services, religious organizations enjoyed only a limited "ministerial exemption." Besides, Bush's respect for federalism ruled out new federal laws or executive orders that preempted or automatically overrode contrary state laws or local ordinances.

In the Jewish tradition, one sometimes answers a question with a question. I had an impulse to ask my questioner, "Do you know why the debate over church-state issues is so needlessly polarized?" But as I opened my mouth to reply, my heart began to pound. For a second I thought that I was having a heart attack. The words caught in my throat and seemed to be choking me. Suddenly, I felt like I was drowning. Ideas and images flooded my brain.

About a quarter-century earlier I had almost drowned for real. It happened when I was a teenager. In the Italian-Irish Philadelphia neighborhood where I grew up, working-class Catholic boys like me typically spent the very first week after high school graduation at a fleabag motel or flophouse "down the shore," meaning the honky-tonk beach towns and boardwalks of southern New Jersey. Drinking, girls, and misdemeanors defined this sacred rite of passage. One steamy afternoon, I went pool-hopping alone. I jumped the fence at a to-me pricey beachside hotel. It was crowded with young families. I was a conspicuous man-child interloper wearing cutoff blue jeans rather than a bathing suit. I darted in between lounge chairs, picked my spot, and dove head first into the big swimming pool. In my haste, I had not noticed the sun-faded marker at poolside indicating that the dark blue water was only four feet deep.

The blow to my head felt no harder than those I had received over the years in street-corner skirmishes. Still, it knocked me partially senseless. I swallowed superchlorinated water. My lungs burnt like hell. I could not swim or get to my feet. I could not see clearly. But my young life did not pass before me. I knew that I was going to survive. I just did not know how. I could not find the way up, but I was serene. Just as my vision cleared, a little kid wearing frogman flippers accidentally bumped my chin to the surface with his kickboard. I simultaneously gulped air and coughed water. But nobody seemed to have noticed my drama. I climbed out of the pool.

My head throbbed. The pool's pretty teenage lifeguard was talking through the fence to a bunch of little girls. She saw me looking at her and smiled wide. Although she had failed to rescue me, I began to conjure up the conditions under which I could more than forgive her. Then I noticed that my silver neck chain was missing. The chain had sported an ornate silver cross. Together the chain and the cross had probably set me back about ten dollars. They were tarnished. Back home in my night table next to my baseball cards, I had a 14-carat gold chain and crucifix that my old-fashioned Italian Catholic grandmother had given to me the previous June as a gift for my "name day" (Saint John the Baptist, June 24). But I resolved to retrieve the cross that lay beneath the water where I had been saved.

"My chain broke," I mumbled to the lifeguard as I stepped slowly back down the stairs into the pool. I immersed myself but could not find it. Then I stood up and felt the cross beneath my right foot. The chain had not broken. It had slipped over my head and come to rest at the bottom. I put it back on. "Come back whenever you want," the lifeguard said with a wink. "Thank you, Jesus," I said to myself.

I did not tell the half-dozen guys in my senior week crew what had happened. Those six guys have been my lifelong friends. They are all now happily married, churchgoing folks with kids (none of whom is allowed to go down the shore for senior week). We often share vacations, tickets for Philly sports teams, weddings, funerals, and religious holidays. Included are a plumber, a pipe fitter, a car mechanic, a civil servant who moonlights as a bartender, and two guys who started work as janitors but who made it big in business together by digging trenches for television cables. I am the only one to avoid real work entirely by being the first person in my family to graduate from college and then becoming (as my friends love to tease me) "a professional student" and "half-assed politician."

What, I thought, would my old Philly friends say in reply to this guy? All expletives deleted, I decided that they probably would say something like, "Not really, chief, but what's it to you?" or "Yeah, boss—you want me to send you on ahead?"

But my mind bounced past their imagined comebacks to a catechetical answer like the ones my Catholic school buddies and I had learned from Philly's good Sisters of the Immaculate Heart of Mary: "Heaven is eternal life spent in union with God and all those who share in God's life. Baptism in Jesus Christ is necessary for salvation, and there are three forms of baptism: baptism of water through the sacrament of baptism; baptism of blood as in the death of martyrs who die before being baptized; and baptism of desire, which applies to infants who die without being baptized and to all people who never hear about Christ or who hear but have not the gift of faith in Him but whose good and innocent lives demonstrate that they have accepted Jesus Christ without, as it were, self-consciously knowing or acknowledging him."

Finally, rather than reply the way my old Philly friends or my beloved Catholic nuns might have, I resolved instead to answer my interlocutor the way my newest Philly friends might. In the 1990s I had gotten to know Christians from the city's black and Latino community-serving ministries. As I regained my bearings and began to speak, I thought of the elderly black Pentecostal preacher who had reinvigorated my own faith by showing me how spiritual commitments can produce civic blessings.

JUST ASK POPS

The barrel-chested Benjamin "Pops" Smith was closing in on 80 years young when I first heard about him in the early 1990s. We were introduced through ministers in other cities, including former street gangsters who decades earlier had been saved by Pops—"Both my soul and my butt," as one put it. Pops was pastor of Deliverance Evangelistic Church in a predominantly black, low-income section of north Philadelphia. As the conservative political columnist and major league baseball fanatic George Will discovered when he visited with Pops and me in 1996, the enormous church was built on the site where Shibe Park, later renamed Connie Mack Stadium, had once stood. Most of the complex was devoted to youth activities and social service programs. Pops had a congregation of about 10,000 members.

During more than fifty years as a minister of the Gospel, Pops could have followed other successful preachers to less troubled city spaces, out to the suburbs, or on to cable television or direct-mail ministry. But each new church that Pops began was in a more blighted neighborhood than the one before it.

I listened to Pops's sermons, both in person and on cassette tapes (they often got me through my hour-long drive from Philly to Princeton University in central New Jersey). His sermons contained two distinct messages. On the one hand, he preached old-time religion. Jesus is Lord. Jesus is Savior. No salvation without Jesus. Salvation by faith alone. Get delivered. Get saved. Come to Jesus. Evangelize. "Don't care who you know, what you know, or what you think you know. Go on out there and tell somebody about Jesus Christ!" My favorite was Pops's standard Mother's Day address. He would whip the crowd into deep sentimentality for deceased mothers, then wipe them out by shouting: "Oh, oh, oh, when mother was here with me! . . . . Well mother ain't here no more, but *Jesus* is here! *Jesus* is all that matters!"

On the other hand, Pops could sound a lot like my old Catholic nuns. As Saint James stressed and as Pope John Paul II often repeated, "Faith without works is dead." Or, in Pops's vernacular, "The time for just having church is over!" He would beckon the church's "soul patrol" to do street ministry. "For Jesus," he himself had walked among gangbangers and other dispossessed inner-city youth. "For Jesus," he had also sparked local economic development projects. "For Jesus," he had forged partnerships with city agencies to provide all manner of youth and family services through the church. "For Jesus," he had sent his disciples out to do the same in other cities.

In June 1998 *Newsweek* put Boston's Reverend Eugene F. Rivers III on its cover with the title "Savior of the Streets." Back in the 1980s and early 1990s Rivers and his mostly Harvard-bred black Pentecostal church members, which then included Mark Scott, my White House office's associate director, had partnered with local police officials to stem the city's youth violence epidemic. But Rivers, an ex-Philly street thug, gave credit where credit was most due: Deliverance, not Harvard.

So, after my eternal pause, I gave the television evangelist the answer that I thought Pops would give him, minus any Catholic caveats (save those muttered under my breath), but with the addition of a plagiarized paraphrase from Saint Paul's Letter to the Ephesians. "Yes, I am, and I know because I know Jesus Christ as my Lord and Savior, and not because of any good works I have done or grace I have merited." As he started to smile, I added: "We must not be blown by every wind of human teaching that corrupts understanding or foments error. Or so I believe."

He seemed delighted. I was about to put the moment behind me forever, but my interrogator added, "Yes. Someone in your position needs to know the right answer to that question."

WHAT WOULD MADISON AND FRANKLIN DO?

Wrong. As a scholar who dabbles in religion, I ought to know what evangelical Christians, Catholics, and other faiths profess. As a U.S. social scientist who does related empirical research, I ought to know how common different religious belief systems are in America. As a cradle Catholic who loves his Church, warts and all, I also ought to know what the basic Catholic answer to my interrogator's question would be.

But no national government official, high or low, needs to know or give any particular answer, or any answer at all, to such a question, or to profess any particular religious beliefs and tenets.

Chapter 1 recovers the founders' faithful consensus about religion and the national government. It does so mainly by reanimating Madison's pivotal place in founding the godly republic as such, including his role in crafting that most blessed compromise with the Anti-Federalists, the Bill of Rights. It outlines how the two First Amendment religion clauses—the Free Exercise clause and the Establishment clause—relate to one another, and how they came to be applied to the states. It explores why, in the first place, Madison and company singled out religion for both special civic benefits and special civic burdens. It thereby challenges both stubborn secular state views and neo-Anti-Federalist Christian nation visions.

After I had drafted the first chapter and lectured from it, a University of Pennsylvania student in my religion and U.S. public policy seminar asked me a question that I had not previously thought to ask myself (Penn students are the best at that). He grasped that the godly republic was an alternative to the secular state and Christian nation ideas. He liked my "middle-ground concept," as he called it. But how, he wondered, did it compare to other such middle-ground interpretations? "No idea," I confessed to him, "but find out!" For his final paper, he discovered a then just-published 2006 book by Jon Meacham, the managing editor of *Newsweek* magazine.[2]

Meacham's excellent book, *American Gospel,* outlines how the U.S. Supreme Court in 1892 came to unanimously declare the false "truth" that "this is a Christian nation."[3] Overall, Meacham's account squares rather well with law professor Philip Hamburger's monumental historical treatise, published in 2002, documenting how church-state separation doctrine resulted largely from the rabidly anti-Catholic forces that held sway in American politics from the 1860s well into the 1940s. The story features national leaders including President Ulysses S. Grant and Supreme Court Justice Hugo Black.[4]

Meacham, however, brings the story starkly into the present. He zeroes in on television evangelists Jerry Falwell and Pat Robertson (neither of whom, for the record, is the preacher who popped the question that I answered in Pops Smith's vernacular). Meacham rebuts the idea that America is "a Christian nation that has lost its way"[5] and transcribes the Falwell-Robertson dialogue that was televised on September 13, 2001.[6]

Meacham describes the dialogue as the Christian nation idea at its "worst" and "grimmest imaginable."[7] In Falwell's words, the September 11, 2001 terrorist attacks on America were divine retribution for "throwing God out of the public square, out of schools" with "the help of the federal court system" and a defiant response to those "who have tried to secularize America" and thereby "mocked" and made "God mad."[8] In reply, Robertson said, "I totally concur" and praised "both houses of Congress" for publicly praying together and disregarding "all the Christ-haters."[9] Meacham notes that the reverends "do not, of course, represent all of evangelical Christianity."[10] Then he adds: "Extreme secularists have not helped matters either, with harsh words designed to wound and deride religious believers."[11]

Amen. Meacham's core concept, "public religion," is a middle-ground concept that comes much closer to capturing the historical and constitutional truth about America than either the secular state view or the Christian nation vision.[12] Still, in certain fundamental respects, it differs from the godly republic interpretation. "Properly understood," argues Meacham, "the God of public religion is not the God of Abraham or God the Father of the Holy Trinity."[13] "Many of the Founders," he maintains, "were influenced by Deism, an Enlightenment vision of religion."[14]

Some were, but many more were deeply influenced by classical Christian beliefs and tenets, and by conventional Anglo-American Protestant ideas and institutions. Look no farther than the prototypically Christian presidential and other public proclamations that Meacham's book so usefully catalogues. Suffice it to say that these leaders, from Washington to Lincoln and beyond, were not talking about Thor, Venus, Vishnu, or any other "God," ancient or modern. They were talking about the God of Abraham as generally understood by Anglo-American Protestants who believed in Jesus Christ's divinity.

Even latter-day leaders from Franklin Delano Roosevelt through Bill Clinton and George W. Bush have explicitly and publicly referenced the God of Abraham, and proclaimed Jesus Christ as Lord and Savior. But the good news is that their Good News has almost always respected the Constitution. Just as the godly republic's first architects intended, America's presidents and other public leaders, whatever their own religious identities, have normally displayed all due regard for religious pluralism and respected settled constitutional limits on church-state collaboration.

This civic miracle was first performed by Madison. As I argue in chapter 1, many patriots and framers mattered, but it is Madison who best represents and embodies the founders' faithful consensus that America was to become the very godly republic that it pretty much is today: Madison, not Witherspoon on his religious right or Jefferson on his religious left; Madison, not the Anti-Federalists on his far religious right or the rare-for-the-day radicals like Thomas Paine on his antireligious left.

And Madison, not Ben Franklin. I love Franklin (almost a job requirement at the University of Pennsylvania, which Franklin founded). This book concludes by going back to my all-time favorite faith-friendly fellow Philadelphian (transplanted, I concede, from Boston). Despite his own lifelong doubts about religion, Franklin in his day did pretty much what I think Jesus would do—and would want all Americans, including secular liberals, to do now—regarding religion, government, and support for the civic blessings bestowed by diverse faith communities. Agnostic but not antireligious in the least, Franklin personally supported multiple community-serving churches, synagogues, and mosques in Philadelphia.

In my earliest drafts and in speeches I gave (like the one in mid-2006 at the University of California at Berkeley that led to this book being published by the University of California Press), I had Franklin, not Madison, as my stand-in for the godly republic's founder-in-chief. But, as I finally had to admit, Franklin was not a typical founder in any way, least of all in his brilliant, and at times playful, disregard for core Christian beliefs and tenets (Christ's divinity, for starters).

A Penn history student shared with me her research on how Franklin had founded the university to be nonsectarian and had beaten back a challenge by the school's first provost, an Anglican minister who tried to turn the place into an Anglican outpost in America. What struck me most was how easy it was for Franklin to take this position: a polyglot genius nonbeliever pushing for Penn to become a nonsectarian school (nobody back then thought to go beyond nonsectarian to strictly secular).

By comparison, with Witherspoon in his right ear, Jefferson in his left ear, and religiously chauvinistic Anti-Federalists in his face, Madison pushed for America to be a godly republic in which a "multiplicity of sects" could survive and thrive, and everyone from orthodox believers to nonbelievers could, at least in constitutional principle, become full-fledged citizens or elected statesmen. Madison is thus the godly republic's civic patron saint, with old Ben in the background saying and doing on religion in the public square pretty much what both he and Madison would have the rest of us say and do on it in America today.

As I revised my thinking from Franklin to Madison, and as I heard from faculty colleagues and others who had read or heard early bits and pieces, I also thought thrice about competing interpretations.

Alas, the secular state view is not completely without serious scholarship to support it. There are some recent and worthwhile works suggesting that George Washington and other founders were less religious than they seemed, or even irreligious beneath it all.[15] Similarly, the Christian nation vision is now backed by more than a few weighty and fairly well-researched tomes insisting that, on the whole, Washington and the other founders were, if anything, more religious than they seemed. There is, for example, more than a little evidence that they trimmed Christianity's role in the constitutional system as little as possible, with pivotal leaders like Washington praying that "the sacred fire of liberty" would burn with a born-again glow in government and the culture forever.[16]

By the same token, I think that Meacham's public religion interpretation lends too much historical credence to secular influences; but, to pluck the beam from my own manuscript, it could be that I overestimate religious influences. In the end, however, the secular state and Christian nation interpretations each seemed so far from the truth as to merit being called "myths"; and the public religion idea, though containing much that is both historically and constitutionally kosher, yet missed America's noblest and most intriguing sacred civic mystery: how true believers in a religious creed that promotes proselytizing have, political generation by political generation, promoted genuine religious pluralism and honored constitutional limits.

At a time when ever more Americans and their leaders, including most elected leaders pursuing 2008 presidential bids, either talk openly about faith in their lives or publicly profess various Christian beliefs and tenets, it is doubly important to get religion's historic place in the nation's civic life right. In the godly republic, we need not reinvent the republican wheel when it comes to fostering mutual civic forbearance on church-state issues, whether in general or between today's Bible-believing Christians and today's secular liberals. We need not reinvent it, but, as chapters 6 and 7 prescribe, we probably do need to retread it for our time.

If chapter 1 makes Madison a civic saint, chapter 2 begs indulgence for the modern-day Supreme Court. It answers two opposing camps of critics of the contemporary Supreme Court's First Amendment religion-clauses jurisprudence. Many orthodox sectarians insist that an antireligious "judicial tyranny" has spread all across the land, beginning with the Court's aforementioned 1962 decision declaring that public schoolchildren may not be required to recite state-sponsored prayers. But the facts support neither the "Godless schools" caricature nor associated claims that the federal courts have forbidden government support for religious institutions. At the other extreme, many orthodox secularists claim that the post-1980 Court has all but endorsed religious "establishments." But the facts about the rabidly anti-Catholic roots of the strict separation doctrine, and the reasoning behind the contemporary Court's ostensibly "pro-religion" decisions, reveal these criticisms to be no more well-founded than those of their main opponents.

The truth is that the Court and the wider federal judiciary have done a commendable, if far from perfect, job of enforcing church-state neutrality principles. Chapter 3 reveals that majority public opinion and bipartisan political sentiment are virtually at one with contemporary Court doctrine and the founders' church-state vision. Certain segments of elite opinion are plainly polarized on religion, government, and faith-based initiatives. But a careful look at the evidence on recent national election voting patterns and opinion dynamics suggests that most Americans are still religious pluralists, not antireligious zealots or religious purists. The same picture emerges from the post-1996 adoption by the federal government of grant-making rules that embody neutrality principles.

Chapter 4 examines the rise and demise of the original Bush plan that advocated greater federal support for community-serving religious nonprofit organizations. The plan unraveled, and the wider consensus was momentarily shattered, when an influential minority of orthodox Christian leaders made policy demands that violated settled constitutional limits on church-state collaboration. But Washington's move toward faith-based initiatives reflected, not created, the public consensus, and the political troubles of the "Bush faith bill" curtailed, not killed, the faith-based social services movement. Even without significantly more help from Washington, grassroots religious groups have continued to deliver social services to people in need. New public-private, religious-secular programs have continued to show special promise—programs like those that put loving adult mentors into the lives of some of the over two million children in America with incarcerated parents.

Chapter 5 summarizes the latest and best scientific evidence concerning the extent and efficacy of faith-based social services. It reprises and retests, in light of fresh and reliable empirical data, several concepts that I first brought into public discourse in the 1990s. Whether measured by association memberships, philanthropy, or volunteering, most "social capital" in America is actually "spiritual capital" supplied by religious institutions that serve nonmembers without regard to religion, race, or socioeconomic status.

Urban community-serving religious nonprofits, especially ones led and staffed by inner-city African Americans and Latinos, are the backbone of America's faith-based social services sector and our most under-resourced and underappreciated repositories of "bridging spiritual capital." Chapter 5 documents that the vast majority of all community-serving religious nonprofits are faith-*based*, not faith-*saturated*.

That is, they are motivated by faith, but they serve people without regard to religion; they do not hire only people who share their particular religious views; and they are ready and willing to work within ecumenical, interfaith, religious-secular, and public-private partnerships. Most are not at all adverse to seeking federal grants. Most are eager to receive technical assistance and capacity-building support from government agencies and secular nonprofit organizations. With or without public or private partners, faith-based organizations' one proven civic comparative advantage is mobilization of volunteers.

Presently, there is no credible research to prove that religious nonprofits that emphasize spiritual transformation succeed where other, religiously motivated or wholly secular programs fail. However, as chapter 5 explains, a sizable body of scientific literature suggests that one or more of three "faith factors" may be associated with many positive social and health outcomes. As it turns out, Franklin was right in believing that, under certain conditions, religion can elicit desirable social behavior, lead to better physical and mental health, and render believers and nonbelievers alike more inclined to help others in need, no matter who they are.

To paraphrase the greatest nineteenth-century foreign observer of American democracy, Alexis de Tocqueville, the world is not led by long or learned demonstrations. Even if I am right about Madison and the founders' faithful consensus, the contemporary Court's approach, recent policy dynamics and administrative developments, and the science of the subject, it is all mere academic musing unless the nation's first "faith czar" can also suggest how we might keep future church-state debates from triggering pitched legal and legislative battles between religious and secular political factions.

Chapter 6 discusses the godly republic's faith-based future, and how deep differences between evangelical Christians and secular liberal elites could be aired and resolved in a more public-spirited fashion than they have been in the recent past. It uses as a case study a live federal court case involving a major evangelical Christian ministry on whose board I once served. It outlines and illustrates three quasi-religious principles for civic engagement on the most contentious church-state questions. And it concludes by emphasizing the one thing on which most people of good civic faith should be able to agree, whatever their stand on religion's public role: America still has a significant poverty problem.

My plea is that we will not permit ideological, political, or other differences to delay, diminish, or derail efforts to help those whom Jesus called "the least of these" among us. We must not substitute cynical partisan gamesmanship for sincere civic action in helping the country's poor and dispossessed by all legitimate means at our disposal. We must resist the temptation to court or prolong legal or legislative conflicts over church-state issues so as to raise more money for "us" from supporters who despise "them," or otherwise worship ideological icons or kneel before organizational self-interest. And my hope is that we will all strive to "think Catholic" when it comes to antipoverty efforts and the common good.

For those without ears to hear, chapter 7 repeats this plea, but in relation to three faith-free principles (or as faith-free as I am capable of making them). It conceives urban faith-based organizations as "civic value stocks" that promise to yield significant social returns on multiple small public and private investments. Reaching back to chapter 5, it documents the special civic strengths and resiliency represented by black churches and argues for focusing the next round of federal and state faith-based initiatives on helping young black urban low-income males. The recipe includes everything from targeted mentoring initiatives for preschool children to targeted prisoner reentry programs for adult ex-offenders. The total price tag, only a fraction of which would need to come from Washington, would be about $10 billion a year, or less than a quarter of what we spend annually on state prisons alone.

As a hedge against having totally missed my mark, and because I think it is the best church-state consensus statement yet drafted by present-day religious leaders, the appendix copies the 1988 Williamsburg Charter.

Obviously, this is a book by an academic, but it is not, strictly speaking, an academic treatise. It is also a book by a former White House official; particularly in chapters 3 and 4, I have drawn on my experience there. Yet this is not an insider or tell-all account.

I am aware that I am many things, or many things all at once, that most citizens are not at all: a working-class character with a Harvard Ph.D. who got tenure early at Princeton; a Democrat who is highly conservative on some issues and quite liberal on others; and a Catholic who, as I noted previously, reclaimed his faith by hanging out with black Pentecostals. Furthermore, as you may see most plainly in chapter 6, my respect and admiration for certain evangelical Christian leaders with whom I have disagreed is so profound that I wish my secular liberal friends would stop cringing at the mere mention of their names. I even hold out hope for mutual civic forbearance so deep that it will permit joint left-right, secular-sectarian advocacy and action to benefit America's most truly disadvantaged children, youth, and families. (I believe in civic miracles.)

All the author's after-tax royalties on this book will be contributed to the following faith-based organizations or programs:[17]

- Amachi
- Evangelicals for Social Action
- The Fishing School
- Habitat for Humanity
- Miguel Schools and People for People Charter School of Philadelphia (Gesu School, La Salle Academy, Hope Partnership, and PFP School)
- National Ten-Point Leadership Foundation
- Nueva Esperanza
- Partners for Sacred Places
- Prison Fellowship Ministries
- Salvation Army
- Teen Challenge
- Urban Promise

I hope that this book sells so well that in some future confession, I must tell my priest that I wish I had not been so generous when thinking about the godly republic.

And I want to reassure my old White House questioner that whether I am generous will not determine whether I see him in heaven.

ONE

The Founders' Faithful Consensus

A GODLY REPUBLIC, NOT A SECULAR STATE
OR A CHRISTIAN NATION

Myth 1   The framers of the U.S. Constitution founded a new government
based on secular Enlightenment ideas that favored a strict and
total separation between church and state.

Myth 2   The framers of the U.S. Constitution founded a new government
predicated on the belief that America was, and should ever remain,
a Christian nation.

TRUTH   The framers of the U.S. Constitution founded a new government
that they hoped would guide America's rise, not as either a secular
state or a Christian nation, but as a godly republic marked by religious pluralism.

ONE NATION, UNDER GOD, FOR ALL

In 1954, the U.S. Congress voted to insert the words "under God" in the
Pledge of Allegiance. On June 6, 2002, the San Francisco–based U.S. Court
of Appeals for the Ninth Circuit, in *Newdow v. U.S. Congress,* ruled that the
Constitution requires that those words be stricken from the Pledge. "In
the context of the Pledge," the opinion asserted, "the statement that the
United States is a nation 'under God' is an endorsement of religion. It is a

profession of a religious belief, namely, in monotheism." "The Pledge, as currently codified," the federal judges insisted, "is an impermissible government endorsement of religion because it sends a message to unbelievers" that they are "not full members of the political community." They held that both the 1954 congressional act adding the words "under God" to the Pledge and local public school practice of "teacher-led recitation of the Pledge" violated the Constitution.

The *Newdow* opinion reflects the view that America is a secular state in which not even interfaith or nondenominational religious expression can receive any public endorsement, and no religious or religiously affiliated organization can receive government financial or other support for any purpose whatsoever, without violating the Constitution and federal laws.

In 1954, the same year that Congress added "under God" to the Pledge, the National Association of Evangelicals (NAE) lobbied for an amendment to the Constitution that included the following words: "This nation divinely recognizes the authority and law of Jesus Christ, Savior and Ruler of Nations, through whom are bestowed the blessings of Almighty God."[1] In the summer of 2002, following the *Newdow* decision, an official NAE publication was headlined " . . . One Nation, Under Jesus Christ." "One question," it proclaimed, "is worth asking: do evangelicals—even through the 'voluntary energies' of our churches—still believe in that vision? If not, then our culture-forming capacity is in doubt."[2]

This NAE vision reflects the view that America is a Christian nation in which Christian religious expression can and should receive special public endorsement, and Christian churches and other Christian organizations can and should receive special government support, without violating the Constitution and federal laws.

The federal judges' opinion is as wrong as the evangelical association's vision is wrongheaded. With regard both to interfaith or nondenominational religious expression and to financial or other support for religious or religiously affiliated organizations that serve civic purposes, the Constitution and federal laws neither enshrine orthodox secularism nor empower orthodox sectarianism.

In America, "God" is mentioned in numerous public songs, including the fourth stanza of the national anthem, "The Star Spangled Banner."

Since 1862, "In God We Trust" has been required under federal law to be printed on the dollar bill and other U.S. currency. To this day, most state constitutions explicitly reference "God" or "Almighty God," often quite reverentially. As noted in the introduction, the Liberty Bell (on daily public display in Philadelphia) is inscribed with words from the Bible's Leviticus 25:10: "Proclaim liberty throughout the land unto all the inhabitants thereof." The U.S. Supreme Court building boasts religious references carved in stone. Both houses of Congress keep chaplains on the public payroll. The White House often hosts National Prayer Day gatherings, and presidents are commonly featured at prayer breakfasts.

Judge Ferdinand F. Fernandez, the lone dissenting judge in *Newdow*, rightly noted that the Constitution and federal laws are not now and never have been "designed to drive religious expression out of public thought." To be sure, the Constitution and federal laws forbid government from supporting some creeds and suppressing others. But they leave ample room for diverse religious leaders and people to be who they are in the public square—even in the hallowed halls of Congress itself. For instance, here is how Senator Barack Obama, Democrat of Illinois, a self-avowed Christian believer, describes religion in the Senate, circa 2006:

> Discussions of faith are rarely heavy-handed within the confines of the Senate. No one is quizzed on his or her religious affiliation. . . . The Wednesday morning prayer breakfast is entirely optional, bipartisan, and ecumenical . . . those who choose to attend take turns selecting a passage from Scripture and leading group discussion. Hearing the sincerity, openness, humility, and good humor with which even the most overtly religious senators . . . share their personal faith journeys during these breakfasts, one is tempted to assume that the impact of faith on politics is largely salutary, a check on personal ambition, a ballast against the buffeting words of today's headlines and political expediency.[3]

As Obama is quick to add, the impact of faith on politics is hardly always so salutary, a point he illustrates by recounting how his first general election opponent for the Senate, Alan Keyes, publicly insisted that Obama's claims to being a Christian were invalidated by the positions

Obama had taken on abortion and other issues.[4] But the broader point is that Obama (who won in a landslide) routinely joins others of both parties, meeting right there in the Senate, in discussing religious commitments and reading biblical verses. Doing so sends no unconstitutional or illegal "message to unbelievers" that they are not full-fledged citizens.

By the same token, through democratically enacted and completely constitutional measures, the national government has long partnered with sacred places that serve civic purposes. In particular, numerous national religious charitable organizations representing diverse faith traditions have for decades received federal grants and contracts to help deliver health care, child care, education, employment, housing, and other social services. This has been especially common in federal programs specifically designed to help low-income children, youth, families, or other people in need.

Such church-state collaboration to promote public well-being is constitutional and consistent with all relevant federal laws, provided that the religious or religiously affiliated organizations serve all citizens without regard to religion; use public support to administer social services, not to conduct worship services or for sectarian instruction or proselytizing; and otherwise follow the identical public accountability and performance rules as all other nonprofit organizations that receive public support.

As *Newdow* dissenter Judge Fernandez stressed, what the Constitution and federal laws require is "neutrality" and "equal protection" so as to ensure "that government will neither discriminate for or against" a particular religion. For instance, for government to promulgate that America is "one Nation, under Jesus Christ" would be tantamount to its endorsing a particular religion and therefore plainly unconstitutional. But, as Fernandez explained, for government to invoke "God," even as in the God of Abraham, the God worshipped by Jews, Christians, and Muslims alike, does not seriously threaten "to bring about a theocracy or suppress somebody's beliefs" and "is no constitutional violation at all."

On April 28, 1952, two years before Congress added "under God" to the Pledge, Justice William O. Douglas penned the U.S. Supreme Court's *Zorach v. Clauson* opinion. Douglas was the modern era's most liberal Court member. But he reminded secular-state-minded jurists (himself included) that the Constitution does "not say that in each and all respects there shall be a separation of Church and State." He recited the "references to the Almighty that run through our laws, our public rituals, our ceremonies." A "fastidious atheist or agnostic," he reasoned, "could even object to the supplication with which the Court opens each session: 'God save the United States and this Honorable Court.'" But, citing constitutional law and precedents and appealing to "the common sense of the matter," he cautioned those who would "press the concept of separation of church and state to these extremes." Americans, he matter-of-factly stated, "are a religious people whose institutions presuppose a Supreme Being," namely, the biblical God of Abraham.

The Constitution and federal laws also require neutrality and equal protection in grant-making and public administration. No less than with respect to citizens' religious expression, neutrality and equal protection are watchwords when it comes to government financial or other support for religious or religiously affiliated organizations. For instance, for government to fund a welfare-to-work program that required beneficiaries to recite a prayer before searching the help-wanted ads or receiving counseling, that used tax dollars to hire only co-religionists, or that exempted itself on religious grounds from complying with program-specific accountability and performance rules, would be plainly unconstitutional and illegal. But for government to fund a faith-based welfare-to-work program that involved voluntary prayer, that exercised the limited right afforded by the 1964 Civil Rights Act and other federal laws to take religion into account in making employment decisions (known as the "ministerial exemption"), and that complied with all program-specific accountability and performance rules just as all other participating nonprofit organizations must do, would be completely constitutional and legal.

The next chapter delves into greater detail concerning the so-called neutrality doctrine and how, according to the U.S. Supreme Court, the Constitution and federal laws are to properly regulate religion's relationship to government in America today. For now, it is more important to understand that the founding fathers, especially those who figured most prominently among the Constitution's framers, agreed from the first that

America should be neither a secular state nor a Christian nation, but instead should rise into a great and godly republic.

A WARM CIVIC WELCOME, NOT A HIGH LEGAL WALL

Start with the framer, the father of the Constitution, James Madison. Born in 1751, the Virginian served in the U.S. House of Representatives (1789–1797) and as America's fourth president (1809–1817). He spent his final decades as a revered senior statesman (he died in 1836 at age 86). For our purposes, however, no period is more instructive than the roughly four years he spent debating, drafting, and defending the U.S. Constitution (drafted in 1787, ratified in 1788) and the Bill of Rights (the first ten amendments to the Constitution, ratified in 1791).

Where Madison is concerned, those who believe that America is a Christian nation (Myth #2) stress such things as his service in Congress on a committee that put Protestant chaplains on the public payroll or his support, as president, for a law that helped to fund a Christian group that distributed Bibles. On the opposite side, those who believe that America is a secular state (Myth #1) emphasize the regrets Madison expressed late in life about supporting such measures or selectively highlight passages from his voluminous writings (such as his 1785 *Memorial and Remonstrance Against Religious Assessments*) wherein he counseled limits on church-state relations.

The truth, however, is that present-day America is blessed to be in religious terms pretty much what Madison and most of the other framers intended it to be. It is a godly republic with governmental institutions that (as Justice Douglas phrased it) "presuppose" monotheistic belief in the "Supreme Being" known to Jews, Christians, and Muslims as the God of Abraham. It is a godly republic that affords a special civic status to nondenominational and interfaith (God-centered) religious expression. It is a godly republic that respects, promotes, and protects religious pluralism: Methodists, Muslims, Mormons, and all other faiths are welcome. It is a godly republic in which both the Constitution and federal laws prohibit government from discriminating against citizens who profess no faith at all (atheists have the same constitutional standing as Anglicans) or who are actively, but peacefully, hostile to all religion or to all church-state collaboration (Americans United for the Separation of Church and State is no more or less entitled to tax-exempt nonprofit status than the National Association of Evangelicals).

Madison and the other framers plainly did not intend for America to become a strictly secular state. They did not wish to exile religion to civic limbo by constitutionally and legally confining religious expression to the private sphere. Neither did they seek to separate religious organizations—churches, synagogues, mosques, or the diverse community-serving religious associations that were already a fixture in the early republic—from any and all collaboration with government institutions.

The words "wall of separation" or "church-state separation" appear nowhere in the Constitution, nor in any amendments to the Constitution, nor in any of the drafts (and there were dozens) of the First Amendment to the Constitution. That is because sentiments and theories favoring strict and total separation of church and state were nowhere in the framers' hearts and minds.

Nor, however, did Madison and the other framers pray for America to become a nation in which either the national majority's religion (then as now Protestant Christianity), or any other particular religion or sect, received preferred civic treatment. Like most of the framers, Madison was a committed Christian in the Reformed (or Protestant) tradition. Yet, almost to a man, the framers firmly believed that their Protestant faith opposed having the national government favor any one religion, including their own, over any other. It would be both morally wrong and imprudent, they agreed, for the new government to tax all citizens to support Christians or to establish any particular Protestant religion as the nation's religion.

Far from etching any Christian nation notion into the Constitution, the framers took multiple measures explicitly to prevent any national religious favoritism or outright religious establishment. For instance, to prevent Christians or other religious people from accruing any exclusive public privileges under the new government, the Constitution (Article VI, concluding paragraph) expressly provides that "no religious test shall ever be required as a qualification to any office or public trust under the United States," period.

In the same civic spirit, in 1791, the framers acted to require the national government to permit citizens to freely exercise whatever religion they might choose and to prohibit it from establishing any particular religion as the nation's religion. To that end, they included two religious freedom clauses in the First Amendment to the Constitution.

As chapter 2 explains, much confusion and controversy has been, and continues to be, wrought by historically off-the-wall decisions regarding religion handed down by the Supreme Court as late as the mid-twentieth century. Today in America, however, the religious beliefs shared and organizations led by Bible-believing Christians are still strongly protected by the First Amendment and by federal laws. So are the religious convictions held, congregations led, and community-serving nonprofit groups sponsored by Jews, Muslims, and American citizens of all faiths. Faith-friendly federal neutrality unto religious pluralism—neither a Christian nation nor a secular state—is precisely what Madison and most of the other framers wanted for America.

The Constitution's no-religious-test-for-federal-office provision and the First Amendment's religion clauses were conceived by the framers as a warm civic welcome, not a high legal wall. They were intended as official public invitations for all American citizens, present and future, to freely exercise whatever religion they might choose—or none at all. They were meant to be a civic guarantee that, with respect to we the people's assorted sacred beliefs, tenets, and institutions, the national government would ever aspire to effect equal treatment, not supply special treatment.

BETWEEN JEFFERSON AND WITHERSPOON: MADISON

In recent decades it has often been asserted that Madison and many of the other framers were not, in fact, committed Christians. Some have even suggested that Madison and company were not Christian believers at all. They assert that most framers were dedicated, not to Christianity or to any particular Protestant sect, but instead to a secular civic creed grounded in ethical and moral precepts only loosely derived from the Judeo-Christian tradition.

The truth is far more interesting. The framers were not, in fact, secular-minded Enlightenment thinkers dressed in religious drag for the sake of political expediency. Most citizens in their day were professed Christian believers. Their constitutional machinery was not intended to run only on secular ethical fumes from the Judeo-Christian moral tradition (a.k.a. the Ten Commandments).

Rather, the framers' plainly expressed preference for religious pluralism is remarkable precisely because, like most other early Americans, most framers did believe what the New Testament taught about the divinity of Jesus Christ as Lord and Savior. As Christians in the Reformed tradition, they believed that coming to Christ was quite literally a matter of eternal life or death. Even many who would not have considered themselves evangelists believed in encouraging others to believe in Christ. At the same time, however, they steadfastly distinguished between "encouraging" and "coercing." They believed that nobody could or should be coerced, least of all by any national government, to believe in Christ. They were certain that both Christianity itself and the republican cause would suffer if the new national government were to privilege Protestantism in any official fashion, up to and including establishing Christianity as America's state religion.

Indeed, the Constitution's no-religious-test-for-federal-office provision was advocated and adopted on the heels of the Christian revival movement known as the Great Awakening. Led by evangelists like Jonathan Edwards and George Wakefield, from the 1730s to the 1770s this revival swept through Britain's American colonies. For the most part, colonial intellectual and political elites favored the movement. All the same, they were just as opposed to sanctioning a religious test for federal office as they were to having the national government grant any titles of nobility (outlawed by the Constitution's Article I, Section 9).

The framers varied in their Christian beliefs and practices. They ranged from the conventionally prayerful George Washington to the supremely heterodox Benjamin Franklin, from the occasionally anticlerical Thomas Jefferson to the unfailingly orthodox John Witherspoon. And the early republic had at least one justly famous antireligious radical, albeit one transplanted in body and spirit to France: Thomas Paine.

Still, the founding fathers arrived at a faithful consensus that America should be a godly republic rather than either a secular state or a Christian nation. Their consensus was captured and codified by the Christian who counted Jefferson and Witherspoon as his two most important mentors and whose work as father and chief defender of the Constitution both men sincerely praised: James Madison.

Before entering public life as a Virginia state delegate in the fateful year 1776, Madison attended Princeton University. The school's founding leaders and faculty members were all deeply committed Christians. Madison's bedrock ideas about the Constitution and hopes for the godly republic were seeded at the college.

Madison's main Princeton mentor was John Witherspoon, a "New Side" Scottish Presbyterian minister and the school's president. Madison affectionately called Witherspoon the "old Doctor."[5] After graduating from Princeton, Madison served with Witherspoon in the Continental Congress (1781–1782). Until recently, Witherspoon was largely a forgotten founder. But his influence on Madison and many other early leaders is beyond serious dispute, as is his role as one who debated and signed both the Declaration of Independence and the Constitution. Witherspoon taught Madison that no republic could survive and prosper without religion. "His formulation might be put this way: no republic without liberty, no liberty without virtue, and no virtue without religion."[6] Most framers, young and old, believed much the same.

For Witherspoon, however, the only religion that could reliably supply the civic virtue necessary to a republic was orthodox Christianity. Regarding the relationship between religion and government, he was "nearer the right bank of the mainstream" than even conservative Christian framers like Washington.[7] Following Reformed Scottish Presbyterian thought, Witherspoon believed "that civil magistrates should have power to advance true religion and punish impiety," and "true religion" for him meant "orthodox Christianity."[8] He would go so far as to claim that "non-establishment and liberty of conscience left room for civil magistrates to promote religion and even to 'make public provision for the worship of God.'"[9]

By contrast, Madison's other dear mentor and fellow Virginian, Thomas Jefferson, inhabited the left bank of the framers' mainstream views on government's relationship to Christianity and religion. Like Jefferson, many well-educated founding fathers knew not only the King James Bible and major Reformed Christian commentaries like John Calvin's *Institutes of the Christian Religion* but also ancient pagan philosophers such as Aristotle and Plato, Enlightenment philosophers such as Montesquieu and Voltaire, and classical historians such as Thucydides and Plutarch. Like Jefferson, several framers also knew more than a bit about experimental science and did more than a little themselves to advance it in their day. Yet few ever vented the hostility to Christianity that, superficially at least, punctuates many private letters authored by Jefferson.

But make no mistake: Jefferson "was no atheist."[10] Rather, he championed religious freedom, and almost every hostile remark he ever made about Christianity or particular Christian sects was made to challenge a religious practice or organization that he believed had "assumed a political character" adverse to both true piety and civil peace.[11] His own religious views "tended toward deism. He believed in one God, not no God, not twenty Gods; but he thought it much better for the human spirit if a country had twenty sects rather than only one."[12]

Jefferson wrote four references to God into the Declaration of Independence. As Virginia's governor, he designated a day for "prayer to Almighty God." As president, he attended church regularly, with services held in the House of Representatives. He permitted the Marine Band to play at worship services. Jefferson even approved a U.S. treaty with Indians that provided, at the Indians' request, federal funds to support a Catholic priest who had begun an outreach ministry to the tribe.

In his youth, Madison seriously contemplated becoming a Christian minister. In his early years and again in old age, Madison sometimes echoed Jeffersonian anticlericalisms. Throughout his life, however, Madison blended and balanced the best thinking on religion and government whispered by Witherspoon on his right and by Jefferson on his left. When all the "evidence is weighed, it is obvious that Madison . . . . was as determined to protect religious believers from an oppressive state as he was to protect dissenting citizens from an oppressive church."[13]

Madison's most enduring civic legacy, however, resides in the beliefs about religion and republicanism in America that he publicly expressed and fought for from the mid-1780s through the mid-1790s.

In 1785 and 1786, the two years immediately preceding the Constitutional Convention in Philadelphia, Madison, then a Virginia assemblyman, battled in the state's legislature for the Act for Establishing Religious Freedom. He corresponded with Jefferson about the controversial act.[14] During the legislative fight, he "scolded Christian conservatives for trying to insert the words 'Jesus Christ' in the bill's preamble."[15] They would, he stated, give "better proof of reverence for that holy name" were they "not to profane it by making it a topic of legislative discussion."[16]

In the mid-1790s, just a few years after the First Amendment and its religion clauses were ratified with the rest of the Bill of Rights, Madison, then a U.S. representative in Congress, became a righteous voice for religious pluralism. For instance, in 1795, "during a congressional debate over naturalization, he bluntly repelled anti-Catholic prejudices."[17] In Catholicism, he stated firmly, "there is nothing inconsistent with the purest Republicanism."[18]

Nowhere, however, is Madison's civic rationale for the godly republic more powerfully and plainly expressed than in the essays he wrote in defense of the proposed Constitution and in the language on religious freedom that he drafted for the First Amendment. Jefferson, Witherspoon, and the many framers whose Christian worldviews lay between the two were most completely at one in admiring Madison's ideas about the godly republic and in endorsing his associated handiwork as father and chief defender of the Constitution.

NO FAITH IS BEYOND FACTION

To help win ratification for the proposed Constitution in the New York state convention, Madison joined Alexander Hamilton and John Jay, under the pen name "Publius," in writing for New York City newspapers eighty-five articles ("op-ed" pieces in today's journalistic parlance) defending the document. Their political essays appeared from late 1787 through 1788. The identity of the authors was kept secret at the time, but we know that Madison authored or co-authored over two dozen of the pieces. Known collectively as the Federalist Papers, they probably played only a small role in securing ratification. But this commentary has since assumed monumental importance as an authoritative and profound explanation of the Constitution.

In his contributions to the Federalist Papers, Madison speaks eternal truth to future power regarding religion's proper role in the American republic. Witherspoon's influence on Madison is abundantly evident in the predominantly Calvinist-Christian worldview that asserts itself on nearly every page and informs nearly every famous phrase.

To wit: Madison writes that "there is a degree of depravity in mankind which requires a certain degree of circumspection and distrust" (No. 55); recommends a governmental structure designed to pit "ambition against ambition" (No. 51); worries that the "infirmities and depravities of the human character" make it exceedingly difficult for even well-meaning citizens to tame "mutual jealousies" or reconcile "discordant opinions" (No. 37); and warns that "enlightened statesmen" dedicated to "the public good and private rights" will be rare because "self-love," even among the wisest and most well-intentioned souls, is normally sovereign over both "opinions" and "passions," and because the propensity to "vex and oppress each other" is "sown in the nature of man" (No. 10).[19]

Madison's bedrock ideas about the Constitution plainly reflect his Calvinist-Christian worldview. James Bryce, an English lord, was among the first observers to duly credit the connection. Next to the Frenchman Alexis de Tocqueville's *Democracy in America* (vol. I first published in 1835, vol. II in 1840), Bryce's *The American Commonwealth* (1888) is arguably the greatest nineteenth-century commentary on American government. Bryce heralds the "hearty Puritanism in the view of human nature which pervades the instrument of 1787. It is the work of men who believed in original sin and were resolved to leave open for transgressors no door which they could possibly shut."[20] True, and Madison's most famous contributions to the Federalist Papers often distinctly echo "the *Westminster Confession*, the creedal authority of English Calvinism," which, in a typical teaching, admonishes that even "a

Christian continues to 'will that which is evil' by 'reason of his remaining corruption.'"[21]

Calvinist-Christian to his intellectual core, Madison thought it foolish to suppose that either Christian beliefs shared by rulers or Christian pieties practiced by the people would prove sufficient to keep the faithful from forming power-seeking "factions" that threatened freedom.[22] Americans, he had no doubt, had been specially favored by Providence in their break with Britain, and America could become an exceptional godly republic. A moment's "pious reflection," he wrote in the third solo-authored article he contributed to the Federalist Papers, would have one perceive "a finger of that Almighty hand" that had been "so frequently and signally extended to our relief in the critical stages of the revolution."[23]

Just the same, Madison admonished, Americans needed to humbly acknowledge that they were no different from any other people with respect to sinful human nature. Americans—both "We the People" and "our Posterity"—were assumed to be no less fundamentally flawed by nature, and hence no more likely to always hear and obediently heed God, than any other people, past, present, or future: "When the Almighty himself condescends to address mankind in their own language, his meaning, luminous as it must be, is rendered dim and doubtful by the cloudy medium through which it is communicated."[24] Only "theoretic politicians" could ignore the civic lesson implied by this spiritual reality, namely, the need to frame the new government in ways calculated to detect, deter, and defeat any faction, whether a majority or a minority, whether religious or secular, that coveted power to serve its members' self-loving purposes.

Thus, as Witherspoon's prize pupil and lifelong intellectual disciple, Madison believed that only "a constitution that acknowledges this fallen nature of humanity and constructs 'checks and balances' to ameliorate its negative consequences can hope to avoid political oppression of one sort or another."[25] Witherspoon's classical formulation about republics, liberty, virtue, and religion was never far from Madison's mind.

Still, neither when Madison was drafting the Constitution nor at other moments did he ever succumb to Witherspoon's view that "true religion" (orthodox Christianity per se) should enjoy a special civic status in America. Neither, however, did he follow Jefferson's claim (in the draft constitution for Virginia) that Christian ministers should be prohibited from holding public office. "Does not," he pointedly replied to Jefferson, "the exclusion of Ministers of the Gospel as such violate a fundamental principle of liberty by punishing a religious profession with the privation of a civil right?"[26]

When it came to religious pluralism, Madison, not Jefferson, was the more orthodox republican precisely because he was also the more orthodox Christian. Original sin, he believed, was real. It had followed the English settlers to the New World. To secure freedom and "a more perfect Union" in America, to translate colonial Puritanism into a national republicanism for the ages, government had to respect, promote, and protect religious pluralism.

Thus, in his two most famous articles, Federalist Papers Nos. 10 and 51, Madison outlined the civic case for founding a new government that he hoped and prayed would guide, not guarantee, America's rise as a godly republic defined by religious diversity.[27]

In No. 10, Madison began by observing that "a well constructed Union" can "break and control the violence of faction." He defined a faction as any group of citizens who attempt to advance their ideas or economic interests either at the expense of other citizens' rights or in ways that conflict with "the permanent and aggregate interests of the community" or "public good." It is, he reasoned, folly to try to defeat factions by removing whatever caused them to arise in the first place. "Liberty is to faction what air is to fire," and to extinguish liberty would be a "cure worse than the disease."

Government could try to make all citizens share the same ideas and economic interests, but the effort would crash against the "diversity in the faculties of citizens"; some are smarter or more hardworking than others. Besides, even if everyone shared the same ideas and economic interests, citizens would still "fall into mutual animosities." Sinful human nature is such that even "the most frivolous and fanciful distinctions" are "sufficient to kindle . . . unfriendly passions" and to "excite . . . violent conflicts." Madison listed a "zeal for different opinions concerning religion" first among the "latent causes of faction" that no government could ever completely erase.

So Madison proposed a second way of defeating faction, not by removing its causes but by "controlling its effects." As America expanded and became home to ever more diverse citizens with widely varying economic interests and ideas, factions could be controlled by having them cooperate or compete with each other under the new government's evenhanded stewardship. The Constitution proposed a form of national government that was likely to serve the public good through the "regulation of these various and interfering interests." The Constitution's sacred civic mission was to "adjust these clashing interests and render them all subservient to the public good." The method to achieve this mission was to establish a republic rather than a pure or direct democracy.

A republic, unlike a pure or direct democracy, is "a government in which the scheme of representation takes place," delegating government decision-making "to a small number of citizens elected by the rest." A pure or direct democracy can only govern a relatively small territory, but a republic can govern a much "greater number of citizens" over "a greater sphere of country." Moreover, in "extensive republics" spread out over vast territories, citizens are less likely to choose as their national representatives men with "factious tempers" colored by "local prejudices" and more likely to "center on men who possess the most attractive merit and the most diffusive and established characters."

There was, however, an even more important advantage to the "extended" republican form of national government proposed under the Constitution. "Extend the sphere," Madison preached, "and you take in a greater variety of parties and interests," thereby making it "less probable that a majority" will find "a common motive to invade the rights of other citizens" or, "if such a common motive exists," rendering the majority faction, whatever its genesis in ideas or interests, less able to enlist the national government's support in exploiting or tyrannizing other citizens.

Fittingly, Madison's first and foremost illustration concerned religiously based factions and prescribed religious pluralism. He wrote, "A religious sect may degenerate into a political faction in a part of the Confederacy; but the variety of sects dispersed over the entire face of it must secure the national councils against any danger from that source."

MADISON'S MULTIPLICITY OF SECTS VERSUS THE ANTI-FEDERALISTS

In No. 51, Madison was even more explicit in linking the new republic's fate to its tendency to respect, promote, and protect religious pluralism. His crowning passage on the multiplicity of sects is as fresh and true today as when he wrote it:

> In a free government the security for civil rights must be the same as that for religious rights. It consists in the one case in the multiplicity of interests, and in the other in the multiplicity of sects. The degree of security in both cases will depend on the number of interests and sects; and this may be presumed to depend on the extent of the country and number of people comprehended under the same government.

Neither Witherspoon the orthodox Christian nor Jefferson the self-styled Deist would have written these exact words. Neither of Madison's mentors would have framed or defended the Constitution precisely as did their protégé and friend. Yet both Witherspoon and Jefferson agreed that Madison was right about the proposed Constitution, right about how the new republic should encourage religious expression, and right about how the national government should seek to seed, sustain, and support religious pluralism.

Witherspoon "approved of Madison's adaptation of his ideas into the new constitution."[28] To a young Princeton faculty colleague, Witherspoon characterized the Constitution "as embracing principles and carrying into effect measures, which he had long advocated, as essential to the preservation of liberties, and the promotion of the peace and prosperity of the country."[29] The most exhaustive studies to date document Witherspoon's "pro-Constitution sentiments and activities, and provide ample proof that Witherspoon was a vigorous Federalist both in and out of the New Jersey ratifying convention."[30] The Old Doctor was genuinely pleased with his Princeton pupil, and died grateful for the godly republic and its "multiplicity of sects."

Madison was more worried that Jefferson, not Witherspoon, would dislike the proposed Constitution. Would Jefferson disdain how "Publius" had defended its key provisions? Would he reject the overarching case for a multiplicity of sects or react against the fact that even orthodox Christian ministers would be free to compete for national public office? Not until the Constitution was ratified did Madison reveal to Jefferson his role in writing the Federalist Papers. As it turned out, Madison had worried in vain. Once Jefferson read the articles, he baptized them the "best commentary on the principles of government which ever was written."[31]

Unlike the more pragmatic Madison, Jefferson harbored theoretical misgivings about any political compact based on popular consent that purported to bind a people to a particular frame of government for more than a single generation (calculated with pseudo-scientific rigor by Jefferson to mean any period longer than 19 years).[32] Still, Jefferson regarded the proposed Constitution as "unquestionably the wisest ever yet presented to men."[33]

During the ratification struggles in Virginia and other states, Jefferson was in France. Among the many leading public figures who opposed the Constitution was Virginia's Patrick Henry, famous for the words "Give me liberty or give me death." In Virginia's ratification debate, Henry made selective and unauthorized public use of some of Jefferson's private letters, using Jefferson's "name against parts of the Constitution which he really approved."[34]

Naturally, Jefferson was upset by such intrigues, but what he really disdained were the factious, party-like clashes over the proposed Constitution. These bitter political battles had broken out between like-hearted patriots who only a decade earlier had clung to each other in the War for Independence. Jefferson declared that he was neutral, not on the Constitution's clear-cut merits, but between the two main contending parties— the so-called Federalists, like Madison, who supported the Constitution, and the so-called Anti-Federalists, like Henry, who opposed it. Were he forced, however, to pick a side, he would stand squarely with Madison, the Constitution, and the multiplicity of sects: "If I could not go to heaven but with a party, I would not go at all. . . . I am not of the party of the federalists. But I am much farther from that of the Antifederalists."[35]

Still, Jefferson shared the Anti-Federalists' concern that, at some future point, the "consolidation of the government" wrought by the Constitution might jeopardize states' rights.[36] In the Federalist Papers Madison had wrestled mightily with this critical concern. For instance, in No. 39 he painstakingly described how the Constitution "is, in strictness, neither a national nor a federal constitution, but a composition of both," creating a "compound" republic.[37] He argued that, even with the Constitution's "supremacy" clause (No. 44),[38] the states, not the national government, would retain most powers unrelated to interstate commerce and foreign relations (No. 45).[39] He intimated that the national government's powers would probably grow as the people became "more partial to the federal than to the state governments," but he insisted that the Constitution would nonetheless perpetually empower the states to stymie the "ambitious encroachments of the federal government" (No. 46).[40]

With such arguments, Madison largely persuaded Jefferson, but he failed to persuade Henry and the Anti-Federalists, among them several other great patriots like Samuel Adams of Massachusetts. Henry, Adams, and other Anti-Federalist leaders worked tirelessly, if unsuccessfully, to prevent the Constitution from being ratified.

The Anti-Federalists' core counterargument was that, for all its power-limiting and power-dividing features, the national government proposed by the Constitution was too strong and too centralized. They predicted that, in time, the compound republic would become the consolidated republic. The national government would absorb powers and functions that once belonged solely to the states. Congress would tax heavily, the Supreme Court would overrule state courts, and the president would come to head a large military establishment.

Since all of these things have happened, and with men like Henry and Sam Adams in their ranks, the Anti-Federalists cannot be ignored or dismissed as cranks or crackpots. Nor can the Anti-Federalists be pigeonholed as men united by narrow regional interests (they drew leaders from every state), by selfish economic interests (although some had land and financial capital, many had very little), or by antebellum solicitude for slavery (abolition-leaning Anti-Federalists, both north and south, would bloody any nose that dared to suggest as much).

Rather, the Anti-Federalists were united by their belief that the Constitution's mechanisms for making "ambition counteract ambition" would not work. They were united, as well, by their fear that the national government's "ambitious encroachments" against the states would prevail. Most profoundly, however, the Anti-Federalists were united by their visceral reactions against the Federalists' forward-looking vision of America as a large national republic encompassing diverse economic interests and a multiplicity of sects. Under this vision, rural life would recede as urban manufacturers rose. Christianity would ever be or long remain most citizens' respected old-time religion but would never be the country's official creed backed by the Constitution and favored by federal law.

Madison proposed controlling all factions including religious groups by having the national government evenhandedly regulate "these varying and interfering interests." The Anti-Federalists, however, were the era's religious conservatives. They wanted a national government that would reinforce such social, economic, and religious homogeneity as characterized each state. "For most Anti-Federalists a republican system required similarity of religion, morals, sentiments and interests."[41] The Anti-Federalists reflexively favored preserving religious homogeneity in each state, not stimulating religious pluralism throughout the land or inviting any present or future multiplicity of sects.

In a typical Anti-Federalist pamphlet, "Agrippa" opposed open immigration to America so that Pennsylvanians and the peoples of other sovereign states could "keep their blood pure" and preserve "their religion and their morals."[42] Even a few founders who were as pro-Constitution and as far removed from religious orthodoxy and romantic localism as the tolerant and cosmopolitan Benjamin Franklin, could on rare occasions stain their otherwise sterling civic legacies with such outbursts.[43] Among the Anti-Federalists were many towering intellects whose Christian morals strictly condemned such prejudices.

Still, the Anti-Federalists "were by and large less well educated and more intensely religious than the Federalists."[44] Too often, xenophobia and zealous intolerance marked their civic discourse about religion and government in America. Even the Anti-Federalists' leading latter-day academic apologist, the University of Chicago's Herbert J. Storing, emphasizes that "Agrippa" and company were against the Constitution largely because they were *for* states preserving their respective homogeneous religious cultures and local moral folkways.[45]

For instance, a Massachusetts Anti-Federalist was among the many who howled at the proposed Constitution's no-religious-test-for-federal-office provision, fretting that it made "a papist, or an infidel . . . as eligible" for national public service as Christians.[46] Similarly, a North Carolina Anti-Federalist protested that "pagans, deists, and Mahometans might obtain offices among us."[47] Another Anti-Federalist asserted that since Christianity was uniquely fit for producing good citizens, "those gentlemen who formed this Constitution should not have given this invitation to Jews and Heathens."[48] Yet another Anti-Federalist declared that without "Christian piety and morals" the Constitution would result in "slavery and ruin," and so urged the national government to institute exclusively Christian "means of education" for the public.[49]

Most Anti-Federalists, however, were willing to compromise: Madison and the Federalists could have their large republic with diverse economic interests (including urban manufacturers) and a multiplicity of sects (including non-Christians and nonbelievers) so long as the national government was constitutionally forbidden from interfering with states' rights. This included the right to keep or establish a particular religion as a state's official religion, if the state's legislators and citizens so desired.

In the proposed Constitution, the Anti-Federalists identified two main threats to states' rights and states' sovereignty regarding religion. One threat, they argued, was immediate: the awesome powers already assigned to the U.S. Congress. The other threat, they insisted, was long term: the insidious powers likely to be acquired by the U.S. Supreme Court. Neither threat, they demurred, had been honestly acknowledged or adequately addressed by Madison and the Federalists.

The Anti-Federalists were suspicious of Madison and many other Federalists, and not without reasonable cause. Alexander Hamilton, Madison's co-author on several contributions to the Federalist Papers, was considered by many Anti-Federalists to be an irreligious "closet monarchist" who favored a unified national government dominated by the executive branch and with sovereign powers over the states. In fact, as a New York State delegate to the Convention, Hamilton had made a long speech arguing for something quite similar to elective monarchy. He favored a consolidated national government that vested great powers in an "energetic" presidency.

In the 1770s, Hamilton was also the primary voice for turning America into the world's leading manufacturing nation, complete with urban workforces and global finances. Having advanced this vision as the nation's first secretary of the treasury under President George Washington, Hamilton was convinced that the many compromises foisted on the Convention by both Anti-Federalists and pro-Constitution delegates from smaller states had almost fatally weakened the national government. He privately called the Constitution "frail and worthless," but in public he defended it with vigor because he deemed all the politically possible alternatives to be even worse.

Madison suffered from more than mere guilt by association with Hamilton. Madison was no monarchist and no siren for a strong executive. Still, he had entered the Convention advocating the so-called Virginia Plan. Under this strong-government blueprint, Congress would have had the power to veto acts of state legislatures. Unlike Hamilton, however, Madison truly warmed to the Constitution that he defended. As the Virginia Plan bled, he bargained. He soon developed a convert's zeal for the compromises necessitated by the political divides of the Convention.

Even during the heated ratification struggles, Madison's Calvinist-Christian rationale for the Constitution resonated with many Anti-Federalists. The passage in the Federalist Papers that best captures this rationale, and best defines American constitutionalism itself, appears in No. 51:

> But what is government itself but the greatest of all reflections on human nature? If men were angels, no government would be necessary. If angels were to govern men, neither internal nor external controls on government would be necessary. In framing a government which is to be administered by men over men, the great difficulty lies in this: you must first enable the government to control the governed; and in the next place oblige it to control itself.[50]

This constitutional credo drew few opponents. Where the Anti-Federalists parted ways with Madison was in insisting that the proposed Constitution did not, in fact, do nearly enough to oblige the national government "to control itself."

The Anti-Federalists' immediate concern was that Congress would enact laws to eradicate powers and functions that had long been enjoyed by the state governments. They correctly noted that the Constitution's Article I (longer than all the document's other sections combined) gave Congress potentially unlimited powers, both in absolute terms and relative to powers assigned to the presidency by Article II. They were sick at the thought of a monarchy-like presidency. And they were certain that the Court would yield black-robed tyrants. But they rightly determined that the Constitution made Congress far and away first in power and authority among the three "co-equal" branches of national government.

After all, in the U.S. Congress were vested the new republic's ultimate powers to lay taxes, spend money, and make all laws deemed by national representatives to be "necessary and proper" to effecting the body's own enumerated powers. Congress also held "all other powers vested by this Constitution in the government of the United States, and in any department or officer thereof " (Article I, Section 8, final paragraph).

Thus, the Anti-Federalists rationally feared that, should Congress ever deem states' rights to be in conflict with the "more perfect Union" referenced in the Constitution's Preamble, then states' rights might suffer in matters ranging from regulating commerce to sponsoring religion, from determining state voters' rights to delineating the rights of criminal defendants. Most thought that this would happen sooner rather than later: Hamilton and his fellow Federalists (many not nearly as sympathetic as Madison to Anti-Federalist concerns or as willing to compromise) were likely to dominate the first Congress and the new Cabinet departments.

MOST BLESSED COMPROMISE: THE BILL OF RIGHTS

Fortunately for all concerned, the Anti-Federalists, the pro-Constitution small-state delegates to the Convention, and the Federalists ultimately compromised in ways that reduced fears about the eradication of states' rights. One consequential compromise resulted in the provision that gave small states like Delaware and Georgia equal representation in the Senate (Article I, Section 3), accompanied by the clause that placed the foregoing provision outside of the normal amendment process (Article V, specifying "that no state, without its consent, shall be deprived of its equal suffrage in the Senate").

The other major compromise wrought by the Anti-Federalists was the Bill of Rights. In the penultimate article of the Federalist Papers (No. 84), Hamilton had given no quarter to the Anti-Federalists' objection that the proposed Constitution contained no bill of rights. He noted that New York State's constitution had no bill of rights, either. He delineated the numerous "particular privileges and rights" already provided in the Constitution's body.[51] He lectured that "bills of rights are, in their origin, stipulations between kings and their subjects" and hence have no place in a Constitution "professedly founded upon the power of the people and executed by their immediate representatives and servants."[52]

Hamilton's most dismissive argument concerned not past precedents but future dangers. He stressed that to include "a minute detail of particular rights" in the Constitution would be perversely to imply that the national government's power extended beyond "the general political interests of the nation" to "every species of personal and private concerns. . . . Why, for instance, should it be said that the liberty of the press shall not be restrained, when no power is given by which restrictions may be imposed? . . . [T]he Constitution is itself, in every rational sense, and to every useful purpose, a BILL OF RIGHTS."[53]

The Anti-Federalists bought little of this. Had they known that Hamilton was behind these arguments, they would have bought even less. Madison, however, quickly relented with but a few reservations. He and other Federalists promised small-state Convention delegates and Anti-Federalist friends that they would personally see to it that the Constitution, immediately after it was ratified in its proposed form, would be amended by a broad bill of rights. By the spring of 1790 all thirteen states had ratified the Constitution, and Madison moved at once to keep the promise. In the first session of the first Congress he introduced a set of proposals, many based upon the existing Virginia Bill of Rights.

The process was hardly simple. Proposals flew from all directions. Both the new Constitution's old friends and its unrepentant foes drafted long, complex amendments and demanded serious hearings for them. In all, nearly two hundred amendments were proposed. Madison took the lead in helping to pen meaningful but concise amendments that were likely to spark consensus. Twelve amendments were approved by Congress; ten of these were ratified by the states and went into effect in 1791.

Nine of the ten amendments that constitute the Bill of Rights can be usefully grouped into three categories: protections against arbitrary police and court action (Amendments 4 through 8), protections of states' rights and unnamed rights of people (Amendments 9 and 10), and protections of specific property rights (Amendments 2 and 3 protect citizens' rights to bear arms and to refuse one's home to troops in peacetime).

Only the First Amendment, however, protects citizens' rights to participate in the political process:

> Congress shall make no law respecting an establishment of religion, or prohibiting the free exercise thereof; or abridging the freedom of speech, or of the press; or the right of the people peaceably to assemble, and to petition the government for a redress of grievances.

Take note: "*Congress* shall make no law. . . . " When and as ratified, the First Amendment, and the rest of the Bill of Rights, did not limit the power of state governments over citizens. Rather, the First Amendment, and the rest of the Bill of Rights, limited only the power of the national government. As stated plainly in the monumental early twentieth-century work on the Constitution by Princeton scholar Edward S. Corwin, the Bill of Rights was originally designed to "bind only the National Government and in no wise limit the powers of the States of their own independent force."[54]

Take note once again: "Congress shall make no law respecting an establishment of *religion*, or prohibiting the free exercise thereof." The First Amendment mentioned religion first, even before speech. It featured two separate religion clauses: an "establishment of religion" clause and a "free exercise" clause. The First Amendment prohibited the national government, not state governments, from establishing a religion or restricting religious practices. As Lord Bryce marveled, it allowed a state to "establish a particular form of religion" and to "endow a particular form of religion, or educational or charitable establishments connected therewith."[55]

The two religion clauses in the First Amendment did not fall from heaven complete and unchallenged. There were drafts upon drafts of proposals. What is striking, however, is that many of the various drafts, whether proposed by Federalists or Anti-Federalists, embodied similar ideas and sentiments about religion and government in the new republic. For instance, Madison's fellow Virginian George Mason attended the Convention but refused to sign the Constitution. Mason, however, is the Anti-Federalist regarded by many as father of the Bill of Rights. Mason drafted Jefferson-like language invoking the natural right to religious freedom and specifying that neither Christianity, nor any particular Christian sect, should be privileged by the Constitution or under federal laws. For the Federalists' part, Madison wanted the First Amendment's religion clauses to read as follows:

> The civil rights of none shall be abridged on account of religious belief or worship, nor shall any national religion be established.

Had either Mason's or Madison's preferred language been adopted, perhaps the secular state and Christian nation myths would have done less to cloud the founders' faithful consensus that America is meant to be a godly republic marked by religious pluralism.

Then again, even the First Amendment's actual religion clauses, obtuse as they are, make plain the framers' desire that citizens' religious rights and liberties must be respected, not reviled, by the national government and that no particular religion may ever be endorsed or established as the nation's official religion, or supported as such by federal officials or tax dollars.

NEO-ANTI-FEDERALISTS VERSUS JUDICIAL TYRANNY

Begat by political compromise, the Bill of Rights promised by Madison quieted "the fears of mild opponents of the Constitution."[56] The First Amendment's two religion clauses satisfied widely respected statesmen on both sides (including the Virginians Mason and Madison) and kept the

Anti-Federalists who had cursed Madison's multiplicity of sects from damning the Constitution. After 1791 only inveterate Anti-Federalists would insist that the national government give special treatment to Christianity and Christian sects. Together with the rest of the Bill of Rights, the two religion clauses were from the first, and remain to this day, a great national blessing. Without them, America would not have become, and could not remain, a godly republic.

Yet the compromise could not hold perfectly, or hold forever. The Anti-Federalists feared Congress and fretted over the presidency, but they hated the Supreme Court and the federal judiciary. It was a hate fueled by fear of the unknown—and the unelected.

The proposed Constitution (Article III) had said little about the extent of judicial power. It gave justices lifetime tenure pending good behavior. It specified the types of cases that the federal courts would oversee. It explicitly tethered and limited the Supreme Court's appellate jurisdiction (its right to hear cases on appeal from lower federal courts) to the legislature's will (Article III, Section 2, paragraph 2). Still, it left completely open critical questions concerning the federal judiciary's role, if any, in deciding whether democratically enacted federal laws were constitutional.

Given the Constitution's language about the supremacy of national law, this silence seemed ominous. Thus, even after the Bill of Rights was ratified, many Anti-Federalists continued to read Article III as a semisecret Federalist plan to assert control over state governments via federal judges. In the Federalist Papers (No. 78), Hamilton had done little more than to pooh-pooh the Anti-Federalists' concerns about the Supreme Court and other federal judges:

> Whoever attentively considers the different departments of power must perceive that, in a government in which they are separated from each other, the judiciary, from the nature of its functions, will always be the least dangerous to the political rights of the Constitution. . . . [The judiciary] has no influence over either the sword or the purse. . . . It may truly be said to have neither FORCE nor WILL but merely judgment.[57]

With pen names such as "Brutus," Anti-Federalist pamphleteers ripped into the Federalists' ostensible plot for judicial tyranny. Some

went so far as to raise the possibility that federal judges would soon shat-
ter the Constitution's checks and balances, outlaw elections, and end by
enthroning themselves as the New World's imperial monarchs.

While the Anti-Federalists' worst nightmares about judicial tyranny
have not been realized, they made three specific predictions about how
the Supreme Court would exercise its powers. Their first two predictions
have proven to be perspicacious; the third, though hardly without any serious merit, has been, and continues to be, exaggerated.

First, the Anti-Federalists predicted that the Court would assume the
power to declare acts of the legislature as well as of the executive branch
unconstitutional and hence null and void. Before the Constitution was a
half-decade old, the Court did just that in *Marbury v. Madison* (1803).
While the Court has used this power sparingly in its history (only a few
hundred laws have been declared unconstitutional in over two centuries),
federal elected officials are ever cognizant of the possibility that a policy
might be deemed unconstitutional and so normally seek before the fact to
avoid any serious clash with the Court.

Second, the Anti-Federalists predicted that the Court would overrule
state laws and use novel arguments to justify doing so. This began to happen after the Civil War. The Fourteenth Amendment, ratified in 1868, provided that no state shall "deprive any person of life, liberty, or property
without due process of law" (known as the "due process clause"). It also
specified that no state shall "deny to any person within its jurisdiction of
the equal protection of the laws" (known as the "equal protection
clause").

In the late 1890s, the Court began to use these two Fourteenth Amendment clauses as a way of applying certain provisions in the Bill of Rights
to the states. On a case-by-case basis, the twentieth-century Court invoked either due process or equal protection, or both, and thereby applied the Bill of Rights to the states. This process, known as selective incorporation (selectively applying the Bill of Rights to the states), is now
largely complete.

To wit: In 1925 in *Gitlow v. New York,* the Court ruled that the First
Amendment's guarantees of free speech and free press applied to the
states. In 1937 in *Palko v. Connecticut,* the Court declared that states must

honor all "fundamental" liberties. In 1940 in *Cantwell v. Connecticut*, the Court applied *Palko* to religious liberties. By the mid-twentieth century, the Court routinely held that the states must observe all fundamental freedoms and rights referenced in the Constitution. The only question was whether the Court deemed a given right or freedom to be "fundamental."

Today, the entire Bill of Rights (all amendments and provisions thereof) is applied by the Court to the states except for the Second Amendment (the right to bear arms), the Third Amendment (the right to refuse your home to troops in peacetime), the Fifth Amendment provision affording a right to be indicted by a grand jury before being tried for a serious crime, the Seventh Amendment provision affording a right to a jury trial in civil cases, and the Eighth Amendment provision banning excessive bail and fines.

So, the Anti-Federalists saw both judicial review and selective incorporation coming. Their third prediction, however, has proven to be less plainly perspicacious. With great alarm, they prophesied that the Constitution's failure to establish America as a Christian nation would eventually lead America to become a secular state.

The specter of judicial tyranny that haunted the Anti-Federalists centered upon the unelected and unaccountable Supreme Court. The misty logic of their civic nightmare went pretty much as follows: Corrupted by its ever-expanding and secretive powers, the Court would engineer a reverse national altar call. Having already kicked Christianity to the civic curb as just one American faith among many, Hamilton's "least dangerous branch," the federal judiciary, would work over time to confine all religions, and such multiplicity of sects as might emerge, to the purely private sphere. The end result for America's godly people, Christian and non-Christian alike, would be national government neutrality and equal protection in name only. Rather, the end result would be legalized hostility and discrimination against the Protestant majority (if there still was one) and all other God-fearing citizens. The faithless would form powerful factions. Federal judges would lead these antireligious minions. In due course, the Court would establish in America a secular Promised Land.

"Experience," counseled Madison in No. 20, "is the oracle of truth."[58] The truth, thank God, is far less sad or sinister, and far more favorable to

America's history and future as a godly republic, than the Anti-Federalists feared and than their present-day neo-Anti-Federalist disciples often seem determined beyond all reason to believe.

Yes, there have been many moments over the past century, some quite shocking and dramatic, when the Supreme Court has spoken as if America was supposed to be a supremely secular state. There have been many lower federal court decisions, such as the one referenced in this chapter's opening pages, that have distorted constitutional history and deified secular ideology. Many federal judges have legislated that government must uniquely restrict public religious expression, aggressively remove religious symbols from public spaces, and wantonly discriminate against sacred places even if they do nothing but serve others in society without regard to religion.

Yet these moments, decisions, and extreme opinions have been, and continue to be, exceptions to the civic rule that are contradicted by prevailing Court doctrine. Just as Madison and the framers hoped, the national government norm on religion remains court-enforced neutrality plus equal protection. The reality is that modern America is the happy home to a multiplicity of sects.

From sea to shining sea, Protestant Christianity remains the majority's religion, and many other religions have gathered strength right alongside the Protestant majority. Roman Catholics, Jews, Muslims, Mormons, and many other religious peoples feel welcome in the godly republic. Albeit imperfectly, the federal government does partner with religious congregations and religiously affiliated community groups to serve the common good. If anything, over the last several decades the federal bench has become more faith-friendly, and Washington's big bureaucracies have become less apt to discriminate unfairly against religious nonprofit organizations. Citizens of virtually every demographic description and representing nearly every socioeconomic status now favor religious pluralism and support church-state partnerships to effect public good. Top political leaders in both parties are openly religious and support neutrality and equal protection. Even the hypersecular, elite academic community has responded to empirical data that proves that faith-based organizations are critical to mobilizing volunteers and helping the nation's needy.

Still, today some religious leaders loudly insist that judicial tyranny has overtaken the founders' faithful consensus. Some have gone so far as to intimate that adverse, antidemocratic court rulings ought to be ignored or resisted by whatever means are necessary. As chapter 2 suggests, this neo-Anti-Federalist cry is not entirely baseless, but it is highly overblown. Or, as Madison might have one say, it prescribes incendiary cures for an imaginary disease.

TWO The Court's Neutrality Doctrine

Myth 3   The U.S. Supreme Court insists that religious expression is strictly prohibited in or around government institutions like public schools, and that government involvement in or support for religious organizations is constitutionally impermissible.

Myth 4   The U.S. Supreme Court insists that religious expression is freely permitted in or around government institutions like public schools, and that government involvement in or support for religious organizations is constitutionally permissible.

TRUTH   The U.S. Supreme Court insists that government must give religious expression and organizations the same basic protections that it offers to nonreligious expression and organizations, and that government must also strive to be neutral when dealing with different religions.

BLESSINGS IN THE BALANCE

On January 8, 2006, some of the nation's best-known conservative religious leaders—Dr. James Dobson and the Reverend Jerry Falwell, to name just two—joined top government officials including Pennsylvania's junior U.S. senator, Rick Santorum, for an open-to-the-press rally inside Greater Exodus Baptist Church in north Philadelphia. The event was billed as "Justice Sunday, III." The church's pastor, Reverend Dr. Herbert H. Lusk III, commenced with preaching that inspired the speakers and fired up the crowd. Sermon by sermon, the speakers urged the Senate to confirm Samuel Alito as a U.S. Supreme Court justice. The time had come, they repeated over and over again, to end the Court's decades-old judicial tyranny against orthodox Christians and their organizations.

If you were to take a look around from the very pulpit where these cries about judicial tyranny rang out, here is what you would see. Just south on the same block is a big community bank owned and operated by the church. Just north on the same street is a public charter school launched by the church's leaders and approved by the state's authorities. In between is a community-serving nonprofit organization, People for People, led by the congregation's faithful. Over the years, to do good works in the surrounding low-income community, People for People has received millions of dollars in government grants as well as much support from private foundations and secular nonprofit organizations. Directly across the street is a building operated by the Salvation Army, a famous international orthodox Christian religious denomination dedicated to serving the needy and neglected. In America, the Salvation Army's adult rehabilitation centers for drug and alcohol addicts and other programs have long received government financial support and technical assistance.

Many in the secular media and the Democratic party blasted the Justice Sunday event, and bashed Lusk, the conservative Republican black pastor who hosted it, for mixing religion with politics. That is something they rarely notice when historically significant urban black churches feature religious progressives and Democratic leaders. One local liberal paper intoned that the event's civic sin was to make it seem that "across racial and economic lines" a national majority supported certain "stands" favored by the visiting evangelical notables.[1] In fact, on same-sex marriage and several other controversial issues, a diverse majority-opinion coalition is closer than not to the Christian conservatives' views.

Silly double standards aside, the event's real civic sin was to bury beneath judicial tyranny rhetoric the truth about the Court's neutrality doctrine. Sincere as they were, the Justice Sunday faithful let the nightmare be father to the thought. They spoke as if the present-day Court's prevailing church-state doctrine was strict and total separation (Myth #3). In reply, their secular liberal detractors vented an opposite and equally baseless nightmare. They spoke as if the contemporary Court was close to razing all remaining constitutional barriers against church-state collaboration and giving religious groups special treatment (Myth #4).

In truth, despite renegade rulings that have been hostile to religious citizens in general and to Christians in particular (first Catholics, then Evangelicals), the Court's prevailing neutrality doctrine protects religious worship as well as wider religious expression. Blessed by citizen-volunteers and public-spirited leaders like those at Greater Exodus Baptist Church and the Salvation Army, community-serving religious or religiously affiliated organizations can and do receive government grants and other public support. From coast to coast, so do myriad other Christian and non-Christian organizations that supply social services. Today, sacred places that serve civic purposes in partnership with government enjoy the same fundamental legal protections, and are subject to the same basic administrative requirements, as tax-exempt secular nonprofit organizations.

As I argued publicly at the time, Alito was a worthy appointment to a Court that still has a few members whose religion-clauses jurisprudence remains stuck in the secular state myth.[2] Still, the Court did not need a new member to exorcise the historically groundless doctrine that the First Amendment's two religion clauses plainly mandate strict and total separation. The Court's decades-old neutrality doctrine was in the works soon after the ink dried on its least defensible mid-twentieth-century church-state decisions. In most religion cases since 1980, the Court has imperfectly but faithfully applied neutrality principles and equal protection logic.

Even acknowledging occasional judicial backsliding from neutrality and equal protection, there is simply no reasonable way to conclude that either orthodox Christians or other religious believers are today beset by judicial tyrants. Godly people in America are not judicially relegated to second-class citizenship. Nor are they wantonly discriminated against when it comes to their organizations' tax-exempt status or treatment by government as nonprofit organizations.

It is nearer to the truth to say that government at all levels—federal, state, and local—has yet to catch up with the Court's neutrality doctrine. Less through active antireligious bias than through outdated ideas about what the Constitution requires, less from ideological contempt for religious institutions than from intellectual confusion bred by real and perceived inconsistencies in Court decisions, government bodies from local public schools to federal Cabinet departments have been slow to internalize and apply neutrality principles. As discussed in the next chapter, this seems especially true for federal and state grant-making government bureaucracies vis-à-vis grassroots community-serving religious groups.

These remaining problems can be largely overcome. The way to overcome them is to follow the founders' constitutional compass on religion and to see to it that the contemporary Court's neutrality doctrine is widely understood by citizens and faithfully followed by government officials, both elected and appointed. The place to begin is with the undeniable and unvarnished historical truth about the secular state myth. The truth is that the wall-of-separation doctrine was erected on a rabidly anti-Catholic foundation by people who wanted to polarize Americans for political purposes.

STRICT SEPARATION DOCTRINE'S ANTI-CATHOLIC ROOTS

As mentioned in chapter 1, the words "wall of separation" do not appear anywhere in the original Constitution or in any amendments to the Constitution. The First Amendment, led by its two religion clauses, reads in its entirety:

> Congress shall make no law respecting an establishment of religion, or prohibiting the free exercise thereof; or abridging the freedom of speech, or of the press; or the right of the people to peaceably assemble, and to petition the government for a redress of grievances.

The "wall" metaphor was penned by Thomas Jefferson on January 1, 1802, in a letter to Baptists in Danbury, Connecticut, a Federalist party stronghold. The Danbury Baptists were worried that their civil rights as a religious minority were being threatened and that the national government might also weigh in against them. President Jefferson's reassuring letter contained this fateful sentence:

> I contemplate with solemn reverence that act of the whole American people which declared that their legislature should "make no law respecting the establishment of religion, or prohibiting the free exercise thereof," thus building a wall of separation between Church & State.

By "their legislature" Jefferson was referring to Congress. Only a strictly off-the-wall interpretation could convert those reassuring words about the national government duly respecting a religious minority into a radical call for strict and total separation between church and state. As discussed in chapter 1, during the Constitutional Convention, the ratification struggles, and the First Amendment debates, neither Jefferson nor any other Framer ever advocated any such thing. Three decades later, during the 1820s, Madison, as an elder statesman, sometimes "used varying phrases that indicated his desire not merely for a conventional disestablishment, but for some broader sort of disconnection between religion and government or between church and state."[3] That, however, is about as close to historical support for wall-of-separation notions as one can get, and it is not close at all. As law scholar Philip Hamburger has concluded, "the constitutional authority for separation is without historical foundation."[4]

As Hamburger details, strict separation as a court doctrine was supported by political strange-bedfellows who were united mainly by anti-Catholicism. The plot thickened in the late nineteenth century. One faction consisted largely of the era's secular-minded liberal elites. They wanted to rid all religious influences from public schools. They also feared that the Catholic Church and its priestly "superstitions" might seduce the modern American masses just as it had seduced medieval European masses. The other faction was made up mainly of Protestant conservatives and associated anti-immigration nativists. They wanted public schools to remain de facto Protestant institutions, complete with Protestant school prayers. They also feared that Catholics would first challenge their religious hegemony over the schools and then challenge their cultural supremacy throughout American society. The two factions entered into an anti-Catholic marriage of political convenience.

National politicians heard, and several embraced, the liberal-nativist faction's anti-Catholic cause. For instance, in December 1875 President Grant "appealed to liberal and nativist sentiment by proposing constitutional amendments in favor of separation."[5] The next week, James G. Blaine, a Maine Republican U.S. House member who was running for president, sank even lower. Blaine rewrote the First Amendment in the way he deemed best calculated to be "most popular with anti-Catholic voters."[6] He drafted "an anti-Catholic measure that still permitted a generalized Protestantism in public schools so long as it was not the Protestantism of any one sect."[7]

Blaine failed to win the Republican presidential nomination; he was beaten by Rutherford B. Hayes. But his strict-separation, anti-Catholic constitutional amendment was featured in the Republican party platform.[8] The "Republicans hoped to transcend sectional divisions by embracing sectarian strife—a strategy that would unite not only liberal and nativist sentiment but also North and South in a campaign against Catholicism."[9]

Blaine's amendment passed in the House (180 to 7) and fell just two votes short in the Senate.[10] Unable to add a "separation" amendment to the federal Constitution, anti-Catholic politicians pandering to the liberal-nativist faction began inserting what became known as Blaine amendments in state constitutions. (Read your own state's constitution—chances are it contains one.)

In the mid-twentieth century, decades after "Nativists, Liberals, and Republicans had demanded separation," the Blaine amendment's strict-separation letter and anti-Catholic spirit were clumsily grafted onto the federal Constitution by Hugo Black.[11] Justice Black, a former Klansman whose "distaste for Catholicism" followed him onto the federal bench, gave the anti-Catholic creed a false claim to constitutional legitimacy.[12] He was the first U.S. Supreme Court justice to "clearly make separation the basis for a decision."[13] The sad and sordid historical details about Black's pre- and post-Klan anti-Catholic shenanigans, and his decision's disgraceful genesis, are beyond serious dispute.[14] Rather than dwell on them, it is more fruitful for our purposes (and, in a forgiving Catholic spirit reflecting "fraternal correction," a bit more charitable to Black's memory) to focus on the decision itself.

Writing for the Court in 1947, Black bent and stretched Jefferson's "wall" metaphor into a faux historical rationale for the view that the Constitution required strict church-state separation. The case, *Everson v. Board of Education of the Township of Ewing*, was brought by a "patriotic organization" in New Jersey that "restricted membership to white, native-born Americans."[15] Its mission statement described it as being for "free education," against "any union of Church and State," and (the most precious part) for keeping "the Public School System" free from "sectarian interference" the better "to uphold the reading of the Holy Bible therein."[16] The nativists objected that a New Jersey township (Ewing) had used tax dollars to reimburse parents for the costs of transporting their children to local Catholic schools.

Black declared that the First Amendment's Establishment clause applied, via the Fourteenth Amendment, to the states. This meant, he ruled, that the government cannot require a person to profess a belief or disbelief in any religion; it cannot aid one religion, some religions, or all religions; and it cannot spend any tax money, however small the amount, in support of any religious activities or institutions.

In the next pen stroke, however, Black "astonished" his Court brethren.[17] He leapt straight from the strict, no-aid separation standard to the conclusion that the Constitution nonetheless permitted New Jersey's subsidized busing. One justice (Robert Jackson) dissented that Black's "advocating complete and uncompromising separation" was "utterly discordant" with his "conclusion yielding support" to church-state "commingling in educational matters."[18]

But Black "understood what he was doing," namely, sacrificing legal logic in the hope that he could thereby "make separation the unanimous standard for the Court while reaching a judgment that would undercut Catholic criticism."[19] He "expected that his disarming conclusion" would fool Catholics into thinking that "they had staved off the practical consequences of separation."[20]

Apparently, Black thought Catholics were not only very dangerous but also quite dumb. He was as wrong as he could be on both counts. His politically calibrated legal illogic rapidly backfired on strict separation doctrine. Catholics were not fooled in the least. In fact, it appears that they saw Black coming. For instance, in 1946, the year before *Everson*, the Catholic Church in America, via the United States Conference of Catholic Bishops, sought and obtained from the U.S. Internal Revenue Service (IRS) a largely open-ended but official federal writ to organize churches, schools, charities, hospitals, and myriad other tax-exempt Catholic nonprofit organizations. Although it has been amended many times, this is the self-same IRS authority that has permitted government-accredited Catholic schools (elementary, secondary, college, university) to grow and flourish and that has legally governed other Catholic institutions in America for the last seven decades.

In order to rule that it was constitutional for the township to pay to bus Catholic children to Catholic schools, Justice Black, metaphorically speaking, had to drive his shiny new separation doctrine around the supposed wall. The surest way around for his five-to-four majority was to declare transportation a religiously neutral activity, akin to providing fire and police protection to Catholic schools. This jurisprudential detour, however, put the Court on the road to thinking about church-state collaboration in relation to neutrality principles. Unintentionally, in opening the public school bus doors to Catholic kids after all, Black opened the jurisprudential door to neutrality doctrine before strict separation doctrine was a day old.

Better still, within just a few years, Black's opinion would collide with the truth about the never-was wall. As summarized in chapter 1, in 1952 ultra-liberal Justice William O. Douglas, in *Zorach v. Clauson*, echoed *Everson's* no-aid separation principle, but clarified that the First Amendment does "not say that in every and all respects there shall be a separation of Church and State," and reiterated the truth that America is home to "a religious people whose institutions presuppose a Supreme Being."

By the early 1960s, a Catholic had been elected president. Older Catholics and their middle-class-bound baby boomers, many well-educated in Catholic schools, were on the way to becoming one in four

Americans and the nation's most politically coveted swing voters. Despite every sanctimonious bigot from Blaine to Black, despite a century-long onslaught by a sinful political coalition, the strict-separation factions failed to contain Catholicism's rise among America's multiplicity of sects.

Their failure is perhaps most evident in the fact that most Catholics today know next to nothing about Know Nothings. In addition to the anti-Catholic Blaine-Grant wing of the Republican party, during the nineteenth century, numerous rabidly anti-Catholic minor political parties were organized by native-born Protestants. The most notorious of these were the Know Nothings, so named "because of their first-degree ritual, in which they swore they would not disclose anything about the organization" and vowed to "vote only for native-born Protestants . . . to the exclusion of all . . . Roman Catholics."[21]

Today in America, the Know Nothings and their ilk are only a dark footnote to American history. Roman Catholics, however, are still making American history headlines. As noted in the introduction, Catholics, at 29 percent, were the single largest religious group in the 110th Congress that assembled in 2007. Indeed, Catholics now come closer than any other large religious group in America to reflecting national political norms with respect to partisanship, ideology, majority opinions, and voting patterns.[22]

LEMON AID STANDS: RELIGION AND EDUCATION

Since the early 1960s, Protestants, not Catholics, have worried most about the Court's stands on such matters as religion's place in the public schools. In particular, evangelical Christians have led Americans in the sentiment that the Court erred badly when it ostensibly decided to ban prayer in public schools.

In 1952, in the aforementioned *Zorach* decision authored by Justice Douglas, the Court had ruled that states could allow students to be released from public schools in order to attend religious instruction. A decade later, however, in *Engel v. Vitale* (1962), the Court ruled that no prayer, not even a nondenominational one, could be recited in public schools. The case involved a law that required New York State school-children to start each school day by reciting a prayer drafted by the New York State Board of Regents.

Justice Hugo Black of *Everson* infamy wrote the six-to-one *Engel* opinion (two justices did not participate). Black's rhetoric was less sweeping than he had used in *Everson*. This time there was no glaring logical disconnect between his general reasoning and his specific decision. Government, he ruled, cannot "compose official prayers" or require "any group" to recite religious prayers. In the lone dissent, Justice Potter Stewart argued that no "official religion" is "established by letting those who want to say a prayer say it" or by giving them "the opportunity of sharing in the spiritual heritage of our Nation."

Many Christian conservatives seem to sincerely believe that since *Engel* the Court has done nothing on church-state issues but rule against prayer in public schools. It is, however, much closer to the truth to say that the post-*Engel* Court has bounced back and forth on religion and education. For instance, in 2000 in *Santa Fe Independent School District v. Doe*, the Court once again echoed and extended *Engel* by declaring that students may not lead prayers before the start of a football game at a public school. Two years later, however, in *Zelman v. Simmons-Harris* (2002), the Court upheld a local voucher program that paid for children to attend religious schools.

It is by no means clear that the post-*Engel* Court has leaned in a decidedly antireligious direction. Setting aside your personal preferences, which of the student religious activities listed below do you think the Court would uphold as being constitutionally permissible in public schools under some or all circumstances?

- Distributing religious literature
- Reading the Bible or other religious texts
- Proselytizing to other students who do not object
- Wearing religious clothing or symbols
- Saying grace before meals
- Prayer by individuals or groups

- Activities with religious content before or after school
- Using school rooms or buildings for religious gatherings if they are provided to other private groups

According to guidelines issued in 1995 by the U.S. Department of Education and distributed to every public school district headquarters in the country, *all* of the foregoing activities are allowed in public schools under prevailing Court doctrine.[23] Public school teachers or administrators are prohibited from leading prayers, teaching a particular religion, or encouraging religious activities. But public school students can preach, teach, greet, meet, pray, display, and otherwise express their religious beliefs and identities in public schools.

It *is* constitutional for students to pray in and around public schools. Examine the fifty-plus, most widely cited post-*Everson* federal opinions that have bearing on religion and education. You will find that, contrary "to popular myth, the Supreme Court has never outlawed 'prayer in schools.' Students are free to pray alone or in groups," but this "does not include 'the right to have a captive audience listen or to compel other students to participate.' What the Supreme Court has repeatedly struck down are state-sponsored or state-organized prayers in public schools."[24] Simply stated, the Court has "never outlawed all forms of prayer from the public schools."[25]

Rather, while the post-*Engel* Court has ruled that "giving state endorsement to prayer" is unconstitutional, it has also consistently held that voluntary prayer, and much other religious expression in and around public schools, is constitutional.[26] So, too, is much state aid to religious schools.

Perhaps you, or others you know, are among the millions of Americans who have received federal financial aid while attending a religious college. Which of the actions listed below do you suppose that the Court also permits?

- Federal aid for constructing buildings on denominational campuses
- States loaning textbooks to parochial-school students for free

- Allowing parochial-school parents to deduct their tuition payments on state income tax returns
- States paying for computers and a deaf child's sign language interpreter at religious schools

The Court has upheld all of these things. It has prohibited requiring that creationism be taught in public schools, rejected a special school district for Hasidic Jews, refused to let states reimburse parents for Catholic-school tuitions, and required Amish parents to see to it that their children receive formal education through at least the eighth grade. But it has hardly acted to erect a "Berlin Wall" (so termed by one participant at the Justice Sunday III event) between religion and public education.

The Court's single most consequential church-state decision related to education came nine years after *Engel*. Although many religious conservatives regarded it as hostile (and still do), the Court's 1971 decision in *Lemon v. Kurtzman* sparked no political firestorm. The case involved laws in Pennsylvania and Rhode Island. In Pennsylvania, the state reimbursed religious elementary schools for personnel, textbooks, and other material used to teach specific secular subjects. In Rhode Island, the state supplemented salaries paid by religious schools to teachers who taught specific secular subjects. In a unanimous opinion composed by Chief Justice Warren Burger, the Court ruled that both states' laws were unconstitutional because they created "excessive entanglement" between government agencies and religious organizations.

The Court's *Lemon* opinion, however, established unequivocally that "establishment" does not occur whenever more than merely incidental church-state collaboration occurs. *Lemon* made plain that there *are* conditions under which government involvement with religion, even direct government financial aid, is constitutionally permissible. Writing for the whole Court, Chief Justice Burger banished Black: "separation, far from being a 'wall,' is a blurred, indistinct and variable barrier depending on all the circumstances of a particular relationship."

Lemon proposed a three-prong test to decide under what circumstances a particular relationship between government and religious activities or institutions is permissible. The relationship is constitutional if it meets these neutrality-principle tests:

1.   It has a secular purpose.

2.   Its primary effect neither advances nor inhibits religion.

3.   It does not foster an excessive government entanglement with religion.

Needless to say, *Lemon* hardly answered every last constitutional question surrounding church-state relations. Constitutional jurisprudence rarely produces easy-to-apply rules. American government teachers, among others, must often strain to explain or reconcile how the Supreme Court and lesser courts have defined and applied these tests or other neutrality principles in different cases. Few would deny that the Court has been somewhat inconsistent, or fail to agree that certain inconsistencies have been almost comical. For instance, the Court has ruled both yes and no to Nativity scene displays on government grounds: no to a Christmas wreath close to a courtroom, and yes to a Christmas tree flanked by a menorah. It has ruled no to paying Catholic schools for maps, but yes to paying Catholic schools for books. As the late great Senator Daniel Patrick Moynihan, Democrat of New York, quipped in reply, "What about atlases?"

In some cases, including recent ones, the Court has singled out religious schools and other religious institutions for special bans or burdens, or let stand state laws that do so. For example, on November 27, 2006, the Court refused to hear *Anderson v. Town of Durham*. The preceding April, Maine's highest court had upheld a state law that permits Maine officials to exclude from its statewide school choice program only those parents who choose religious schools. For decades, Maine had paid parents in small towns to send their children to the school of their choice, public or private, religious or secular, in Maine or in other states. In 1980, however, the state radically changed its policy to exclude religious schools. Lawsuits challenging that policy were brought in 2002. Five years later, the Court simply shrugged off a lawsuit challenging the notion that the federal Constitution allows state governments to wantonly discriminate against parents who choose religious schools and against the schools themselves.

Still, since *Lemon*, the Supreme Court has only rarely echoed the notion that the First Amendment's religion clauses ought to be interpreted as requiring strict or no-aid separation, or a high and thick wall between

church and state. While this or that court decision may cheer or chill orthodox secularists, on the one hand, or orthodox sectarians, on the other,
the Court has for the most part struggled honestly and intelligently to
apply neutrality doctrine in virtually every religion-clauses case that has
come before it since *Lemon*.

This assessment applies especially to the post-1980 Court, most especially to the Court during the last decade or so that Chief Justice William
Rehnquist presided. Rehnquist joined the Court in 1972 and led it from
1986 to 2005. Consider two post-2000 Court decisions that appeared on
the surface to go in opposite directions, the aforementioned *Zelman v.
Simmons-Harris* in 2002 and *Locke v. Davey* in 2004.

In *Zelman*, the Court upheld a Cleveland program that gave low-
income, inner-city parents vouchers that could be used to send their children to nonpublic schools, including religious schools. The Cleveland
program, the Court ruled, did not violate the Establishment clause.

In *Locke*, the Court upheld Washington State's constitutional exclusion
of a devotional theology degree from its otherwise-inclusive state scholarship aid program. The Washington State program, the Court ruled, did
not violate the Free Exercise clause.

Writing for *Locke's* seven-to-two majority, Rehnquist observed that the
two religion clauses "are frequently in tension" and noted that the Court
has "long said that 'there is room for play in the joints' between them."
There are, he explained, "actions permitted by the Establishment Clause
but not required by the Free Exercise Clause."

Regarding the Establishment clause, Rehnquist noted that "the link between government funds and religious training is broken by the independent and private choice of recipients." This was the core constitutional rationale for the Court's pragmatic *Zelman* decision. To wit:
Cleveland's program affords vouchers to parents who are defined by financial need and residence in a particular school district. Those beneficiaries may choose to use the public funds at duly accredited nonpublic
schools (which may happen to be religious in character) that the parents
believe to be better educationally for their children.

Not surprisingly, *Zelman* drew some intellectually serious, wall-of-
separation-minded academic critics, including law professor Gary J.

Simpson. But, like Simpson, most informed critics agreed that the Court had hinged its decision (correctly or not) on "the program's neutrality."[27]

Zelman is predicated on the principle that unless a given government program "sends a message that one religion is favored over another or that religion is preferred to no religion," government aid is presumptively okay constitutionally.[28] Simpson laments *Zelman* as "at the very least the culmination of two decades of Supreme Court precedent" and cites *Zelman*'s most impassioned dissenter, Justice David Souter, noting that "doctrinal bankruptcy has been reached."[29]

But Justice Souter (whose *Zelman* dissent suggests that he has not really read his Madison) underlines my point: love it, like it, or loathe it, strict, no-aid separation doctrine, which never really had much constitutional currency, is long since out of active circulation. *Zelman* was not a pro-religion decision, but another (whether well or poorly reasoned) pro-neutrality one.

Locke posed different religion clause conundrums than did *Zelman*, but it was resolved by applying the same basic neutrality principles in the same way. *Locke* was not an anti-religion decision, but another pro-neutrality one, arguably harder to nitpick than *Zelman*. As Chief Justice Rehnquist reasoned in his majority opinion, for better or worse, many states have long "had in their constitutions formal prohibitions against using tax funds to support ministry." Washington State's constitution draws "a more stringent line" in defining "antiestablishment interests" than does the U.S. Constitution itself.

Given their anti-Catholic genesis, there is no moral justification for Blaine amendments or their like. Still, states' rights precedents permit them to exist, and federalism precepts allow for interstate and federal-state legal differences to persist. Besides, as Rehnquist observed in *Locke*, that "a State would deal differently with religious education for the ministry than with education for other callings . . . is not evidence of hostility toward religion," for "religious instruction is of a different ilk." The Washington State program, he noted, funds "students to attend pervasively religious schools, so long as they are accredited." This does not violate the Constitution's Establishment clause. The same program, however, does not fund students to train in a particular theology and become clergy. This does not violate the Constitution's Free Exercise clause.

Neutrality principles apply, and were duly applied, in "anti-religion" *Locke*, in "pro-religion" *Zelman*, in most post-1980 religion cases involving education, and in virtually all other church-state decisions rendered during Rehnquist's last decade or so leading the Court. The contemporary Court's neutrality doctrine has resulted neither in religious establishment nor in strict separation. Rather, it has resulted mainly in faith-friendly equal protection for the godly republic's multiplicity of sects.

FREE EXERCISE VERSUS INDIRECT ESTABLISHMENT

As Hamburger stresses, those early Americans whose concern for religious freedom led them to endorse the First Amendment's intertwined religion clauses "no more wanted a separation of church and state than they wanted an establishment."[30] There have been, and continue to be, "myriad connections between religion and government that do not amount to an establishment, let alone a full union of church and state. . . . Happily, some commentators have noticed that union and separation are overgeneralizations between which lies much middle ground."[31]

Of course, the most influential of these commentators today are federal judges, starting with those on the Supreme Court. So, imagine that you were offered a seat on the Court and that your only job would be to weigh in on cases involving religion. Forget, for the moment, what you know so far from reading this book—Madison and company will forgive you. The first thing that you should do is read the Constitution, and study the First Amendment, with an amateur's passion for the obvious.

When you do, Mr. or Ms. Justice, you will notice that the Constitution singles out religion. The First Amendment's first two clauses do not mention philosophy. They do not deal with ideology. They reference only religion. Go ahead then and fixate on the First Amendment's first two clauses. One protects religious "free exercise." The other prohibits "establishing" a religion.

Before long it will occur to you that the two religion clauses, whatever each means exactly, must always be somewhat in tension. For instance, churches, synagogues, mosques, and other religious properties, including religiously affiliated schools, pay no property taxes. Most function as tax-exempt nonprofit organizations so that, subject to guidelines in the IRS code, people can legally deduct charitable gifts to congregations on their federal income taxes.

There have always been some citizens, though ever a tiny minority, who want America to be a purely secular state and so would like to tax religious properties and also to forbid tax deductions for donations to religious organizations. But, as the famous maxim goes, the power to tax is the power to destroy. Less dramatically, the power to tax (or to nix tax deductions) is the power to deter or discourage. On the one hand, to tax religious institutions or to deny their private donors tax credits, might lead government to trim religious expression or trifle with religious freedom or "free exercise." On the other hand, not taxing religion for free exercise's sake or allowing tax relief for tithing, might put government on the slippery slope to "establishing" religion.

Without the advantages that come from professional legal education or the knowledge of competing constitutional theories, if you keep thinking along these lines, you will soon be asking yourself the essential religion-clauses questions that the modern Court has been asked to decide authoritatively for the world's most demographically diverse democracy. For instance, is not taxing religion tantamount to publicly subsidizing it? Yes, the Constitution's framers forbade European-style "establishment" (the national government taxing all citizens to support an official state religion), and the Court has since outlawed this practice in the states, too. But what about "indirect establishment" by the national government—like giving religious expression greater protection than other expression, or endorsing one religion over others, or favoring religion over nonreligion? What *can* those clauses mean? How *does* the Constitution single out religion for special protections and restrictions, and how, if at all, *should* it?

Look around the next time you drive to work or take a crosstown trip. Your confusion could give way to a minor empirical epiphany. In many places, houses of worship are about as numerous as gas stations, and maybe more so. Your windshield survey will tell a well-documented truth: churches, synagogues, mosques, and other religious buildings are virtually everywhere in America. Not that they are as ubiquitous in one state as the next or evenly distributed by denomination in every city. There are more Catholic churches in Philadelphia, Pennsylvania, than there are in Philadelphia, Mississippi; more big mosques in Detroit than in Dallas; and more synagogues in New York than in New Mexico. But religious people and their organizations are in every state and every county. America today is home to scores of different religions, over 350,000 religious congregations, and untold numbers of religiously affiliated nonprofit organizations that supply social services to members and nonmembers alike. And no matter where in America you bought this book, stores there must accept as legal tender money with "In God We Trust" printed on it by the U.S. Treasury Department.

The run-up to your hypothetical Court duty complete, you already know something about "church-state jurisprudence" so obvious that it is often overlooked, yet so important that it must never be ignored: whatever the prevailing constitutional principles, whatever their arcane details or academic twists, they have made Madison's multiplicity of sects a modern-day reality, and America is a thriving federal republic wherein the national government itself acknowledges God.

Of course, even before you bought this book or explored the subject in other ways, you probably already knew that Congress could not pass a law prohibiting Catholics from celebrating Mass, requiring atheists to become Anglicans, or preventing Jews from holding a bar mitzvah or Quakers from holding a meeting for worship—at least not without drawing a swift rebuke from the Court for violating the Constitution. From this book's first chapter, you also know that, courtesy of the post-1925 Court's selective incorporation process, state governments cannot pass such laws either.

What you probably may not yet fully understand is that the contemporary Court treats religion and its "free exercise" pretty much the same way it treats free speech. As an American citizen, you can usually do and say, preach and practice, what you like so long as it does not unduly harass or cause serious harm to others. If you happen to be an American citizen acting as a government official, your religious freedom may be constrained when you are exercising public authority on the job, especially if your beliefs would have you use public authority to discriminate on purely religious grounds against others or favor your own co-religionists. But not otherwise.

By the same token, if you happen to be an American citizen acting as a religious leader or believer, your religious freedom is virtually absolute. The Court has even sometimes gone so far as to exempt religious believers from public laws that apply to everybody else: Seventh-Day Adventists who were denied unemployment compensation under state laws because they refused to take an available job that required work on Saturday (forbidden by their religion) and Amish parents who wanted their children partially exempted from minimum compulsory age requirements to be in school, have both prevailed in the federal courts.

Similarly, the Court has unanimously upheld provisions in the 1964 federal Civil Rights Act and in subsequent federal laws that grant religious organizations the right to take religion into account in making employment decisions. The so-called ministerial exemption is absolute when it comes to religious organizations functioning in their purely religious capacities relating to religious worship or sectarian instruction (mosques need not hire Mormons, Baptists need not ordain Catholics). It also applies, albeit in a more limited way, to religious organizations that seek and accept public funds to administer government social service delivery programs.[32]

The Court, however, does not read the Constitution to mean that any right or freedom is so fundamental as to be absolute. In its First Amendment jurisprudence, the Court today almost always applies neutral principles to church-state questions with results that normally betoken, not special treatment for religious people or groups, but equal protection for all, religious and nonreligious alike.

Take, for example, the well-known "conscientious objector" justification for refusing combat duty. As interpreted by the Court, religious reasons can justify a conscientious objection exemption from laws that mandate military service—but *not only* religious reasons. As the Court declared in the 1970 case *Welsh v. United States*, citizens can be exempted even if they have no religious beliefs, so long as their "consciences, spurred by deeply held moral" or "ethical" beliefs "would give them no rest if they allowed themselves to become part of an instrument of war."

Even public laws, policies, or programs that do not appear on the surface to apply to religious individuals or institutions are unconstitutional if their enforcement by government imposes special burdens on them. For instance, many people dislike door-to-door salesmen. There is nothing prima facie unconstitutional about laws that restrict such public solicitations. But government may not target religious groups for special antisolicitation restrictions or burdens. Thus, as far back as 1938, in the case of *Murdoch v. Pennsylvania*, the Court has held that a state cannot apply a license fee on door-to-door solicitors only when the solicitors are peddling religious tracts.

Similarly, although those who handle animals are subject to public laws and regulations covering everything from food manufacturing to laboratory research, killing animals is generally not illegal. Subject to governmental guidelines and restrictions, animals are killed for many different purposes. In 1993, in the case of *Church of the Lukumi Babalu Aye v. City of Hialeah*, the Court ruled that the City of Hialeah, Florida, acted unconstitutionally when it banned animal sacrifices by members of an Afro-Caribbean religion called Santeria, because the ban in this case had outlawed actions by citizens that were otherwise legal if undertaken for nonreligious purposes. (To be facetious, the Court was silent on whether Public Broadcasting Service television stations could run *I Love Lucy* reruns without violating the Constitution, since the famous 1950s sitcom often featured the Santeria "Babalu Aye" ballad sung by Ricky Ricardo, the show's Cuban-born co-star and director, Desi Arnaz, Sr.)

Neutrality doctrine respects religious freedom but avoids indirect establishment. Take the Court's support for the aforementioned ministerial exemption to federal antidiscrimination laws governing employment. The exemption fosters free exercise by directing the national government to permit religious congregations to use religious criteria in deciding who to hire, thereby "discriminating" against people who do not share the congregations' religious beliefs and tenets. Sacred places that also sponsor social service delivery programs (after-school programs, homeless shelters, etc.) with *private* funds and charitable donations retain this religious free-exercise exemption.

But in this case neutrality doctrine simultaneously avoids indirect establishment by requiring government to treat all nonprofit organizations, whether religious or secular, the same when it comes to seeking, receiving, and disbursing *public* funds with which to administer *government* programs. Under neutrality doctrine, whatever the particular beliefs and tenets of a religious nonprofit organization, if it wishes to implement a public program with public dollars, then it must comply with all program-specific rules and regulations governing personnel selection, financial accountability, and performance protocols.

For example, without violating neutrality doctrine, north Philly's Greater Exodus Baptist Church can spawn a community-serving ministry such as its People for People nonprofit social service organization. Pastor Lusk's church-related nonprofit can have a mission statement that plainly reflects and embodies its parent church's religious beliefs and tenets. It can even use prospective staff members' solidarity with that mission as one factor among others in deciding whom to employ with funds that come in whole or in part from a government grant program.

But just as Pastor Lusk's church-spawned *public* charter school cannot require faculty, staff, or students to be Baptists, his church's community-serving nonprofit organization cannot use *public* funds for proselytizing, sectarian instruction, or worship services that are integrated into its delivery of tax-supported social services. Nor in that self-chosen public trust capacity can it legally refuse to serve otherwise eligible program beneficiaries or summarily deny employment to otherwise qualified program staff, strictly to satisfy its sectarian character or religious preferences. To do those things would plainly violate neutrality doctrine and trip all three *Lemon* wires (use public funds only for secular purposes, neither promote nor inhibit religion, and avoid excessive church-state entanglement).

In sum, under neutrality doctrine, respecting religious free-exercise rights does not require the government to make special accommodations or grant extraordinary exemptions that constitute indirect establishment or violate other citizens' free-exercise rights. The Constitution explicitly singles out religion, not philosophy or ideology, for national government protections and restrictions. More often than not, the contemporary Court consistently interprets the First Amendment's two religion clauses to require government neutrality and equal protection, not strict separation or special treatment.

BLAME THE FOUNDERS, THE ANTI-FEDERALISTS,
AND THE PEOPLE

Of course, not everyone is happy with the church-state balance that is struck by neutrality doctrine. Some citizens who favor strict separation and want to rebuild the wall assert that so-called neutrality doctrine is a euphemism for national government policies that unfairly treat nonbelievers as second-class citizens and unconstitutionally give religious organizations tax-supported benefits. They blame the Court for keeping America from being a secular state.

Cornell University legal expert Steven H. Shiffrin offers to the advocates of the secular state view wise and balanced counsel. Given the plainly faith-friendly yet "pluralistic foundations of the religion clauses," Shiffrin observes, the Establishment clause "cannot be fairly read to preclude all action by politicians that favor religion any more than the Free Exercise clause precludes all state actions with a negative impact on religion."[33] Elsewhere he adds:

> Proponents of a high wall between church and state . . . are wishing for a country that does not exist and probably never will. Our Constitution must be interpreted in the light of our evolving traditions—like it or not. So we make compromises and today can say "In God we trust" on its coins but not "In Christ we trust". . . . When government acts, it does so for civic reasons, not because God has something to say about the subject.[34]

Equally unhappy with neutrality doctrine, but for the opposite reasons, are those citizens who believe what the Justice Sunday III faithful profiled in this chapter's opening pages believe, namely, that the Court has wrongly interpreted the Constitution to rid religion from the public square. They blame the federal government's "judicial tyrants" for foisting so-called neutrality doctrine upon what one Justice Sunday III participant, Reverend Falwell, once famously called America's "moral majority."

Obviously, both groups cannot be right. In fact, neither is right. However, for me at least, it is easier to understand why many orthodox Christians sincerely believe that their far-reaching complaints about the federal courts are justified. After all, how "godly," how genuinely prone to respect religious believers and organizations, is the republic when the national government singles out religion in the "neutral" way described in this chapter?

Here is what I hear from the most reasonable "judicial tyranny" voices: The national government acknowledges God, but it now limits all such official acknowledgment largely to symbolic gestures. Religious congregations retain tax-exempt status, and donors to religious nonprofit organizations can still get tax breaks. But Washington will generally not pay to help preserve or restore even historic or architecturally significant religious properties, and at a time when over 50 million Americans live in private homeowner associations (condominiums, cooperatives, gated communities, and other forms) organized around myriad secular purposes including recreation, religion in most cases remains a "prohibited category" in federal housing law. And what about cases like that recent one in Maine where the Court let the state give tuition money to parents to choose any school they liked excepting only religious ones?

They continue: Prayer was never outlawed in public schools, but "voluntary" prayer and other religious expression in and around public schools remains highly regulated and thereby marginalized and discouraged. The *Lemon* standards permit church-state collaboration and reject strict separation, but if sacred places want to participate in government programs, they must not only agree to use any public support strictly for secular purposes but also to use it in ways that do not promote or favor their own religious beliefs and tenets. Yes, the Rehnquist Court issued many faith-friendly majority opinions like *Zelman,* but it also ruled (per Rehnquist's own aforementioned *Locke* opinion) that "religious instruction" is of "a different ilk" than, say, instruction in secular humanist values, utilitarian philosophy, or what some orthodox believers regard as virtual anti-religion religions such as Darwinism, Marxism, or Freudianism.

They thunder: What, then, is "neutral" about denying public funds for graduate study to people who want to teach that the Bible is true but not to people who want to teach that the Bible is false? Similarly, why should a liberal secular nonprofit group like, say, Planned Parenthood, be permitted to receive federal funds and discriminate in hiring against citizens whose conservative religious convictions require them to be pro-life and to condemn abortion, while, say, an evangelical Christian nonprofit pregnancy counseling group is not permitted to receive public funds and discriminate in hiring against citizens whose liberal secular ideology leads them to pro-choice moral absolutism and related "proselytizing"?

However one answers these questions, understand that the Court's neutrality doctrine, loathe it or love it, *has* reflected both the founders' original church-state vision *and* the will of the national majority. If one is inclined to strongly disagree with the contemporary Court's religion-clauses jurisprudence, know that one is also thereby at odds with what the framers advocated in the late eighteenth century, and with what most Americans today agree is the right church-state balance.

The framers, not the latter-day federal courts, chose to single out religion for specific constitutional protections and limitations. For three reasons, they hoped that the national government would work to balance free exercise rights and antiestablishment interests.

First, as is discussed in chapter 1, Madison and the other framers believed that religion was vital to sustaining certain civic virtues without which no republican government could long last. For them, however, religion meant a multiplicity of sects in a large federal republic, wherein all including nonbelievers could hold national office.

Second, Madison and most other framers believed that history had taught that religion was uniquely valuable as a force for individual beneficence, social good, and civil peace, but also uniquely volatile as a force for destructive zealotry, social division, and civil war. They knew that religion was hardly the only belief system or human institution that embodied these large positive and negative potentialities. They lived before the various secular "isms" of our age. The word "ideology" had yet to be coined. But they knew ancient pagan philosophies, secular Enlightenment creeds, and, just two years after drafting the Constitution, radical French revolutionary ideas. Yet they purposely created, and the Court has largely maintained, a constitutional system in which only *religious* beliefs, practices, and organizations that touch government, even if only to the slightest degree, are automatically marked "handle with care."

Third, whether Federalist or Anti-Federalist, the early republic's leaders agreed that any central government that did not acknowledge a Supreme Being would not long acknowledge limits on its supreme powers, either vis-à-vis states or with respect to citizens' inalienable rights. "Inalienable" rights as in God-given rights, not government-granted rights. So, they compromised their way to a "compound" godly republic that forbade the national government to establish a religion, required it to respect citizens' fundamental religious and political freedoms, *and* disposed it to defer to the states in many matters pertaining to "church and state."

Blame (or credit) the framers and the Anti-Federalists, but to this very day, within broad boundaries of federal neutrality doctrine, the states continue to represent diverse approaches to religion and government. State constitutional provisions vary on at least seven church-state counts: (1) whether they contain any references to God, Providence, or a Supreme Being; (2) whether they have a non-Establishment clause, and, if so, how stringently it is worded; (3) whether they have a no-aid or no-funding clause prohibiting funding of religious organizations and, if so, whether it applies mainly or solely to religious congregations or missions; (4) whether they have, either in addition to or without a general no-aid clause, a specific prohibition against funding religious schools, like the anti-Catholic so-called Blaine amendments adopted widely in the nineteenth century; (5) whether they have clauses specifically prohibiting either direct state aid for religious organizations (grants or contracts), indirect state aid for religious organizations (vouchers or certificates), or both; (6) whether they exempt religious organizations from state laws forbidding hiring discrimination on religious grounds; and (7) whether any religious hiring rights exemption is lost or rendered wholly or partially inoperative in the context of religious organizations receiving public funds.

Without regard to often subtle but important differences in wording and without even attempting to estimate how faithfully the state's public agencies follow any given provision in practice, differences in state constitutional postures on these seven church-state counts, circa 2005, can be summarized basically as follows:[35]

- 42 state constitutions reference God, Providence, or a Supreme Being
- 10 of the 50 state constitutions have a non-Establishment clause
- 37 of the 50 state constitutions have a generic no-funding clause
- 29 of the 50 state constitutions have a specific no-education funding clause, many born as anti-Catholic Blaine amendments
- 10 of the 50 state constitutions have a clause distinguishing between direct aid and indirect aid
- 45 of the 50 state constitutions exempt religious organizations from some or all state laws prohibiting religious discrimination in hiring
- 20 of the 50 state constitutions render religious hiring rights exemptions either completely or partially inoperative when religious organizations receive public funds, and other state constitutions either have no provision or language so ambiguous or self-contradictory that even nonpartisan experts cannot agree on what they mean

To put it mildly, it is treacherous to assume that either a state's present-day political posture on church-state issues, or its recent record in responding to federally led initiatives favorable to faith-based organizations that wish to compete for public funds, or both, bear any clear-cut relationship to what its state constitution allows or forbids. By the same token, however, it is a big mistake to assume that the states' respective constitutional postures on church-state matters have no effect on what they do today on faith-based issues.

By 2006, for example, about two-thirds of all states had enacted some type of law or program akin to the faith-friendly charitable choice laws enacted by the federal government in the late 1990s, and most states also had established one or more offices akin to the White House Office of Faith-Based and Community Initiatives established by executive order in 2001 (details on those federal actions are provided in chapters 3 and 4). But which states did so, what the changes meant in reality rather than only on paper, whether the changes have yet resulted in any actual increases in state grants or contracts with faith-based organizations, and whether state constitutional provisions to the contrary will exercise a latent veto power over any additional changes or themselves be changed, are all questions that cannot be answered except by examining the situation on an ongoing, up-close, state-by-state basis.

By comparison to the diversity and complexity of the states, the federal Constitution and federal laws, and the Court's prevailing doctrine, are crystal clear on church-state matters. Begat by the framers and carried on by the Court, neutrality doctrine, love or loathe it, *does* require the *national* government to justify any special burdens, intentional or not, that it places upon religious individuals or institutions—justify them or work to eliminate them. It *does* require that U.S. citizens not be treated by the *national* government as second-class citizens because they hold certain religious views or harbor religious motivations. It also forbids *federal* agencies from reflexively relegating religious citizens and organizations to a limbo of lesser civic significance when it comes to participating in the *federal* grant-making process and delivering vital social services funded partly or entirely by the *national* government.

Most present-day Americans favor neutrality principles. They do not agree with the strict separation zealots, but neither do they echo the religious ultra-conservatives. From opposite extremes, each group has asked loaded but legitimate questions about the Court's neutrality doctrine. Most twenty-first-century Americans answer these questions much the way that Madison and the other framers would answer them. They do not crave strict or total church-state separation, but neither do they carp about judicial tyranny. They are faith-friendly and tolerant toward citizens whose religious beliefs differ from their own or who profess no such beliefs. They support changing the country's church-state status quo only so long as any changes make government more, not less, likely to respect religious freedom while avoiding indirect establishment.

As is discussed in chapter 3, on religion and government, America's actual moral majority is pluralistic and pragmatic. The Court's neutrality doctrine, and the wise and workable church-state balance to which it aspires, is backed by mass opinion and bipartisan sentiment. Neither strict secularists nor religious purists represent what we the people love most about our godly republic. In particular, neither extreme reflects how willing most citizens are to have their national political leaders in Washington help local community-serving religious organizations to help children, youth, and families in need.

THREE

The People's Charitable Choice

Myth 5   Religious conservatives have somehow succeeded in getting the national government to do their bidding on church-state issues and, more generally, in polarizing partisan elites and the mass electorate.

Myth 6   Secular liberals have somehow succeeded in getting the national government to do their bidding on church-state issues and, more generally, in polarizing partisan elites and the mass electorate.

TRUTH   Most Americans are religious believers who respect other citizens without regard to religion and whose consensus on church-state issues national leaders have generally heeded by enacting bipartisan laws and faith-friendly programs.

BIPARTISAN BELIEFS

A prominent national politician has made numerous statements about religion and government. On January 19, 2005, this politician preached to inner-city clergy in Boston:

> But I ask you, who is more likely to go out onto a street to save some poor, at-risk child than someone from the community, someone who believes in

the divinity of every person, who sees God at work in the lives of even the most hopeless and left-behind of our children? And that's why we need to not have a false division or debate about the role of faith-based institutions, we need to just do it and provide the support that is needed on an ongoing basis.

On December 17, 2001, during a panel on religion and government in a New York City church, this same leader argued:

> The Founders had faith in reason . . . faith in God, from which the ability to reason is a great gift. . . . Government works in partnership with religious institutions . . . to promote public purposes—feeding the hungry, sheltering the homeless. Faith inspires these good works, to be sure. But tax dollars are properly used to channel the energies of the faithful in a direction that helps our society as a whole.

Senator Hillary Rodham Clinton, Democrat of New York, made these two statements.[1] Just as President George W. Bush has often been wrongly associated with the view that America was founded and ought to function as a Christian nation (Myth #2), so Senator Clinton has often been wrongly associated with the view that America was founded and ought to function as a secular state (Myth #1). As President Bush has been mistakenly lumped together with partisan supporters, mostly conservatives, who insist that judicial tyrants have vanquished religion from public life (Myth #3), so Senator Clinton has been mistakenly lumped together with partisan supporters, mostly liberals, who insist that federal judges have gone overboard in protecting religious expression and permitting government to collaborate with religious institutions (Myth #4).

On July 22, 1999, Texas governor George W. Bush delivered his first presidential campaign speech, "The Duty of Hope," before inner-city clergy in Indianapolis:

> In every instance where my administration sees a responsibility to help people, we will look first to faith-based organizations, charities, and community groups that have shown their ability to save and change lives. . . . Sometimes the armies of compassion are outnumbered and outflanked and outgunned. . . . It is not enough to call for volunteerism. Without more support—public and private—we are asking them to make bricks

without straw. . . . We will keep a commitment to pluralism, not discriminating for or against Methodists or Mormons or Muslims, or good people of no faith at all. Government cannot be replaced by charities, but it must welcome them as partners, not resent them as rivals.

On the morning of January 29, 2001, the first day of his first full week in office, President Bush, by executive order, created the White House Office of Faith-Based and Community Initiatives (OFBCI) and authorized OFBCI centers in five federal cabinet agencies.[2] In his opening remarks at the signing ceremony, he stressed that "We will not fund the religious activities of any group, but when people of faith provide social services, we will not discriminate against them." Bush's executive order creating the OFBCI read in part: "The delivery of social services must be results-oriented and value the bedrock principles of pluralism, nondiscrimination, evenhandedness and neutrality."

Despite the many profound political differences between them, President Bush and Senator Clinton share a belief that America was founded and ought to function as a godly republic. On church-state issues, both have often disappointed partisan and ideological supporters. Former governor Bush has never embraced the notion that America's religious citizens are disrespected by a government that is dominated by secular liberal elites (Myth #6). Former first lady Clinton has never embraced the notion that America's nonreligious citizens are disrespected by a government that is dominated by religious conservative elites (Myth #5).

The 2000 presidential contest between Bush and Vice President Al Gore suggested as much. The contest was hardly a love fest. It ended even more bitterly than it began. One consensus point, however, was consistently struck by the two candidates. Both Bush and Gore called for faith-friendly national laws forbidding grant-making federal government agencies from discriminating against otherwise qualified community-serving religious nonprofit organizations.

Bush and Gore were not breaking new common ground. The first law of this sort appeared as a provision (Section 104) of the Personal Responsibility and Work Opportunity Reconciliation Act of 1996, better known as the 1996 federal welfare reform law. The provision was termed "charitable choice." It had two fundamental purposes: first, citizens who received federal aid were henceforth to have wider choices among federally funded providers of financial aid or social services, including religious charities and other religious nonprofit organizations; and second, otherwise qualified faith-based organizations, even small, grassroots, community-serving ministries like the ones that both Bush and Gore would later tout during the 2000 presidential campaign, were henceforth to be permitted to administer federal antipoverty and other social services programs on the same basis that all other nonprofit organizations were permitted to do so. A second charitable choice provision was added to the Community Services block grant program when it was reauthorized in 1998. In 2000, a third charitable choice provision was added to the Substance Abuse Prevention and Treatment block grant, and a fourth one was added to the Projects for Assistance in Transition from Homelessness program.

In the U.S. Senate, the main architect of the first charitable choice provision was Missouri Republican John Ashcroft, who later became Bush's first U.S. attorney general. Widely and rightly regarded as a staunch religious conservative, Ashcroft, whom I first got to know in the mid-1990s, was nonetheless a centrist when it came to church-state issues. "It's my religion," he liked to say, "not to impose my religion on others."

From the first, Senator Clinton and many other top Democrats were warmer than not to charitable choice. Later in this chapter, charitable choice laws are explored in some depth, including the reasons for their stunted, but not stillborn, implementation in 1996–2006. For now the salient fact is that back in 1999 and 2000, Vice President Gore, Governor Bush, First Lady Clinton, and Senator Ashcroft all had basically the same positive message about faith-based programs and charitable choice. On May 24, 1999, two months before Bush's maiden "The Duty of Hope" speech in Indianapolis, Gore spoke at a Salvation Army center in Atlanta, Georgia. The Democrat declared that America's "severest challenges are not just material, but spiritual":

> I believe strongly in the separation of church and state. But freedom of religion need not mean freedom from religion. . . . Some past national leaders have asked us to rely on a patchwork of well-intentioned volunteerism

to feed the hungry and house the homeless. . . . In contrast, faith- and values-based organizations show a strength that goes beyond "volunteerism." These groups nationwide have shown a muscular commitment to facing down poverty, drug addiction, domestic violence and homelessness. And when they have worked out a partnership with government, they have created programs and organizations that have woven a resilient web of life support under the most helpless among us.

For the most part, the Democratic party's secular liberal elites hated Gore's Salvation Army speech. They sniped at the message and the messenger all the way to and through the 2000 Democratic National Convention. However, the 1996–2000 charitable choice laws, which President Bill Clinton was happy to sign, had many important Democratic champions besides Gore, including several with impeccable liberal credentials. One of these, Andrew Cuomo, the son of former New York governor Mario Cuomo and the Clinton administration's secretary of Housing and Urban Development, reached out to diverse religious leaders and took creative first steps to explain, publicize, and implement charitable choice laws.

Bush's "Duty of Hope" speech drew a similar negative reaction from his party's right wings, both the tax-cutting libertarians and the Bible-believing sectarians. The speech went through at least sixteen rewrites that involved more than disputes about grammar and syntax. Many Republican conservative activists hated the center-hugging "compassionate conservatism." Others favored it, but only as a rhetorical Trojan Horse. If a "compassionate conservative" was actually a government-shrinking libertarian in religious drag, then fine. But, if Bush really meant what he said, Gore-like, about volunteerism not being enough, about the "armies of compassion" not simply being unleashed but getting more government aid, about expanding federal-state programs like Medicaid for low-income children, or about rejecting as "destructive" the Reagan-tested idea that government itself is the main problem, then many conservative Republicans would not suffer it.

In particular, Bush risked the wrath of religious conservatives who had supported Ashcroft-sponsored charitable choice laws as better than nothing but who deeply resented them as weak tea supposedly brewed to suit the tastes of antireligious liberal Democrats including, they absurdly asserted, Gore and his running mate, Connecticut U.S. senator Joseph Lieberman. Lieberman, a man of the center-right and an orthodox Jew, was chastised repeatedly in 2000 by the party's liberals for engaging in too much "God talk."

During the 2000 presidential campaign, these Bush critics on the religious right remained quiet. But in late January and early February 2001, several weeks before Bush's first executive orders on faith-based and community initiatives went into effect, they badgered Bush's political advisors and finally, in frustration, went public with their demands. Essentially, they wanted the new president, a fellow evangelical Christian, to frontally assault the Court's neutrality doctrine. They wanted Bush to change charitable choice laws to permit federal funds to be used for proselytizing and to pass new federal laws that would permit proselytizing with federal funds. They wanted him to give religious nonprofit leaders an unqualified right to use federal funds in social service delivery programs employing only persons who profess and practice the religious nonprofit leaders' own religious beliefs and tenets. They wanted Bush to override or preempt, by legislation or by executive orders, any contradictory state or local laws and, also by legislation or by executive orders, to convert federal educational and other programs by the hundreds into voucher programs—programs that dispense benefits directly to eligible individuals who can then purchase services pretty much wherever they wish, rather than dispense them through grants administered by qualified organizations.

Since the political fur flew over these demands in 2001, not much has actually happened. Despite strong challenges, the original charitable choice provision was retained when the 1996 federal welfare law was reauthorized in 2005. Between 2001 and 2006, no major new charitable choice laws were passed, save for certain provisions in legislation like the 2005 Hurricane Education Recovery Act. While the amount of federal funds trickling down to community-serving religious nonprofit organizations increased slightly at least by some measures, no substantial progress was made in forging public-private partnerships with the literally thousands of grassroots religious groups from coast to coast that help people in need. On the other hand, while Bush signed several executive orders that seemed to radically expand religious hiring rights, the measures' fine print left the relevant pre-2001 federal employment discrimination laws intact, neither expanding nor contracting the so-called ministerial exemption that has been on the federal books for decades.

As Wheaton College political scientist Amy Black and others have dispassionately chronicled, "religious purists," as Black aptly termed them, momentarily shattered the charitable choice consensus in Washington in 2001.[3] But these religious purists are constitutionally entitled to their church-state views. Besides, they did not undermine the mass public consensus about religion and government that charitable choice laws reflected, *not* created. Nor did they permanently set asunder the bipartisan beliefs on church-state issues shared by President Bush, Senator Clinton, and many other national leaders.

When it comes to helping truly disadvantaged Americans, President Bush, Senator Clinton, and many of their peers in the federal government are basically sincere, responsible, and well-meaning people. They are also, at bottom, smart, savvy, and well-practiced politicians. They know that, whatever their respective well-organized partisan and ideological supporters want, most Americans are neither religious purists nor strict secularists. They know, without pollsters having to tell them, that most Americans believe in God, profess a particular faith, and at heart are public-spirited religious pluralists.

Most Americans favor faith-friendly but pragmatic approaches to church-state issues. In Washington, each party's church-state ideological faction exercises enormous sway, but neither ever comes close to carrying the day, either in legislation or in court. For all the pardonable pandering to their respective party extremists, most national political leaders, like President Bush and Senator Clinton, ultimately speak truth to power about religion and government in America.

Most Americans, thank God, are still more stirred by such bipartisan beliefs in action than they are incited by rank ideological appeals. For all the post-2000 and post-2004 punditry about red (Republican) versus blue (Democratic) states, for all the pseudo-sophisticated talk about the yawning religious divide in national electoral politics (the most religious vote Republican, the most secular vote Democratic), today's American public majority still instinctively revels in Madison's multiplicity of sects and intuitively embraces the Court's neutrality doctrine.

PURPLE PEOPLE ON CHURCH-STATE

Both in absolute terms and relative to their civic cousins in most European democracies, Americans have been, and continue to be, a religious people. Wide popular majorities, no matter their socioeconomic status, demographic description, or geographic jurisdiction, say they believe in God (96 percent), never doubt God's existence (79 percent), pray daily (75 percent), and think that religion can solve all or most of today's problems (61 percent).[4] And most Americans, not only orthodox Christians or other religious conservatives, feel sure that the civic state of the union depends critically on the religious state of the union.[5]

Americans' persistent religiosity has not become synonymous with New Age spirituality or Judeo-Christian sensibility. Constitutionally, America is not a Christian nation, but most Americans are Christians. By percentage, religious affiliation in America today breaks down pretty much as follows:[6]

Evangelical Protestant	33.6
Mainline Protestant	22.1
Catholic	21.1
Unaffiliated	10.8
Black Protestant	5.0
Jewish	2.5
All other religions	4.9

Even the one American in ten without any religious affiliation is somewhat religious: 62 percent believe in God, 31.6 percent pray occasionally, and 11 percent believe in Jesus Christ's divinity.[7] Among all Americans, between 1975 and 2005, there was an increase in those never going to church, but there was also an increase in those going to church weekly or more.[8]

America at the twenty-first century's dawn may or may not be in the grip of another Great Awakening, like the Christian revival movement sympathetically witnessed by Princeton's Reverend John Witherspoon and many other founding fathers. However, America is undoubtedly closer to another Great Awakening than it is to any full-scale retreat from traditional religious identities or, as is discussed in the concluding chapter, any European-style descent into purely secular civic isms. If anything, America will probably be more predominantly Christian, and more orthodox in its Christian cast, by the mid-twenty-first century than it was in the mid-twentieth century.

As has been true for decades, today between 40 and 50 percent of adult Americans identify themselves as "Bible-believing," with most preferring to describe themselves as "born again" Christians rather than as "Evangelicals."[9] Over the last several decades, mega-churches (5,000-plus members) representing diverse Protestant denominations have sprung up in just about every metropolitan region.

Meanwhile, the country's Catholics have become a diverse national religious community and swing-voting bloc, but about a third of today's Catholics would count as "traditionalists."[10] Nobody is sure how inmigration will affect the sectarian breakdown, but it is clear that the Mexican masses and other Latino populations who have been resettling America below the Mason-Dixon line are predominantly Christian. As politicians wonder whether the nation's growing Mexican Hispanic minority (now larger than its African American minority) will decisively break Republican or Democratic in the years to come, Catholic bishops wonder whether it will remain largely Catholic or (as it has in Latin America) trend toward evangelical Christian, Pentecostal, or other Protestant churches.[11]

African Americans remain predominantly Baptists (roughly half), about a tenth identify as Methodists, and an estimated 4 to 5 percent identify as Catholics. But the nation's fastest-growing African American churches are probably ones such as the Church of God in Christ and various other Pentecostal or quasi-Pentecostal churches. As discussed in chapter 5, by many measures, African Americans are the most religious people in America, both with respect to Christian beliefs and in relation to community-serving deeds that put their beliefs into action.

Thus, most Americans today are what most Americans were in the nineteenth century when they so amazed the French observer Alexis de Tocqueville. Most are Christian believers who routinely profess, even if they do not consistently practice, a particular faith. But make no mistake: while Christians predominate in America and the trend toward traditional Christianity is real, Christian America remains a Protestant patchwork quilt featuring different denominations by the dozens, flanked by ethnically diverse Catholics, and friendly toward citizens claiming many other faiths. This is true for every major U.S. metropolitan region. Mormons are no longer confined mainly to Utah. Muslims are a small but significant presence in Michigan. Korean American Evangelicals shop alongside third-generation Italian American Catholics in Philadelphia's Italian market district. And so, gloriously, Madison's multiplicity of sects still grows all across America's godly republic.

It is therefore not surprising that the American mass public favors faith-friendly church-state approaches and public policies. Most secular liberal elites in America who once trivialized or simply denied this reality have come to understand, even if they do not gladly accept, that America is a representative democracy where many more people think that angels are real than think that God is dead. This is a federal republic where the Protestant majority witnessed the election of a Catholic president, John F. Kennedy, in 1960, but where, even today, most Protestants, Catholics, and other citizens uniformly agree that they would not vote an avowed atheist into the Oval Office.

America's secular liberal elites, concentrated primarily on the East and West coasts, are still frequently late to recognize a phenomenon like *The Purpose-Driven Life*, the best-selling book by evangelical Christian pastor Rick Warren that as of this writing has sold about 30 million copies. As I can attest personally, even the best and brightest among them can be "shocked, shocked" when an Ivy League professor freely admits to having read this book and fondly praises its author—and God.[12]

Still, only tenured radicals who inhabit the isolated nonbeliever bubbles known as elite secular universities, off-campus Marxists (both of them), and journalists who work in newsrooms dominated by secular liberal elite dogmas (hundreds of them) keep waiting for the mass American public and its leaders to forget God and forsake religion.

They do not have a prayer. Most Americans are religious pluralists and political centrists. When pushed, they are more inclined to sing with the center-right choir than they are to skip church with the center-left minion. Or, as an old Philadelphia Democratic party hack put the point to me some years ago, most working-class and middle-income Americans like neither party's national activists, ideological mouthpieces, or celebrity elites; but, if forced to choose, they would rather "leave their children with Jerry Falwell" (the late Moral Majority leader and religious-right icon) than "with Jerry Garcia" (the late Grateful Dead leader and drug-culture icon).

When Gore and Bush both touted faith-based programs in 1999 and 2000, the "mainstream" media were slow to understand that the politicians were merely holding up a mirror to between-the-extremes mass public preferences. Numerous post-2000 national surveys probing Americans' attitudes on religion and government paint a faith-friendly but decidedly centrist picture. Here is a small but representative sample:[13]

- Two-thirds think that America's historical roots and traditions render it a "Christian nation" and over two-thirds believe "liberals" have "gone too far" in "keeping government out of religion," but 49 percent also say that "Christian conservatives" have "gone too far" in "imposing their religious values."

- Two-thirds, encompassing millions who are regular churchgoers, believe that "the will of the people" should "have more influence on U.S. laws" than "the Bible."

- Only 7 percent identify themselves with the "religious left," and only 11 percent identify themselves with the "religious right."

- Two-thirds to three-quarters support government funding faith-based organizations to supply social services and think that religiously motivated social service providers tend to be more caring and compassionate than other social service providers (and more cost-effective to boot).

- But support for government funding faith-based organizations to supply social services ebbed as the idea became associated with funding pervasively sectarian activities and as the number who thought that President Bush talked too much about religion and prayer doubled (from 14 percent in 2003 to 28 percent in 2005).

America's overwhelmingly faith-friendly majority is nonetheless pluralistic and pragmatic when it comes to religion and government. The majority's support for public-private partnerships involving religious organizations is conditional on government ensuring that public funds do not support proselytizing or discrimination against beneficiaries or paid workers. Thus, the same surveys that report faith-friendly leanings also find four-fifths agreeing that one can "be a good American" without either Judeo-Christian or other religious faith. And about three-quarters are *opposed* to government support for faith-based programs that require beneficiaries "to take part in religious practices" or that "only hire people of the same faith."[14]

The faith-friendly but pluralistic and pragmatic majority also agrees that even "deeply religious elected leaders" *should* compromise with "elected officials whose views are different" on hot-button political issues like abortion (57 percent), gay rights (60 percent), the death penalty (60 percent), and welfare programs (68 percent).[15]

Most Americans are not divided between pro-religion red-state conservative Republicans and anti-religion blue-state liberal Democrats. Rather, most Americans neither see red nor feel blue; instead, most prefer the combination of red and blue, or purple.[16] It is true that the country is undergoing an elite culture war. Per this book's introduction, I have some political and rhetorical scars, several administered by each side, to prove this point. But neither the nation's people, nor even its most prominent national political leaders, are deeply polarized on religion and government.

There are four much-invoked arguments to the contrary. One is that the nation's born-again Christian population clusters on the Republican right. A second is that most recent national elections have been nip-and-tuck contests between tradition-minded churchgoers, who mostly vote Republican, and weakly religious or nonbelieving citizens, who mostly vote Democratic. A third is that grant-making federal bureaucracies wantonly discriminate against religious people and organizations. A fourth is that the centrist people and their leaders have let partisan and ideological extremists on each side dominate the church-state debate, block their best-laid legislative plans, turn efforts to aid poor children into fights over issues like gay rights, and derail partnerships that empower faith-based organizations to help more people in need.

Each argument contains a valid empirical point or two, but each also folds facts into faulty inferences that beget false generalizations. The first three arguments are dealt with below, and in the next chapter, the fourth argument is analyzed mainly in relation to the politics that surrounded faith-based initiatives in Washington from 2001 through 2006.

TURNING RED OVER RELIGION?

When it comes to public opinion, partisan affiliation, and voting patterns, evangelical Christians are often large outliers, as compared to other religious groups. In 2004 Evangelicals figured prominently as loyal Republican "moral-values" voters who favored Bush over Kerry, even when compared to conservative Catholics.[17] On hot-button issues such as gay rights, Evangelicals are more uncompromising (principled!) than other sects: three-quarters of Catholics and 60 percent of the general public, but just over a third of Evangelicals, agree that even deeply religious elected leaders should be willing to compromise with other elected officials whose views on gay rights are different.[18] Similarly, compared to Catholics and the general public, Evangelicals are about 50 percent more likely to agree strongly that school prayer "is an especially effective way to improve the values and behavior of today's young people," half as likely to disagree strongly with that view, and half as likely again to agree strongly that school prayer "violates the Constitution."[19]

This is all true. But it is perilously far from the truth to say that evangelical Christians are virtually all ideologically conservative Republicans who put moral values first in deciding how to vote—and that by "moral values" they mean only their own traditional religious beliefs applied to gay rights and other controversial topics.

For starters, Protestants can be found in both parties (Methodists President Bush and Senator Clinton, for two), and born-again Protestant believers know no one denomination. Baptist, Lutheran, Presbyterian, and many other Protestant churches claim as members people who consider themselves to be either born-again or evangelical Christians.

I may be the country's only self-described "born-again Roman Catholic," but the over 40 percent of all adult Americans who say they are born again are cut from many different denominational cloths that do not cluster geographically any more completely than they cluster theologically. In recent decades, certain religious geography facts have changed but little. For instance, Catholics are still the nation's single biggest religious denomination, and the single largest in each of twenty-eight states; evangelical Christians remain concentrated among Baptist churches that claim more adherents than any other religion in most southern states; Utah is still predominantly Mormon; and non-evangelical Lutheran churches still dominate in the Dakotas. But one of the states where Catholics predominate is Texas; both Baptist and other evangelical Christian churches are more common than ever above the Mason-Dixon line; Mormon populations are up in many states; and Lutherans calling themselves "evangelicals" are not hard to find in many cities far from the Dakotas.

Among evangelical Christians, as among all Americans, there are important gender and generational differences in politically salient beliefs. These and related intragroup differences are behind the ongoing ferment at many orthodox Christian colleges and universities (Baylor University in Texas, Calvin College in Michigan, Wheaton College in Illinois, and many others).

At some institutions, the ferment has meant pitched battles among and between faculty and administrators. Some want to preserve or reinstate traditional religious controls over curricula and hiring; others want to do precisely the opposite. At Baylor University, for example, since 2000 there have been highly publicized faculty fights over requiring professors to sign faith statements and over the traditional policy against employing scholars, no matter how vaunted their professional standing, who profess other faiths or none at all.

Regardless, Boston College political scientist Alan Wolfe was right when in 2000 he observed that "the rest of America cannot continue to write off conservative Christians as hopelessly out of touch with modern American values."[20] For good or ill, the "opening of the Evangelical mind," as Wolfe's essay phrased it, has already left important national political marks that are hardly old-time religion footprints.

Some such marks have been left in high places. President Bush's chief speechwriter, Michael Gerson, graduated from Wheaton College. While the media have nominated many others for this distinction (myself included), Gerson was truly the principal intellectual and rhetorical architect behind Bush's compassionate conservatism and the main mind involved in crafting the president's faith-based and community initiatives.

After years as Bush's top wordsmith, during Bush's first term, Gerson suffered a heart attack at age 39. But he kept his position, fortunately recovered, and returned to the White House to serve as the president's top advisor on all compassion agenda items, including faith-based programs. He was also the only longtime Bush White House senior official to be celebrated for his wit and wisdom by secular liberal elites, both during his service and after he announced his resignation in mid-2006. Reflecting his own core convictions as an evangelical Christian and the president's as well, all Gerson's rhetorical roads and policy paths on compassion led not to the Christian nation or to the secular state, but to and from the godly republic.

More Evangelicals think like Gerson (and Bush) than the predominantly secular-minded (no-Evangelicals-need-apply) D.C.–New York–L.A. elite media corps realize. Perhaps the best example of this point concerns the church-state issue that has riled orthodox Protestants for over forty years—school prayer. As I noted previously, Evangelicals are far more convinced than Catholics and the general public that school prayer is socially desirable and completely constitutional. What, however, do most Evangelicals recommend that government do now about prayer in schools?

By 2001 most evangelical Christians (53 percent), an identical percentage of the general public (53 percent) and a slightly larger Catholic contingent (57 percent) preferred that public schools have "a moment of silence." About a quarter of Evangelicals, matching a quarter of Catholics and a fifth of the general public, preferred instead having "prayers that refer to God but to no particular religion." And just 12 percent of Evangelicals, versus 6 percent of the general public and 4 percent of Catholics, wanted the public schools to have children "say a prayer that refers to Jesus."[21]

Most evangelical Christians, like most other Americans, are nearly as purple-as-thou on church-state issues, albeit with red highlights. Their most widely noted and incessantly quoted religious leaders, like the Reverends Jerry Falwell and Pat Robertson, rarely sound at all purple. But their younger and upcoming religious leaders, like the aforementioned Reverend Warren, while no less theologically conservative, are far more prone to search for common ground on controversial issues. They are also far more likely to display their particular spiritual beliefs by performing civic good works. And their baby-boomer-bred civic and political leaders, like Gerson, are ideologically conservative yet as committed to religious pluralism as most other leaders.

Like Warren's domestic and international antipoverty missions, like Charles W. Colson's Prison Fellowship Ministry (for which Gerson, not coincidentally, once worked), and like numerous other evangelical Christian outreach programs, most evangelical ministries today serve people in need without regard to religion. One could also cite in evidence the present-day Salvation Army's programs (Salvationists are an orthodox Christian sect) or the "theology of the hammer" represented by the Christ-centered but ecumenical Habitat for Humanity. Millions upon millions who identify themselves as either born-again or evangelical Christians support such programs with their time, their backs, their money—and their prayers.

Ironically, secular liberal elites are probably the only people in America who still think that Reverend Pat Robertson and his gray-to-the-gills *700 Club* cable television show represent the beliefs of most American Evangelicals, or represent them better than a Reverend Rick Warren and his antipoverty ministries. Too many top journalists still relish the easy-to-get controversial "Christian Right" quote. Too many still prefer to peddle utterly outdated nonsense about orthodox Protestants than to actually get out and meet, survey, work—or worship—alongside them. Too many would rather shadowbox with a religious conservative straw man on creationism than engage someone like, say, the evangelical Christian Francis Collins—the biologist who led the international humane genome project—on intelligent design (he eschews it) or theistic evolution (he extols it).[22]

TWO ELECTORAL EXTREMES EQUAL ONE-THIRD

Many "mainstream" analysts, activists, and others miss or misconstrue the mass consensus on religion in American civic life because they exaggerate—often, it seems, purposely—the religious divide in national electoral politics. The voting divide is real, but it is not new, and it does not involve most voters. Studies dating back decades have suggested that tradition-minded voters who attend church regularly tend to cluster together in presidential, gubernatorial, and senatorial elections as well as in voting on issue referenda.[23] For instance, there is ample empirical evidence that, from 1992 through 2004, church attendance has been strongly associated with presidential voting.[24]

Stanford University political scientist Morris P. Fiorina has amassed evidence that Americans are far less polarized politically than we so often hear. But Fiorina agrees that the "stronger relationship between religiosity and voting that has developed recently appears to be genuine and not a spurious reflection of other factors. . . . So, religion in the sense of personal commitment has become an important cleavage in recent American elections, consistent with the arguments of those who believe in the culture wars."[25]

Likewise, a 2005 Pew Research Center report stressed that voters who attended church regularly were far more likely to vote Republican in 2000 and again in 2004.[26] It correctly noted that various statistical tests find church attendance to be a uniquely powerful predictor of presidential voter preference and that this variable was even "more important in 2004 than it had been in 2000."[27] It also outlined the plausible, though far from proven, case that "so-called moral issues—prayer in school, abortion, homosexuality, gay marriage—have tended to push the religiously more observant into one political corner and the more secular into the other."[28]

James Q. Wilson, an eminent scholar of American politics and public policy, has challenged Fiorina's case that the culture wars are a myth. Still, Wilson has stressed that the religious divide in presidential voting is easily exaggerated and that it does not, in any case, betoken similar divides in voting in other elections, in mass views on religion and civic life, or on particular policy issues.[29] As he has observed, based on national exit polls, it appears that in the November 2004 elections, nearly two-thirds of the people who said they attended church more than weekly voted for Bush. Of the voters who said they never attended church, two-thirds voted for Kerry and a third voted for Bush. The church-going group, however, made up about one-sixth of the electorate. The no-church group made up roughly one-seventh of the electorate. Thus, together, the "churched" versus "unchurched" electoral extremes made up a third of the electorate.

As Wilson has concluded, religion makes a difference, but very religious and very irreligious voters are only a minority of the electorate. The religion gap in voting is real and important: Bush received 61.1 percent of all votes cast by people who attend religious services regularly, but only 44.3 percent of all votes cast by people who do not attend religious services regularly, for a religion gap of 16.8 points (61.1 minus 44.3). But there were six other statistically significant voter gaps in the 2004 Bush presidential vote:[30]

Race gap (whites 58.7% vs. nonwhites 27.6%)	31.1
Religion gap (weekly attendee 61.1% vs. less than weekly 44.3%)	16.8
Income gap ($50,000/yr. and up 57% vs. under $50,000/yr. 44.7%)	12.3
Region gap (South, Midwest 55.2% vs. Northeast, West 46.6%)	8.6
Location gap (suburbs or rural 54.5% vs. cities 46.9%)	7.6
Gender gap (male 55.5% vs. female 48.2%)	7.3
School gap (some college or less 53.1% vs. college or more 49.9%)	3.2
All voters (Bush 51.5% vs. Kerry 48.5%)	3.0

The race gap was far larger than the religion gap. When subjected to closer statistical analysis (called a binary logistic regression analysis), the school gap and the gender gap loom larger, but the religion gap remains a distant second to the race gap. As even analysts who have stressed religion's role in deciding recent elections have admitted, "President Bush could not have been reelected without the support he received from less-frequent worshipers" while Kerry would have been trounced had he "not received substantial numbers of votes from frequent worship attendees."[31] This is not to say that the two religious electoral extremes, equaling roughly a third of the mass electorate, do not matter. Over a decade ago, Jeffrey Bell, a respected Republican pro-life movement leader and political consultant, explained "the rise of value politics." [32] Nobody can now reasonably doubt that Bell was dead right.

But the electoral politics of moral values and related symbolic (or, as political scientists term them, valence) issues is more complicated and dynamic than we often hear.[33] For instance, as Wilson has noted, in the November 2004 national elections, the fraction of all voters who said that moral values were the most important issue for them was lower in 2004 than it had been in 1996 and 2000. In 2004 terrorism and Iraq were the most important issues to most people. In sum, Wilson concluded, religion makes a difference in elections, but so do many other factors.

In 2004, Bush won largely because his chief political strategist, Karl Rove, was absolutely right in surmising that several million Evangelicals who might have voted for Bush in 2000 stayed home instead. Rove was relentless in focusing his party's political machinery on getting these Americans to the polls on Election Day 2004. As the same 2000 and 2004 exit poll data cited by Wilson indicated, self-identified white Evangelical and born-again Christian voters, who comprised an estimated 14 to 17 percent of the electorate in the 2000 national elections, comprised an estimated 23 percent of the electorate in the 2004 elections. In 2004, evangelical Christian voters favored Bush over Kerry by about a 57-point margin—about 78 percent for Bush to 21 percent for Kerry, compared with the electorate at large, in which 51 percent voted for Bush and 48 percent voted for Kerry.

The Evangelicals were not alone. Non-evangelical Christians, including swing-voting, tradition-minded Catholics registered as Democrats, also heard and heeded the Rove-tailored messages about Bush's opposition to gay marriage. They helped to tip the election to Bush. Some experts on both sides believe that Kerry, a self-identified Catholic whose sudden nostalgia for his days as an altar boy was communicated alongside his staunch support for keeping abortion legal under all circumstances, might have won Ohio and the election had he kept more fellow Catholics in his column.

Maybe, but Kerry lost because most voters, not just Evangelicals, felt that the war on terror and Iraq mattered more than any moral values issue did. On these two top-tier issues, he was judged less worthy than Bush by most voters. Kerry did not lose because he lost Evangelicals, swing-voting Catholics, or other religious voters on religious or moral values issues. He lost because, even with a huge Democratic turnout in both red states and blue states, Bush beat him on the red, white, and blue issues that mattered most to those Americans who went to the polls.

And Bush beat Kerry for other reasons that go deeper, reasons that preceded 9/11 and even the first Iraq war by several decades. Since the Democratic party championed civil rights in the 1960s and since Republican Richard Nixon's "law and order" campaign turned the Democrats' moral values on civil rights into an electoral vice, no Democratic presidential candidate has won a majority of white votes in the South. The white-black partisan divide was with us well before anybody zeroed in on how religion affects national election outcomes. Simply stated, the race gap remains bigger than the religion gap because most churched blacks still vote with unchurched whites for Democrats.

By the same token, in 2006, Republicans lost both the House and the Senate to Democrats. A prominent theme in the instant analyses offered by some television talking heads was that the shift reflected a significant Republican loss of support among evangelical voters. Actually, exit polls showed that 2006 Republican congressional candidates drew 72 percent of the evangelical vote, compared to 75 percent in 2004 and 74 percent in 2002. Republicans lost just a bit more ground among all voters who attend religious services weekly: 53 percent in 2006, compared to 57 percent in 2004 and 57 percent in 2002. To the limited extent that the Republicans' loss was related to religion rather than to public displeasure with Bush's Iraq policies displaced onto his party's congressional candidates, it was Catholic voters in Pennsylvania and several other states who swung to Democrats.[34]

In sum, although we now often hear that religion matters most in national elections, for at least two-thirds of all Americans, it simply does not. In American politics, religion is not the alpha and omega variable. Scholars and pundits who once ignored religion are now exaggerating its political importance. What Fiorina teaches about the culture wars applies with special force to faith and public policy in America today: "Disagreement,

division, polarization, battles, and war make good copy. Agreement, consensus, moderation, compromise, and peace do not."[35]

PROXY GOVERNMENT GETS RELIGION, 1996–2000

Whatever the truth about political polarization, government is as government does. Voters elect leaders and leaders make laws, but government agencies translate those laws into administrative action. Representative democracy begets government bureaucracy. Government policies
and programs are enunciated in rhetoric; public administration decides
what government policies and programs mean in practice.

Unfortunately, if understandably, most people find public administration boring. Even experts who know a lot about public policy (say, federal health care policy) or a particular federal program (say, Medicaid),
often know very little about how the program is actually executed or
funded, or how it actually performs.[36]

Among nonexperts, while almost everybody learns at least a little free-
market economics in high school or college, practically nobody learns
anything about how government actually works. Public administration,
the academic field in which I myself have most often worked, remains a
rather low-status academic specialty. Its only best-selling book was by
nonacademics, who radically oversimplified things.[37]

Not surprisingly, certain fundamental realities about how the American national government actually works are therefore not widely understood by many otherwise politically knowledgeable people. This includes
most Washington pundits and even veteran journalists. In relation to the
claim that the federal government wantonly discriminates against religious people and their organizations, the single most important such reality concerns so-called government-by-proxy.[38]

Simply stated, since the Second World War, the federal government
has directly administered virtually none of the domestic programs (and,
in recent decades, increasingly few of the international and even military-
related programs) that it funds in whole or in part. As University of Pennsylvania public administration scholar Donald F. Kettl was the first to

document definitively, today the federal government administers most policies and programs via grants and contracts with state and local governments, for-profit firms, and nonprofit organizations.[39]

Why the federal government has come to work via government-by-proxy is a complicated story that would take us far beyond the phenomenon's importance to the church-state questions before us (and far beyond the reader's patience as well, no doubt). In bare outline, the rise of the proxy-government system coincided with the post–World War II expansion in the size and scope of the federal government.

Ask almost any American how to address a social or economic problem, and he or she will express an opinion about what the president and Congress should do. Today, Americans expect Washington to address crime, abortion, drug abuse, campaign finance, gun control, school quality, the environment, and the homeless. But none of these issues was even on the national government's policy or program agenda as recently as the 1950s.

Now all of these issues and many others (the most recent major addition being homeland security) are on the federal policy and program agenda. Each issue that has been added in the last half-century has had its laws as well as its bureaucracies, in all cases many of each. The expansion has continued unabated without regard to which party controls either the White House, or Congress, or both.

Republicans won seven of the ten presidential elections from 1968 through 2004. Republican presidents, most notably Ronald Reagan, talked about abolishing major federal government agencies (Reagan targeted Education and Energy) but abolished none. Nor did any Republican president significantly decrease federal spending as a percentage of gross domestic product or reduce the federal civilian workforce. All endorsed various new federalism plans. All affirmed a devolution revolution in which Washington would give state and local governments a greater say in how domestic federal policies and programs were designed, funded, and administered. But, apart from coining new concepts for incumbent realities, the only effect of this Republican rhetoric was to expand the existing government-by-proxy system.

The Oval Office Democrats did the same. In the late 1970s, the Carter

White House launched various federal government reform plans, but they had little impact. One such Carter-era reform, in 1979, created the Federal Emergency Management Agency, or FEMA. New Orleans and Gulf Coast citizens got a tragic crash course on that bureaucracy and its proxies, including the American Red Cross, after Hurricane Katrina struck in 2005. Led by Vice President Gore, in the 1990s the Clinton White House launched the so-called National Performance Review (NPR), better known as the "reinventing government" initiative. It achieved some notable successes, and it was associated with a nontrivial reduction in the federal civilian workforce. Even its biggest fans, however, do not contend that it succeeded in its publicly proclaimed goal of making most federal agencies "work better and cost less." The NPR did nothing significant to roll back government-by-proxy.

But the main credit or blame for the proxy-government system belongs to Congress. Essentially, government-by-proxy has grown out of the desire, shared by post–World War II congresspersons in both parties, to respond to new public demands while not appearing to spend much more public money and without appearing to create big new federal government bureaucracies.

Without regard to party or ideology, the proxy-government system suits most congresspersons' political self-interest. As University of Virginia political scientist Martha Derthick has explained, "Congress loves action—it thrives on policy proclamation and goal setting—but it hates bureaucracy and taxes, which are the instruments of action. Overwhelmingly, it has resolved this dilemma by turning over the bulk of administration to the state governments or any organizational instrumentality it can lay its hands on whose employees are not counted on the federal payroll."[40]

Despite a half-dozen major post-1950 federal government reform initiatives, nothing has yet happened in Congress to put the proxy-government genie back in its pre–World War II bottle. As even many knowledgeable small-government conservatives and libertarian Republican loyalists admit, the 1994–2006 Republican ascendancy in Congress resulted mainly in federal government "business as usual."[41] Thus, by 2006 for every one federal civil servant, there were nearly seven government-by-proxy employees (state and local government workers, for-profit con-tractors, and nonprofit grantees) administering federal policies and pro-grams, and paid entirely or mostly with federal dollars.

Government-by-proxy has been plagued by problems. The famously flawed Hubble Space Telescope, massive fraud in Medicare, the floods of criticism that have followed FEMA's responses to natural disasters—scratch the surface of these and countless other federal government fail-ures, and you will find proxy-government mismanagement, waste, and abuse staring back at you.

Now, the really bad news. For decades, many state governments have exploited major federal-state programs like Medicaid in ways that ex-plode program costs without generating any offsetting benefits. Although many public officials have sincerely tried, no one has ever been able to fix such intergovernmental messes. Similarly, complaints and scandals in-volving the federal government's for-profit contractors, military as well as domestic, make headlines and fill volumes but persist.

For our purposes, the single most significant proxy-government failure is how the system has favored a relatively small set of large nonprofit or-ganizations. It has favored them with renewable, multiyear grants even though most of these sizable (and often politically well connected) or-ganizations have never been subjected to a single independent perfor-mance evaluation or systematic performance audit.

Large national nonprofit organizations, *including* faith-based mega-charities, have long been a part of the government-by-proxy system. Not so, however, most small- to medium-sized community-based social ser-vice delivery organizations. Whether religious *or* secular, these grassroots groups have faced multiple barriers to participation in the federal grant-making process—barriers largely or entirely unrelated to their organiza-tional histories or performance records.

Where government-by-proxy is concerned, a "relatively select group of large social-service and health non-profits" have "long received the bulk of public funding."[42] All together, large religious nonprofit organi-zations have received tens of billions of dollars in government grants. The sacred and the secular have also mixed for many decades at religious col-leges and universities that have received public money, including federal funds, for multiple educational and infrastructure purposes.[43] Tax-funded "religiously tied social service organizations have always played a big role in American society," and the "long history of collaboration between government and religious institutions . . . is still going strong."[44]

But that long history of collaboration has a missing chapter: grassroots community-serving religious organizations. For decades now, many citizens who lead grassroots nonprofit social service organizations—especially small urban religious groups that serve primarily low-income Latino and African American children, youth, and families—have maintained that they and their organizations are given short shrift by government agencies, both with respect to funding and with respect to technical assistance.

Their complaints are sometimes exaggerated but, in the main and writ large, they have merit. Some grassroots religious groups receive funding from larger, more-established religious nonprofits. Some receive token funding from local governments, and occasionally attract private foundation or corporate dollars. For the most part, however, grassroots community-serving organizations, both religious *and* secular, receive little or no public money, as well as little or no corporate or philanthropic support.

In relation to community-serving religious nonprofits, the corporate and philanthropic communities can answer for themselves and are free to do pretty much as they please. Not so, however, the federal government.

Constitutionally, the Court's neutrality doctrine is not supposed to end where federal public administration begins. Government-by-proxy is constitutional, but discriminating against prospective proxy-government agents because they happen to be religious in character is not. Proxy government is legal, but tilting the grant-making process against faith-based organizations that are otherwise qualified to participate in accordance with all policy- or program-specific rules and regulations is not.

The half-century-old proxy-government system is teeming with compliance, oversight, and accountability problems; but it is unethical, as well as unconstitutional and illegal, to take these problems seriously only when government-by-proxy appears, as it were, in religious drag. And it is doubly wrong to selectively insist that small local faith-based organizations adhere in every particular to fiscal, administrative, and performance standards that have been largely ignored (or worse) for decades where the system's large for-profit and nonprofit players are concerned.

The persistent problem is that small urban faith-based organizations receive last priority (at best) or are unfairly discriminated against (at worst) when it comes to receiving federal financial support or related government technical assistance. This occurs even when grassroots religious organizations supply the bulk of available social services to their needy neighbors; even where they tend to the youngest, the neediest, or the most difficult-to-serve populations in their own communities without regard to beneficiaries' religious orientations; and even when they boast long-standing working partnerships with local government agencies or secular nonprofit organizations. It occurs even in cases where they have been subjected to rigorous independent performance evaluations or audits that most large and well-funded nonprofits always manage to escape, and even where they have achieved, or declared a willingness to achieve, Internal Revenue Service section 501(c)3 nonprofit status.

To cite just two typical examples, studies document that local criminal justice agencies partner extensively with urban grassroots religious groups to deliver court-mandated education, employment, and other services to minority youth who have gotten into serious trouble with the law.[45] Yet in 2001 the U.S. Department of Justice awarded only one-third of 1 percent—.003 percent—of its discretionary grant funds to faith-based organizations, and virtually nothing to minority-led youth outreach street ministries.[46] Likewise, studies find that local faith-based programs supply a significant fraction of urban welfare-to-work services, but they are denied public funding at three times the rate that otherwise comparable secular nonprofits are rejected and receive, on average, so much less funding than do their secular counterparts that "a *prima facie* case can be made that discrimination is going on."[47]

In the mid-1990s I and a few other scholars began to focus wider academic and media attention on growing empirical evidence that diverse urban sacred places were serving multiple civic purposes and functioning as critical social service delivery agents in America's poorest communities. At the same time, many local religious leaders began to address themselves publicly to what some have called the "grassroots-govern-ment funding gap."

As press attention mounted, many politicians in both parties became more interested in talking about faith-based programs. For Democrats, discussing faith-based programs promised to reinvigorate the public dis-course about poverty and social welfare in America. For Republicans, faith-based programs underlined the need to go beyond traditional big-government approaches to poverty and social welfare in America.

Before the decade was out, bipartisan beliefs favoring faith-based pro-grams left four federal legislative marks, namely, the four aforemen-tioned charitable choice laws. As noted previously, in 1996 Senator Ashcroft crafted the first charitable choice law. In 2002 David Kuo, the su-pertalented young Ashcroft aide and evangelical Christian who had co-drafted the provision, became deputy director of the White House Office of Faith-Based and Community Initiatives under the office's second di-rector, Jim Towey.

Kuo, who I first met in the early 1990s through ex–drug czar and Edu-cation secretary William Bennett, had been a Bush speechwriter in 1999. He was known as a brilliant wordsmith with a "who's who" D.C. rolodex that included everyone from religious conservatives like Christian Coali-tion wunderkind Ralph Reed, to Republican heavyweights like Bennett, to leading journalists like Joe Klein and E. J. Dionne. With encouragement from other senior staff members, I recruited him to work in the new of-fice a few months after it had opened. In 2003 he suffered a major health malady and left the office some months thereafter.

Then, in 2005 and 2006 Kuo came to public attention. He argued that the West Wing had cheaply politicized the president's compassion agenda and self-critically warned fellow born-again believers to eschew "pastor-in-chief" power politics.[48] Gerson and other Bush loyalists volleyed back, as did assorted GOP operatives, religious leaders, and radio jocks. But reports by research organizations seemed to back him.[49] So did a federal (Western District of Wisconsin) lawsuit by the Freedom From Religion Foundation charging Towey and others with unlawful po-litical activities pursued in violation of the Establishment clause.

Nonetheless, Bush critic Kuo, Bush loyalist Gerson, and most others who had been midwives at the faith-based creation, never stopped touting charitable choice, and for good reason. The charitable choice laws were intended to ensure that religious nonprofit organizations, including small ones based in low-income urban communities, received equal treatment, *not* special treatment, from the federal government. The laws were designed to be completely consistent with the Court's neutrality doctrine. In particular, they were tailored to tap the bipartisan sentiment and majority support for forging church-state partnerships to help achieve antipoverty goals and related civic objectives.

Together, the four 1996–2000 charitable choice laws were meant to level the federal proxy-government grant-making playing field for grassroots and other religious nonprofit groups. The intent was to level the playing field, *not* tilt it in favor of faith-based organizations. All told, the four laws applied to tens of billions of grant-making dollars, flowing through dozens of social programs and policies across many different federal cabinet departments and agencies. The four charitable choice laws embodied four constitutionally correct public administration neutrality principles, each one favored by most Americans and leaders in both parties:

- *No funds for proselytizing, sectarian worship, or religious instruction:*
  Diverse partnerships between government and religious organizations are entirely permissible, provided that faith-based organizations use public funds only to fulfill social service goals or other civic or secular purposes, as directed by public law and relevant grant-program-specific terms and conditions. The language to this effect was quite explicit. The 1996 law's section headed "Limitations on Use of Funds for Certain Purposes" reads as follows: "No public funds provided directly to institutions or organizations to provide services and administer programs . . . shall be expended for sectarian worship, instruction, or proselytization."

- *Do not treat religiously motivated volunteers as second-class citizens:*
  The leaders, employees, and volunteers of faith-based programs are eligible to administer public programs and supply social services, and they may do so on the same basis as all other citizens, to be neither included nor excluded, neither advantaged nor disadvantaged, because they are religious, too religious, or practice the "wrong" reli-

gion. The 1996 law's section headed "Nondiscrimination Against Religious Organizations" provided ample safeguards against any government official, federal or state, forcing a religious nonprofit to "alter its form of internal governance" or "remove religious art, icons," or other "symbols" in order "to be eligible to contract to provide assistance, or to accept certificates, vouchers, or other forms of disbursement under" the relevant federal programs.

- *Respectfully serve all clients or beneficiaries without regard to religion:*
  In administering programs supported in whole or in part by public funds, religious organizations may not discriminate against any individual on the basis of religion, a religious belief, or refusal to participate in a religious practice, and government must guarantee that a wholly secular alternative is available to any beneficiary who prefers one. The 1996 law's section headed "Nondiscrimination Against Beneficiaries" was crystal clear on all these and related counts.

- *Faithfully follow all existing civil rights laws governing employment:*
  As noted in chapter 2, in their capacities as houses of worship, faith-based organizations, most notably churches, synagogues, mosques, and other religious congregations, have a near-absolute constitutional right to take religion into account in making employment decisions (for example, synagogues need not interview priests). Likewise, in supplying social services without any public funds, their right to hire on religious grounds remains near absolute. But, when supplying social services with public funds, they must honor all existing federal civil rights laws governing employment and may be subject to other federal, state, and local employment antidiscrimination laws. The 1996 law explicitly directed that "a religious organization's exemption provided under section 702 of the Civil Rights Act of 1964 . . . shall not be affected by its participation in, or receipt of funds from," the relevant federal programs.

NO BUSH VERSUS GORE ON "FAITH-BASED"

Between 1996 and 2000, charitable choice laws did little to quiet the claim that federal government agencies wantonly discriminate against religious people and institutions or to turn down the volume on neo-Anti-Federalist barbs about judicial tyranny. Part of the blame belongs to the Clinton White House, which was not terribly astute or aggressive about implementing charitable choice laws or monitoring their results.

The laws came to fruition during Clinton's second term. That term was badly hamstrung by the sex scandal involving the president and a White House intern, Monica Lewinsky. The scandal set asunder well-laid Clinton-Gore plans on many issues far more politically salient, socially important, or globally consequential than recalibrating federal public administration to make it more fully consistent with church-state neutrality principles. Some observers believe that the guilt-by-association vote cost Gore the 2000 presidential election in several states that he and Clinton had carried in 1996, including Gore's own state, Tennessee.

That is debatable, but nobody doubts that the scandal stole steam from many policy and program initiatives, both major and minor. The scandal begat political dynamics unfavorable to Clinton's centrist leanings. As the media pressure mounted and congressional impeachment proceedings unfolded, Clinton rallied the party's liberal congressional leaders, and its liberal base voters, to defend him against conservative opinion-makers and Republican attackers. Accordingly, he trimmed his centrist or New Democrat positions on multiple matters, domestic and international.

Liberal Democrats were never comfortable with charitable choice laws in the first place. As several well-placed senior Clinton administration officials confided to me at the time, and again after Clinton left office, charitable choice implementation never got any real traction as a White House priority. Said one, "You can't expect him to be Nixon opening China when Nixon suddenly needs the party's anti-communist [zealots] to defend him. Besides, this isn't China. Except to policy wonks . . . it's a small and totally invisible issue." Following the 2004 presidential election, the same official updated and modified this insight: "What nobody really understood in 1999 or even in 2000 was how, by doing nothing, by appearing to be dragged into . . . [faith-friendly] positions, Gore and the whole [Democratic] party conceded the 'God issue' to Bush and the Republicans."

Another former Clinton-Gore aide lamented that "[Democrats] do this all the time. Clinton talked about God, and mentioned Jesus Christ, more than Bush did [in his first term]. . . . Clinton signed every [charitable choice provision] that got to his desk. . . . [During the 2000 campaign], the liberals yelled at Gore for invoking religion and wanted [his running-mate] Lieberman to stop mentioning God all the time. . . . [After the September 11, 2001 terrorist attacks on the United States], Lieberman was the first person in Washington to propose having a new department for 'homeland defense'. . . . But [Democrats] gave away religion in 2000 and gave away security in 2002."

It is true that Clinton actually engaged in more God talk, and used more explicitly Christian language, than his successor did. But it is not so clear that Gore conceded religion to the Republicans. As noted previously, in 1999 Gore gave a major speech touting church-state collaboration and faith-based programs two months before Bush did the same. In 2000 he and Lieberman (who continued to use religious rhetoric) made some faith-friendly noises in the Democratic party platform.

The Democrats' top party faithful, however, remained largely lukewarm on religion. Whether as a strategy for reinventing government, a tactical campaign ploy, or a point of personal conviction, on church-state issues and charitable choice ideas Gore could never win over all those in his own inner circle, let alone his party's liberal elites.

To some extent, Gore tried. As *Time* columnist Joe Klein has rightly observed, in 1999 Gore made "a thoughtful and sometimes even courageous display of policy expertise" and "risked disapproval from the party's base with his . . . support for government funding of poverty programs run by religious organizations."[50] But as Gore's 2000 campaign strategy mutated, it became progressively more Old Democrat in tone, striking familiar class-based economic themes favored by the party's progressive wing and making only episodic attempts to cut into the Republicans' support among God and guns voters.

Gore bested Bush in the popular vote but lost in the electoral college. The morning after the election, a constitutional crisis loomed over the Florida vote-count controversy. The Supreme Court stepped in and decided the matter in Bush's favor.

At least initially, the Court's five-to-four majority opinion in *Bush v. Gore* drew the expected partisan and ideological reactions: most Republican conservatives loved it, most Democratic liberals loathed it. The Court's conservatives with Republican pedigrees endorsed the decision, its liberals with Democratic pedigrees dissented. I was, at the time, the only person to write a morning-after essay condemning the Court's reasoning in a major conservative magazine (albeit condemning it for being hypocritically contrary to conservative precepts respecting law and precedent, federalism, legislative authority, and local custom).[51]

To a degree that has yet to be duly appreciated even by careful observers, the Florida vote-count controversy and the uproars that followed the Court's conservative-liberal split decision favoring Bush, affected the pre–9/11 Bush White House politically and did so in a manner very similar to how the Lewinsky scandal had affected the outgoing administration.

Bush had sought the office as a centrist "compassionate conservative" who had distanced himself explicitly from the "destructive" idea that merely cutting government was next to godliness. Upon entering office in January 2001, he faced a no-honeymoon Congress. Many Democrats, even centrists, were in full partisan attack mode. Congressional Republicans and their conservative loyalists were ready to rally to the new president's defense. They did, but at a price.

In record time, Capitol Hill Republicans passed Bush's massive tax-cut bill. Soon thereafter, they let him be a "uniter, not a divider" by passing his No Child Left Behind education bill. They did so even though the bill, drafted largely in concert with liberal Democratic senator Ted Kennedy of Massachusetts, contained no voucher provisions and had built in significant federal spending increases on (so-called Title I) public schools where low-income urban children are highly concentrated.

But these legislative successes were the extent of congressional Republican support for any major component of Bush's compassion agenda. Especially during the first 180 days, Republicans were prepared to back Bush against Florida-frenzied Democrats, but only so far, and only if the education bill was the first and last major bipartisan compromise (or "sell out," as some Republican leaders who ballyhooed the measure in public bashed it in private).

As one Republican congressional strategist stated matter of factly in a February 2001 meeting that I attended, on anything having to do with religion, all that "really matters" is keeping Democrats on the political "defensive." Far from capitalizing on bipartisan church-state sentiments and mass support, faith-based initiatives, the strategist summarized, should contain proposals that "force [Democrats]" into opposition and make it easier to depict Democrats in Congress, even the faith-friendly centrists among them, as America's "anti-God squad." (To this day, remembering the moment and recalling the phrase gives me a knot in my stomach.)

But it takes two not to tango. For their part, congressional Democrats were not about to give Bush so much as a rhetorical victory, let alone any actual legislative or administrative victory, on any issue that might show him to be above politics or sincere in his bipartisan sentiments about certain social policy issues. As one liberal Democratic leader in Congress lectured me in February 2001, "I don't care if [you] re-type Clinton's stuff and give Gore credit. Hell, I don't care if he [endorses my own bill] or promises us [support on home-district projects]. . . . This president is getting nothing else fast, no matter what." (A second stomach knot followed this conversation.)

Even if the "compassion is real," a centrist Democratic leader in Congress told me apologetically in July 2001, even if the White House were to supply policy "details by the bucket" that make good sense and "strike the right balance," and even if the main beneficiaries would be "poor people who normally vote Democratic anyway," there is no "desire to let the president get credit or win big through compromise." The "charitable choice consensus," this Democrat predicted, would remain "buried for some time to come." Initially because "of [the Florida vote-count controversy] and now because [the White House staff] has played real hardball on everything except education . . . whatever the president says about [faith-based programs], the focus through 2004 will be on what the people on his right [in the House] and other extremists say about them." An aide to this leader confided, "Look, both sides now feel they . . . just have to continue the food fight and keep their base supporters fired up and lined up. Frankly, I hate to say so, but I wish [he] would do the same. . . . The center on this thing is a lonely and risky place to be."

The aide was perhaps more right than she knew. The saga of President Bush's faith-based initiative from 2001 and my tenure as the nation's first "faith czar" through 2006, and the appointment of my second and third successors, is a story of a political center that did not hold. Partisan and ideological extremists on each side, at both ends of Pennsylvania Avenue, and in the media stopped the original Bush compassion plan before it got started. Sinfully, they turned reasonable disagreements about implementing charitable choice laws and complicated questions about what Washington should do to help more faith-based organizations to help more people in need, into inside-the-beltway, base-rallying battles over issues like gay rights.

As chapter 4 chronicles, President Bush began in 2001 with a bipartisan plan that respected religious pluralism and promised substantial increases in federal support for community-serving religious nonprofits. But literally before the new office was opened, the original plan was political compost and, as 2007 began, most grassroots faith-based organizations remained unwelcome total strangers to the federal proxy-government system, just as they had been a decade earlier before the first charitable choice law passed in 1996.

But this past need not be prologue. The political center on church-state issues can be made to hold. The empirical truth about how most faith-based organizations serve people in need, with or without public support, can begin to free us from each extreme's factions. Chapter 5 summarizes the latest and best scientific evidence bearing on community-serving religious nonprofits and how various faith factors promote social well-being. The two concluding chapters examine how the godly republic's faith-based future can be made brighter than its recent past for all including the nation's most severely at-risk urban children and youth.

FOUR The President's Bipartisan Prayer

FAITH-BASED WITHOUT WORKS IS DEAD

On April 27, 2006, my first successor as faith czar, Jim Towey, stood with me at the pulpit of a packed church in Philadelphia. It was to be his last public appearance as a White House official. We were both there to celebrate the fifth anniversary of Amachi, a national program for mentoring children with incarcerated parents. Amachi is an Ibo-Nigerian word meaning "Who knows but what God has brought us through this child." I had helped to hatch the program in the late 1990s. I was there to receive an award from the program's two main sponsoring organizations, Big Brothers Big Sisters of America and Public/Private Ventures. Jim was there to echo the praise that President Bush himself had heaped on the program over the years, including during several events with Amachi leaders, volunteers, and beneficiaries in Philly. He touted the president's Mentoring the Children of Prisoners program, which had dedicated $150 million over four years to this mission.

A little over four years earlier, before he started as director in February 2002, Jim had spent several hours with me in Philly. We had not met before, but we were both pro-life and pro-poor Catholic Democrats (he had once worked as Mother Teresa's legal counsel). We both knew more than we should about professional wrestling circa the 1960s. We both liked a good (or bad) joke, too. That made it all the easier to answer his questions about what (and who) he was truly up against, and what might actually be accomplished, come what may.

Sitting in my university office in west Philly, I told Jim that I believed the president was completely sincere in wanting faith-based initiatives to achieve real and substantial civic good works, most especially for low-income children, youth, families, and communities. The president, I half-kidded, "is a closet Catholic—he believes that faith without works, or at least faith-based without works, is dead." Not only that, I added, but Bush truly wanted to keep the office and the effort as far above partisan politics as possible and as far away from serious constitutional challenges as possible.

During my White House tenure, President Bush had consistently stressed that his compassion agenda, most especially "faith-based," should remain bipartisan. Sure, sometimes the stress was situational. For instance, in late May 2001, after Senator Jim Jeffords, Republican of Vermont, bolted from the GOP, the president took to reminding reporters that his "faith guy," as he sometimes referred to me, was a Democrat: "I haven't checked his party affiliation," he told one media gaggle, "because he understands that this is not an initiative to try to gain political gain." No, the president emphasized, it was really all about making "America a better place." (A few years later, with a few exceptions made, White House personnel, including in my old office, would be told in no uncertain terms that they needed to be registered Republicans in order to keep working there; but in 2001, that would have seemed impossible.)

Yes, I confided to Jim, the West Wing's political warriors and their friends on Capitol Hill had played partisan games on the issue, and the Democrats had more than returned the disfavor. Still, all told, my experience had confirmed my conviction that the president himself really wanted to keep the office close to bipartisan politics, far from constitutional challenges, and positioned to produce real blessings for people in need.

With his slight build, silver hair, soft-spoken manner, lawyerly locutions, and (the ultimate giveaway) sweater, Jim looked and sounded far more like a prototypical Ivy League academic than I did. He would be coming to the director's post as a deputy assistant to the president rather than as a member of senior staff. And his office would be "outside the gates," across the street from the White House at Jackson Place. He had worked as Florida's health and human services chief. He had strong ties to the president's brother, Florida governor Jeb Bush. I advised "the professor" that his single best shot for sustained presidential attention, senior staff support (or at least no senior staff subversion), and follow-up action from the West Wing to Capitol Hill would probably be new money for Amachi-type programs.

As I recounted for Jim, in 1999 and 2000, in my first one-on-one briefings with then Texas governor Bush, I had used these programs to illustrate what real-world civic-good faith-based and community initiatives could help to achieve while staying within church-state limits and breeding bipartisan sentiments.

The nation, I had tutored the future president, had over two million children with parents incarcerated. Innocent children in low-income, crime-torn inner-city neighborhoods with parents behind bars were America's most severely at-risk children—at extreme risks for everything from school failure to delinquency to chronic unemployment to premature death. Yet nobody had focused much serious attention on them. Mentoring was a proven way to improve life prospects for even the most truly disadvantaged youngsters. The social science research on its efficacy in reducing extreme risks was overwhelming. But, research aside, most efforts to actually mobilize mentors to serve this especially challenging population had fallen far short or failed. For one thing, even the best mentoring programs relied on the parent or guardian to take the first step by contacting the organization. Thus, to get impoverished inner-city children with imprisoned parents a mentor, it would be necessary for the program to take the first step, including working from inside the prisons out.

Or, as Bush once eagerly quipped back to me, "If this thing's gonna work, we just gotta go on out and get 'em." Exactly, and not only that, but the mentors would need to be people with extra-special dedication, willing to get up close and personal with often deeply dysfunctional families residing in blighted, high-crime places.

Enter the inner-city black churches and other local churches, from which the mentors could be mobilized wholesale to help their own needy young neighbors. Enter partnerships among and between the churches, other religious congregations, secular nonprofit organizations, private foundations, and government agencies. And enter a hoped-for billion-dollar federal compassion fund to match a quarter to fifty cents of each dollar spent on duly structured and evaluated mentoring programs for this purpose. The average mentoring match made by gold-standard organizations like Big Brothers Big Sisters cost about $1,000 a year. A billion bucks a year from private foundations, charities, and local governments could fund a million matches. Match that nonfederal compassion kitty with federal funds for proven programs, and the outside potential and promise would be two million matches a year. Next to literacy, mentoring was the civic purpose that drew the fewest ideological, partisan, or church-state gadflies. "Big John," the president said to me more than once, "let's make this work."

It did not work; but, as Jim Towey truthfully told the church crowd, President Bush from day one had remained steadfast in his desire to have Washington help expand high-quality mentoring programs for children with incarcerated parents. Together with Jim, a few key White House aides had remained steadfast, too. But, as I had warned Jim in Philly four years earlier, unless he proved to be a miracle worker (or a hell-raiser), faith-based actions, even on Amachi-type programs near and dear to the president's heart, would be confined mainly to occasional speeches, symbolic gestures, base-pleasing executive orders, and conferences that supported public liaison purposes, served as legislative bargaining chips, or squared with campaign politics priorities.

By way of typical example, I recounted for Jim a hastily arranged 2001 Roosevelt Room "compassion" photo-op session in which the president and the First Lady met with leaders from Lions, Rotary, Optimist, Kiwanis, and Big Brothers Big Sisters of America. I had no role in scheduling the event, but I was called in to moderate it. The meeting was to announce "the million mentors initiative." Million? What? Who? How? Huh? It was too late to pull the plug on the gathering. And it was too late for me to get in to see the president before he and the First Lady came to the table and risked slight embarrassment. But in the few minutes with the guests before the cameras rolled in, the president caught my furtive glances. Perceptively, he lobbed me a question that permitted me to admit, on his behalf, what the leaders already knew, namely, that we had no plan or program in place but aspired to do good and to make good. The president was candid, too.

After the million mentors meeting, he told me to tell Andy Card, then the White House chief of staff, what had happened. Mixing the president's Texas vernacular with my own Philly vocabulary, I told Andy that such "half-assed stuff on faith-based" had better stop. I also reiterated how certain well-intentioned West Wing colleagues, senior and junior, kept trying (albeit unsuccessfully, save in one case) to back me and my office into hyper-partisan, GOP-only public events that raised hackles even among our most understanding Democratic allies, such as Ohio representative Tony Hall and Connecticut senator Joe Lieberman. Andy listened, agreed, and even asked me to tell the cautionary tales to all at the senior staff retreat held on July 9, 2001. I did, and the reactions were predictably defensive. But I finished my president-certified sermon. Better, I preached, to say and do nothing at all than to say and do things calculated for message edges or partisan advantages.

In 2003 some substantive White House action on faith-based and community initiatives was triggered by much-publicized criticisms that I had made in late 2002 about the administration's failure to put any actual flesh on the bones of so-called compassionate conservatism.[1] I had praised the president but harshly blamed the "Mayberry Machiavellis" on his staff. The phrase and the critique caught media fire. Even though I immediately apologized, retracted my broad-brushed barbs, and did no media whatsoever myself, the president called senior staff to account. This momentarily forced "faith-based" back on to their to-do lists.

Thereafter, the West Wing rapidly resurrected certain compassion agenda proposals, most notably the push for Amachi-type programs that became the Mentoring the Children of Prisoners (MCP). Still, to move this program from rhetoric to reality, John M. Bridgeland, the former Domestic Policy Council chief who became the president's first director of USA Freedom Corps, had to battle almost daily.

From election season 2004 through mid-2006, the president's bipartisan prayers for faith-based and community initiatives, his hopes for achieving major civic results by mobilizing the "armies of compassion," seemed like little more than minor historical footnotes in waiting. But I continued to believe that the bipartisan vision could be realized, if not by or before 2008, then thereafter. On the same day that Jim and I were together celebrating Amachi at the Philly church, I said so in a full-page op-ed in a local newspaper.[2] Therein I reiterated my view that the president had honestly wanted faith-based and community initiatives to achieve real civic results in a bipartisan spirit and with a clearly constitutional writ.

But I also criticized the West Wing (my first such public criticisms since late 2002) for talking from both sides of its mouth, most blatantly on the Mentoring the Children of Prisoners program. Specifically, the White House's 2007 budget fact sheet praised the program and boasted that $40 million of the $150 million was slated to be distributed to worthy grantees; but, simultaneously, its ExpectMore.gov website sentenced the MCP to budget cuts by placing it on a "results not demonstrated" list, ostensibly because, as the website asserted, it had "yet to achieve its ambitious goal of establishing 100,000 matches."

Through 2006, the MCP program's slower-than-expected progress on 100,000 matches was begat mainly by dumber-than-dirt decisions made by the grant-making federal agency (like selecting as grantees several groups with zero track record as mentoring organizations) and by the White House's own funding shell games (the $150 million for mentoring had been redirected in part to other worthy purposes). But, through early 2007, the MCP was still the single most impressive new domestic program to result from the president's faith-based and community initiatives. As such, it was at once a credit to the president and a measure of just how far short of his original prayers, hopes, and plans the effort had fallen.

In August 2006 Jim Towey, who was promoted to senior staff just after the president's reelection, was succeeded at the deputy assistant level by the well-regarded Jay Hein, former head of a policy research institute in Indiana. In 2003 through early 2007, I was called or contacted by senior and other White House officials, invited to come in for various advisory purposes and events, and asked to address certain policy ideas or proposals on paper. When I responded, I did so in writing or by phone rather than in person or by revisiting the West Wing.

As I have consistently maintained, both in public and in private, both to Bush loyalists and to Bush critics, given constitutional fidelity, administrative true grit, and adequate funding, faith-based and community initiatives can yet measurably help millions of people in need without playing partisan games or violating the Constitution. Standing with Jim Towey and celebrating Amachi before a church crowd containing many of my hometown's most dedicated community-serving clergy, my mind turned back to early 2001, to President Bush, and to the bipartisan road paved but not yet taken.

THREE STEPS TO THE ROAD NOT TAKEN

On January 29, 2001, the new administration's first Monday in the White House, President Bush announced that he was nominating former Indianapolis mayor Stephen Goldsmith, the well-respected moderate Republican who had been Bush's chief domestic policy advisor during the 2000 presidential campaign, to become chairman of the Corporation for National Service (CNS).[3] Next, he announced that he was appointing me, a university professor and a Democrat who had studied and worked closely with many local and national faith-based organizations, to be a White House senior advisor (an Assistant to the President, sitting alongside Assistants Karl Rove, Karen Hughes, Condoleezza Rice, and others), and director of the new White House Office of Faith-Based and Community Initiatives (OFBCI).

The two personnel appointments were not coincidental. Goldsmith, in consultation with speechwriter and domestic advisor Michael Gerson and other senior Bush campaign hands, was to lead the administration's compassion agenda during the president's first term. Initially, Goldsmith was to exercise this leadership as CNS chief and as a member of the president's domestic policy kitchen cabinet. In due course, it was widely assumed, he would exercise it more formally as secretary of a domestic cabinet department (probably Health and Human Services or Housing and Urban Development). I was a longtime friend of Goldsmith's. I had first gotten to know him when he was the mayor of Indianapolis. I also knew many senior and junior Bush White House aides.

Before 2001, I had met several times with Bush. I liked him. I had publicly argued that his faith-friendly compassionate conservatism, if properly developed into a workable governing philosophy, had a fighting chance to succeed in making the government-by-proxy system perform better, especially in administering antipoverty programs. I harbored both high hopes and serious doubts.[4]

But I was, indeed, a Democrat, albeit a pro-life Catholic one with conservative credentials on some issues. I also liked Gore, mainly from work on government reform that I had done in the mid-1990s via the Brookings Institution and from contacts with him in 1999. I had worked with both the Bush and Gore campaigns, though more extensively with the former.[5] But I had endorsed neither candidate. As noted in chapter 3, I had publicly criticized the Supreme Court's *Bush v. Gore* decision that ended the Florida vote-count controversy in Bush's favor.

Also, I had only recently switched universities and launched new research programs on religion. As I publicly stated at the time, I agreed to serve in the new Bush White House but only for six months, or just long enough to help the OFBCI complete a multiagency review of grant-making procedures (officially due in 180 days) that was mandated by executive order.

The six-month plan for 2001 called for the CNS and the OFBCI to begin to work jointly and incrementally to put charitable choice rhetoric into practice. Specifically, the original compassion-in-action plan as it related to faith-based and community initiatives had three bipartisan objectives: studying and implementing existing charitable choice laws, match-funding model religious-secular or public-private partnerships, and seeding OFBCI counterparts in mayors' offices across the country.

Studying and Implementing Existing Charitable Choice Laws

In 2001, four years after the first charitable choice law had taken effect, not many community-serving religious organizations had applied for federal grants. The aforementioned review mandated by executive order was intended to examine the extent to which the federal government itself posed barriers to the full and effective participation of these groups in the application process. Led by my office's Stanley Carlson-Ties, a half-dozen agency aides co-produced the mostly factual report. It met my basic specifications for the (rushed) audit. With help from my office's David Kuo, I edited it into shape, entitled it *Unlevel Playing Field,* and touted it in speeches and op-ed articles. It was released on time in August 2001.

As noted in chapter 3, as of early 2007 the report was still available via the White House website (www.whitehouse.gov, OFBCI link). I resigned when the staff work neared completion and publicly announced my resignation immediately following the press event, held at the Brookings Institution, on the day that the report was released. The president reluctantly accepted my resignation in a two-page, heartfelt handwritten letter dated August 17, 2001.

As the report reckoned, there was already ample evidence to suggest that faith-based organizations in urban neighborhoods were especially active in delivering a very wide range of social services to low-income children, youth, and families. Studies had also intimated that, even without any public funds, most of these organizations operated in ways that would likely pass muster under charitable choice: there was no proselytizing, they served all without regard to religion, they did not hire only co-religionists, and they had or were willing to establish separate, IRS-sanctioned 501(c)3 entities. But while many urban ministries apparently wished to consider applying for grants, it was widely thought that most probably needed technical assistance such as targeted notifications of funding availability, grant-writing assistance, financial accounting training, and more.

Whether or not these grassroots religious social service groups ever received any federal grants, such technical assistance, long enjoyed by other proxy-government nonprofit organizations, could prove highly valuable. Technical assistance could help them to apply for private foundation support, build computer-assisted personnel and fiscal management systems, and so on. Large national faith-based nonprofit organizations like Habitat for Humanity, a personal favorite of mine, had relied on the CNS, specifically AmeriCorps staff and Senior Corps volunteers, "to recruit, manage, and organize" faith-motivated and other "traditional volunteers."[6]

But grassroots religious groups and other local faith-based organizations had rarely benefited from such federal help. Charitable choice laws, on the books since 1996, had produced civic results that were ambiguous or, as some maintained, practically nonexistent. As I had told the future president in 1999 and 2000, antireligious bias by bureaucrats and the like undoubtedly figured in the story, but it could not possibly be the whole story. Both then and in early 2001, he agreed with enthusiasm that the right first step would be a breathtakingly academic one: dispassionately studying the public administration and intergovernmental relations that had been associated with the laws to date, devising multiple and competing detailed plans for how best to improve their implementation, and assessing the civic results before any new such legislation was proposed.

Match-Funding Model Religious-Secular and Public-Private Partnerships

Charitable choice laws are concerned with the public administration of federal programs, *not* the total amount of money or types of grants available. Least of all do they involve any financial "set asides" for religious programs. In fact, among my first official acts as OFBCI director was to identify a Clinton-era program (a $5 million grant operation within the Department of Health and Human Services) that had functioned, de facto, as a financial set-aside for religious organizations, and direct that it be ended forthwith. (It was.)

The whole point of charitable choice was to rid the proxy-government system of any arbitrary regard for the religious character, or lack thereof, of the prospective nonprofit grantee. All religious, political, or other considerations unrelated to an organization's capacity to meet program-specific administrative and performance protocols were to be minimized or eliminated. But neither in letter nor in spirit did charitable choice laws promise any organization, religious or secular, for-profit or nonprofit, national or local, a single new or additional penny in federal funding.

Some secular liberal critics and others carped that charitable choice implementation, even if constitutionally correct and politically even-handed, might result in faith-based organizations getting slices from existing federal funding pies that formerly went to other organizations. Arithmetically, at least, they were quite right. But, ethically and legally, that possible result was beside the point, which was to produce the best civic results possible by making the proxy-government system equally open to all qualified citizens and organizations. Besides, my own prediction, shared by several others in the administration (including, interestingly, then Office of Management and Budget director, the faith-friendly

Mitch Daniels) was that, if there were any changes in grant distribution, their net effect would be to redirect federal grants from for-profits to non-profits. This had already happened, it seemed, in some state and local jurisdictions that had begun independently to reform their public administration systems and play fair with all nonprofits including faith-based groups.

And our bipartisan hope was that, if a critical mass of new faith-based *or other* nonprofit grantees emerged and the system's results improved, then the political appetite for increasing federal funding would grow correspondingly. If, for example, proxy-administered federal housing rehabilitation dollars starting leaving more habitable homes than blighted or boarded-up buildings in their wake; if federal welfare-to-work funds found more women working in living-wage jobs with truly decent health benefits than in minimum-wage or temporary jobs with few or no benefits; if federal support for state prisoner reentry programs became associated with reductions in recidivism and increases in long-term employment among recent parolees; and so on, then the value of faith-based and community initiatives would be apparent. Accordingly, the first op-ed I wrote as faith czar was entitled "Know Us by Our Works."[7]

The plan did call for at least one big new pot of federal money. The original idea for the Compassion Capital Fund was to provide new federal matching funds to legitimate public-private or religious-secular initiatives that research had shown could tackle critical but unmet social needs on a citywide or national scale. The working assumption was that the federal match would normally amount to not more than a quarter to half of total program costs.

Inside the White House, in early 2001, Compassion Capital Fund figures ranging from $500 million over five years to $2 billion over ten years received serious attention. A mention of $700 million actually made it into President Bush's first speech before Congress in February 2001.

The original Compassion Capital Fund plan reflected the "coordination" language in the executive order that created the OFBCI and defined its director's mission. The OFBCI, the CNS, federal agency field offices, mayors' offices, secular nonprofit organizations, faith-based organizations, foundations, and private donors would all be involved in identifying exemplary faith-based and community initiatives and in coordinating efforts, public and private, national and local, to support their expansion, document their operations, monitor their performance, and measure their impact.

Amachi-type mentoring programs were just one example. As is examined more definitively in the next chapter, faith-based organizations, especially across urban America, have partnered extensively with each other (often across religious lines), with secular nonprofit organizations, with private foundations and philanthropies, with both religious and secular colleges and universities, and with government agencies to deliver vital social services to people in need. They were partners in welfare-to-work programs, juvenile delinquency and crime prevention programs, housing rehabilitation and antihomelessness programs, public health programs, literacy and antitruancy programs, drug treatment and counseling programs, and scores of other programs as well. But they were uniquely the "unpaid," and often the unacknowledged, partners in these civic ventures, even when and where, facts be told, they did most of the actual work. Nobody in government knew this better, or had more stake in changing it for real so as to expand the faith-based role in addressing urban needs and problems, than the mayors who served big cities and medium-sized ones.

Seeding OFBCI Counterparts in Mayors' Offices across the Country

As is noted in chapter 3, state and local governments are far and away the most significant players in the government-by-proxy system. Most federal social service dollars are administered through state and local governments, not via competitive grants. Well before charitable choice language debuted in the *Federal Register*, some cities administered social service delivery programs funded in whole or in part with federal dollars in conjunction with local religious congregations and other faith-based organizations. Unfortunately, many of these programs functioned in ways that left much to be desired: inadequate funding, shoddy accounting procedures, politically tinged selection processes, and so on.

Thus, our original plan called for the U.S. Conference of Mayors and other groups to begin to foster OFBCI counterparts within city govern-ments. The federal government would assist by creating new and reliable databases, seed-funding new city-led projects, and the like. Local OFBCI offices would be dedicated to helping small but qualified community-serving programs, religious or secular, access additional public *and* pri-vate support with which to better serve their own needy neighbors.

Most U.S. Conference of Mayors members are Democrats. Fearing that they might use any occasion to bash President Bush, some senior White House staff strongly opposed this critical, city-focused prong of the faith-based and community initiatives program. The president himself, how-ever, consistently supported it.

In June 2001, President Bush spoke in Detroit at the annual meeting of the U.S Conference of Mayors. The conference, led by its then-incoming president, Democrat Marc H. Morial, mayor of New Orleans, formally en-dorsed Bush's original, bipartisan plan for faith-based and community initiatives. Morial, a former Penn classmate of mine who now serves as president of the National Urban League, watched as over a hundred may-ors signed on. There was no Bush bashing. The local leaders, both Dem-ocratic and Republican, were quite willing to work with the White House in good faith.

NEUTRALITY CHALLENGES: THE BUSH FAITH BILL

Purposely absent from this three-step, incremental, bipartisan plan was any early push for new legislation that might deliberately or inadver-tently undermine or inflame the charitable choice consensus. Purposely absent from the plan was any proposal that went beyond what, in chap-ter 2, is discussed as the Court's neutrality principles. New legislation might eventually be recommended—for instance, to reflect findings in the mandated federal grant-making review or to establish the Compas-sion Capital Fund. But in early 2001 no new legislation was necessary or advisable.

Most journalists were completely unaware that Clinton-Gore era char-itable choice laws were already on the books. Few were interested in learning more or would suffer more than a minute's lecture on government-by-proxy. But they recognized that Gore had endorsed the faith-based idea in his campaign. They saw his running mate, Lieberman, welcome the original Bush plan—he appeared with Bush and me at a D.C.-based, grassroots youth outreach ministry the day after the CNS-OFBCI announcement. They heard rumors that over a dozen Democrats in the Senate had immediately climbed aboard as well. One, New York's newly elected Democratic senator Hillary Rodham Clinton, seemed to be singing from the same faith-friendly hymnal as Bush.

Still, many in the press (including many who knew better) either ignored or underplayed these complicated, consensus-bearing facts, the better to splash the conflict-laden church-state story that they (or, as several sheepishly confided to me, their editors) wanted to write or broadcast. Many stories that made it into circulation were less journalism than sensationalism: Bush was breaking entirely new ground; billions in federal funds were to be set aside for religious organizations; my office would soon have scores more people on staff; the "Christian Right" was about to raid the federal Treasury; secular civil liberties groups were bound to sue (starting with me); the federal courts would soon need to resolve the conflict; and so forth.

The media were aided and abetted in this misinformation or disinformation process by liberal and conservative academics whose overnight expertise on the subject did not prevent them from having strong views, and whose fake connections to the actual decision-makers (myself included) inflated their pretense of possessing inside information.

Yet the media and their unreliable sources only deserve a small part of the blame. Literally within a few hours of Bush's January 29, 2001 announcement, ideological factions within each party were spoiling for any excuse to spotlight and fight over controversial issues only superficially related to aiding the poor or improving social policy administration via faith-based and community initiatives.

In the run-up to the January 29, 2001 announcement, the West Wing took special pains to dampen any impression that President Bush would seek or support legislative challenges to settled church-state limits, or otherwise act to weaken, challenge, or negate the Court's neutrality doctrine.[8]

During the first 180 days after the CNS-OFBCI announcement, numerous public statements by President Bush himself plainly reiterated and
underlined that position. The day after the announcement, speaking at the
Fishing School, a local community-serving ministry in Washington, the
president underscored the fact that government, "of course, cannot fund,
and will not fund, religious activities." At the National Prayer Breakfast
on February 1, 2001, he stressed that our "plan will not favor religious
over nonreligious institutions. As president I'm interested in what's constitutional, and I'm interested in what works." At a press conference on
February 23, 2001, he answered a pointed question by saying "I strongly
respect the separation of church and state—I am a secular official."

Similarly, speaking before Congress on February 28, 2001, Bush
reprised key passages from "The Duty of Hope," his July 22, 1999 maiden
campaign speech in Indianapolis: "Government cannot be replaced by
charities or volunteers. And government should not fund religious activities."

Sitting in the gallery that night next to the First Lady was Philadelphia's faith-friendly Democratic mayor, John F. Street, the second African
American in the city's history to hold that high office. The president ad-
libbed the line I had penned for the speech, about Street helping Gore to
beat him by several hundred thousand votes in Philly. This gesture reflected the bipartisan aspirations for truly helping people in need through
the original faith-based and community initiatives plan.

In sum, the regard for religious pluralism and support for neutrality
principles that President Bush demonstrated in his "Duty of Hope"
speech continued unabated in the weeks following the CNS-OFBCI announcement in January 2001. From his May 2001 commencement address
at the University of Notre Dame to his June 2001 speech before the U.S.
Conference of Mayors, President Bush never publicly—nor, in my presence, privately—retreated one inch from these principles.

But before the OFBCI opened its doors in mid-February 2001, the
House Republican staff began to circulate various drafts of Bush "faith
bills." They shared portions of these drafts with selected members of the
Washington media and the Christian press. The bills contained several
provisions that directly challenged the constitutional neutrality principles

embodied by charitable choice laws. By March 2001, these Hill-led shenanigans, countenanced by some within the White House who viewed the president's compassion agenda rather cynically, had largely eclipsed the original three-part, bipartisan plan outlined above.

As Wheaton College political scientist Amy Black and her colleagues have recounted, the final draft bill, which became H.R. 7, the Community Solutions Act of 2001, presented myriad problems to charitable choice-minded religious pluralists and pragmatists in both parties and at both ends of Pennsylvania Avenue, including me.[9] Both privately, in numerous memos to key senior staff colleagues and in briefs at senior staff meetings, and publicly, as in a March 2001 speech, "Compassion in Truth and Action," before the National Association of Evangelicals in Dallas, I had made no secret of my view that trifling with neutrality principles was a mistake. As I repeated, challenging neutrality principles was wrong constitutionally and shortsighted politically. And it was almost completely contrary to fulfilling what the president had sincerely called his special "charge to keep"—encouraging Washington, in a bipartisan spirit, to help diverse religious congregations and faith-based organizations help people in need.

Through June 2001 the House bill, and several related proposals floated by its supporters, reflected three neutrality challenges favored by Black's religious purists: (1) permit religious nonprofit organizations to receive federal grants for programs that proselytize, promote spiritual transformation, or are otherwise indivisibly conversion-centered; (2) permit religious nonprofit organizations to receive federal grants for programs that hire as paid staff only co-religionists who share the organization's specific religious "beliefs and tenets" (as the draft bill phrased it into June 2001); and (3) summarily change how most federal social programs are financially administered, from disbursements to qualified organizations (such as grants and contracts) to disbursements to eligible individuals (specifically, vouchers or certificates).

Only in June 2001 did my public and private concerns about the House bill's controversial provisions briefly become, as it were, the White House party line. This occurred after certain Republican House leaders and veteran House and Senate Judiciary Committee staff in both parties took a closer look at the bill's fine print. These Republican congressional leaders told other senior White House advisors, and at least one bluntly told the president himself, that if the bill were to have a fighting chance of passing in the House, it would need to drop the proselytizing and employment discrimination provisions and take care that any voucher language was tepid or toothless.

A few weeks before a mid-July vote on the bill was scheduled, the aforementioned Bridgeland, then still director of the president's Domestic Policy Council, and I met with the relevant Republican House staff on Capitol Hill. Bridgeland had previously worked in the House as chief of staff to Ohio Republican representative Rob Portman (the same Portman who later became the president's third director of the Office of Management and Budget). By the time of our meeting, the West Wing had already let the relevant Republican Hill staff know that I was no longer the only White House official who thought the bill needed a major overhaul. Bridgeland chatted up the charitable choice precedents that I had been citing for months and told the *New York Times* and other media outlets that the bill needed to be brought "back into line with the Constitution."

That proved relatively easy with respect to proselytizing. The bill's language was modified to make it clear that beneficiaries who chose a religious charity could refuse to participate in any expressly religious components of the program. A few vocal religious purist critics insisted that, as one memorably phrased it, it was simply "Christophobic" to oppose using tax dollars for expressly religious activities. But nobody who actually mattered much politically fought against the change.

It was somewhat harder and more complicated to modify the bill with respect to religious hiring rights. Federal laws including Title VII of the 1964 Civil Rights Act and a 1972 statute already afforded religious organizations a limited ministerial exemption in hiring. The House bill contained language that would give religious nonprofit organizations a virtually unlimited right to hire only congenial co-religionists and pay them with public funds. Related beliefs-and-tenets proposals in the bill asserted that state and local laws to the contrary, including those that forbade employment discrimination based on sexual orientation, were to be automatically trumped by the new national law.

Having set out to build on bipartisan charitable choice laws that empowered religious groups to partner with government in serving the poor, H.R. 7 turned the debate over the Bush faith bill into a surreal clash about religious organizations being somehow coerced by federal law into hiring gays and lesbians who rejected their beliefs and tenets. Many civil libertarians, liberal Democrats, and homosexual rights organizations took the political bait. Their equally surreal counterargument was that the beliefs-and-tenets language would somehow legalize race-based employment discrimination. They also argued that steering billions of dollars to faith-based programs (nobody, save a few dial-a-quote Christian conservatives without any real West Wing clout, had actually proposed a penny in set-aside or "religion-only" grants) would divert money from distressed public schools that disproportionately served the poorest (so-called Title I) pupils. In fact, whatever its other problems (and they proved to be many), the only big Bush legislative initiative that was relevant to public education (the No Child Left Behind law) had increased federal spending on such public schools by billions of dollars.

Even experts who disagreed on other church-state matters agreed that giving religious organizations a constitutional *carte blanche* to practice employment discrimination with federal funds was overreaching. In 2001 a panel of diverse experts with signatories and draftees ranging from the National Association of Evangelicals to a former legislative counsel to Americans United for Separation of Church and State, had concluded:

> Federal law does not prohibit religious organizations from taking religious beliefs and practices into account in making decisions about hiring, promotion, termination, and other conditions of employment. The Supreme Court has not addressed whether a religious organization retains the liberty to make employment decisions on the basis of religion in the case of employees who work in programs or activities funded (in whole or in part) by, or paid with, government money. Although the law is not settled in this area of government-funded positions, we agree that religious organizations retain their ability to use religious criteria in employment for those positions in nongovernmental programs that are wholly privately funded, regardless of whether other programs or activities of the organization receive government funds.[10]

By mid-July 2001, the beliefs-and-tenets language had been stripped from the bill. Repeated efforts to reintroduce it were blocked. On July 10, 2001, a front-page *Washington Post* story summarized a Salvation Army internal document which claimed that the White House had entered into a secret deal with the Salvation Army. Allegedly, this arrangement granted the organization a federal waiver exempting it from state and local employment antidiscrimination laws covering sexual orientation. It soon became clear that this document contained misinformation and that no such deal had been contemplated, let alone cut.[11] Still, the media frenzy surrounding the story put on hold the religious purists' push for White House action favoring unlimited religious employment rights.

The voucher demand survived the redrafting process. But the voucher provision that was inserted into H.R. 7 in the eleventh hour was worded in ways that rendered it, as one White House colleague from Texas quipped, "all hat, no cattle." The final H.R.7 bill also contained a few provisions that cultivated consensus (for example, its food bank and charitable tax-credit provisions), but its real and perceived challenges to neutrality principles alienated many otherwise faith-friendly Democratic supporters.

H.R.7 passed the House in July 2001 with all Republicans but only fifteen Democrats voting in favor. By passing the bill in the Republican-dominated House, the president had avoided receiving an embarrassing political black eye. For that much at least I was grateful. But, as even some Republican House staff members who had gone along with the bill's partisan "anti-God squad" tactics admitted to me years later, the bill's challenges to neutrality principles were perverse from the start and proved disastrous. Regardless, everybody knew that the bill was dead before its arrival in the Senate.

Shortly after the House vote, I invited Republican senator Rick Santorum of Pennsylvania and Democratic senator Joe Lieberman of Connecticut to the White House. To help get that meeting arranged and approved at my end of Pennsylvania Avenue, I circulated to key West Wing colleagues fresh copies of memos dating back to February and March 2001. In these memos I had delineated the problems with H.R.7 and had accurately predicted both its legislative fate and the collateral public communications fallout. The two senators met with President Bush in late July, and both agreed to work with the OFBCI over the summer to draft a new charitable choice–type bill.

Immediately after the Oval Office meeting, Senator Santorum told reporters what had been agreed upon. He quickly drew criticism from some who had coveted the controversial proselytizing and religious hiring provisions. Nonetheless, work on the new bill proceeded, and the mandated OFBCI report on grant-making was released in mid-August.

I was to brief the president regarding the progress on the new bill and related matters (mainly regarding Latino church leaders) on the afternoon of September 11, 2001. I was sitting in the West Wing with Bridgeland and David Kuo when the attacks occurred. Of course, that particular briefing never happened, but the effort to bring faith-based and community initiatives back into line with neutrality principles, charitable choice precedents, bipartisan sentiment, and the president's own publicly stated and privately reiterated compassion vision nonetheless proceeded apace.

In order to complete the report on federal grant-making mandated by executive order, I had agreed to stay on at the White House for two extra months. In July 2001 Andy Card asked me whether I would agree to remain in the job for at least another year if I was permitted to move the OFBCI headquarters to Philadelphia. In reply, I told him what I had told the president, namely that, much as I still hoped that the original plan might be revived and achieved and much as I believed in the president's bipartisan compassion vision, I wanted to stick as close as possible to my public pledge to serve for only about six months. Besides, I wanted get back to my new students at Penn, reconnect with my friends and family in Philly, take better care of my health (certain chronic problems had gotten worse while I was in Washington), and resume working from suites-to-streets on faith-based and community initiatives in low-income urban communities.

The overly generous letter that the president sent to me from Crawford, Texas, in response to my resignation letter had left the door wide open. Still, I resigned as planned, going public with the news via an exclusive interview with Rebecca Carr. She worked for Cox News Service, which published papers nationally and was especially big in Texas. I was thereby rewarding Carr as one of the few journalists who I thought had done a highly responsible job of reporting on church-state issues and the Bush faith bill throughout my tenure. White House senior colleagues and other staff members showered me with warm notes, most with a please-just-stay plea or subtext. Bridgeland described me as a "sage and a saint," a phrase that several White House communicators echoed. Even West Wing colleagues with whom I had frequently disagreed wrote or spoke many kind words, both in private and in public.

Karl Rove was no exception. There was between us, then and thereafter (including after my much-publicized 2002 criticisms that centered on his dominant West Wing role), no personal animosity but only the deep policy disagreements to be expected between a Philly-bred, self-styled New Democrat public intellectual on a civic-religious mission and the most capable Republican national political operative in a hundred years. Back in August 19, 2001, he told the *Atlanta Journal-Constitution*, and repeated to others, that I was the main reason, next to the president, why "faith-based had advanced at all." He called me "the guiding spirit of this" and predicted that I would continue to play "a big, important role."

For several months after I left the White House, I continued to help shape and support the effort.[12] By October 2001 press reports suggested that a scaled-back White House proposal was in the works. If truth be told, the new proposal more closely reflected our original plan.[13] In early February 2002 a Santorum-Lieberman-led bill was drafted, and press reports correctly noted that it included charitable choice–bred language, new tax breaks for charitable giving, and more money for social services block grants (for day care and other services), but not new provisions for proselytizing, hiring rights, or indirect aid (voucher) provisions.[14] One newspaper offered this headline: "Accord Reached on Charitable Aid Bill after Bush Gives In on Hiring."[15] That was about half-right: Bush had agreed to support the new bill, but up to that point, the administration had never officially supported any legislative proposal or executive order that challenged neutrality principles.

In announcing Jim Towey as my successor in February 2002, President Bush repeated what he had often said when discussing faith-based and community initiatives, namely, that "there are things more important than political parties."[16] In his 2002 State of the Union Address, the president had launched USA Freedom Corps, naming Bridgeland as its first director. Charged with volunteer mobilization and related tasks, Bridgeland's new office was tied to the old CNS. Although the Goldsmith-DiIulio/CNS-OFBCI plan was by then ancient history, Towey now reported to Bridgeland, an assistant to the president, thereby linking the two White House offices. For all the controversy surrounding the Bush faith bill, something like the original bipartisan Bush compassion-in-action agenda suddenly seemed to have a new lease on life.

BELIEVERS ONLY NEED APPLY?

It was not to be, however. The 9/11 national unity moment lasted only a few months in Washington. Homeland security became a partisan issue in the November 2002 midterm congressional races. In both parties, political campaigning focused on core—or base—issues, and constituencies became even more pronounced than they had been in 2001. On church-state issues, House Democrats, egged on by the party's secular liberal faithful, threatened to kill existing charitable choice laws and to strip existing religious hiring rights from the federal books.

The secular liberal Democratic push against existing charitable choice and religious hiring rights laws was met by a religious purist Republican shove. Now, however, the White House, not the House Republicans, was in the lead on faith-based and community initiatives. In December 2002 the OFBCI organized a speech by President Bush at a Philadelphia church. The president unveiled new executive orders. When he referenced a new provision that supposedly gave faith-based organizations unlimited freedom to favor members of their own religious sects for employment, the crowd roared on cue.

Actually, the new executive order's provision was less far-reaching than it sounded and has proven to be far less consequential than it seemed at the time. In effect, the provision exempted faith-based organizations from a pre-Bush executive order that forbade religious discrimination by any organization that receives federal grants or contracts. That previous executive order was already widely believed to be overruled by other federal laws, including the aforementioned ministerial exemption provisions of the 1964 Civil Rights Act. It was also obviated by other post-1964 federal legislation that favored limited religious hiring rights for faith-based organizations and that had repeatedly survived federal court scrutiny. As one senior Washington official close to the action later confided to me, "We sort of knew that the new order was only giving [them] pretty much what they already had, but . . . it was politically irresistible."

Had the White House really wanted to tether itself to the religious purists' case on religious hiring rights, the same executive order would not have begun with black-letter language reiterating that no federal grantees can use any federal funds for any "inherently religious" purpose whatsoever. "That," a White House junior aide admitted several years later, "was our hedge or loophole against any possible court challenge, as well as our answer to [Democrats'] public attacks that the president had given the initiative over to the religious right."

In June 2003 the OFBCI released *Protecting the Civil Rights and Religious Liberty of Faith-Based Organizations.* In some respects, it echoed the *Unlevel Playing Field* report that I had overseen and released in August 2001. For instance, the 2003 report reiterated President Bush's oft-stated view that religious organizations supplying social services should be free to compete for federal funds on the same basis as all other nonprofit groups— provided they "do not discriminate against any persons receiving a public service," do not require "participation in religious activities as a condition for receiving services," and do not use tax dollars "to support inherently religious activities."

However, the same June 2003 OFBCI report also matter-of-factly asserted that faith-based organizations were "reluctant to administer Federally funded programs" because they "could be subject to different Federal, State, or local rules and regulations" governing whether they can "hire according to [their] religious beliefs." This, the report declared, "has discouraged many effective faith-based providers from competing to provide government-funded services."

Bridgeland, the original Bush compassion agenda's best friend still on senior staff, resigned in December 2003. As the 2004 presidential election loomed, the White House contradicted its earlier claim that inadequate religious hiring rights had discouraged many effective faith-based providers from competing for federal grants. It asserted instead that more groups than ever had applied and that more federal money than ever was going their way. Specifically, in 2004 and again in 2005 the OFBCI released public statements indicating that, in each of the latest years for which competitive nonformula grants data were available, about $2 billion in grants had been awarded to hundreds of faith-based organizations.

But, even if one looks as far from January 2001 as January 2007, the data on federal grants to faith-based organizations, so far as a truly objective rendering of them is possible, are not encouraging. Scholars agree that the "substantial majority of federal support for [social services] is in contracts or grants awarded by state and local governments . . . and few public programs record whether . . . contractors are faith-based."[17] Four things in particular are clear.

First, since 1996 the total amount of federal funds that has gone to proxy-government organizations involved in social service delivery has been in the hundreds of billions of dollars. Even $2 billion a year in federal grants to faith-based organizations represents a relative pittance.

Second, there is no way of knowing which faith-based groups—the old and well-practiced federal grant-receiving religious mega-charities or the new-to-the-process and smaller local community-serving ministries—received what share of that pittance, or via precisely which federal money pots. In 2006 two Penn undergraduates spent a summer in Washington as Brookings Institution interns trying to get the facts about just one small program (the Drug-Free Communities Support and Mentoring Program, awarded via the Substance Abuse and Health Services Administration). They were forced to conclude what many a veteran public administration scholar already knows, namely, that the "federal government cannot track where its money goes in the grant process," least of all with respect to faith-based initiatives.[18]

Third, by 2002 the original compassion capital concept of matchfunding model programs that tackled specific social needs via partnerships with religious nonprofits had mutated into an amorphous new human services grant-making program. Repeated press claims that the funds were being steered to politically connected groups were less compelling than observations that the fund's grant-making seemed to have no pattern at all. Grantees ranged from a university in Hawaii to groups that had specialized in consulting. The application process required "experience" but no particular problem-solving focus, and the compliance oversight process required no independent performance evaluation.

Fourth, even if we had reliable and meaningful data with which to answer the question of how much money had been distributed, "How much money?" is hardly the only or the most important question to ask.

The object of charitable choice, like the purpose of the president's original faith-based and community initiatives plan, was never simply to increase the amount of government money that would be given to religious nonprofit organizations. The purpose was to ensure that sacred places and faith-based groups that served civic purposes were free, if they chose, to participate fully and fairly in federal proxy-government grant-making and technical assistance programs. It was not assumed that all, most, or even a large fraction would opt to participate. For good theological or other reasons, many would not. Nor was it assumed that every faith-based organization that chose to apply would be worth funding or assisting. Nor, finally, was there any desire to create faith-favored, rather than to ensure faith-neutral, federal grant-making and technical assistance norms.

Consistent with court doctrine, public opinion, and bipartisan sentiment, the purpose was to level the playing field. That might or might not result in more money being made available to faith-based organizations. Given the aforementioned program-specific, not aggregate, preliminary funding pattern data on justice, welfare-to-work, and other federal grant-making programs, the best bet back in 2001 was that implementing charitable choice would, over time, result in more money being allocated to religious nonprofits. But not overnight, not on political command, and not unless enough qualified organizations opted to work with Washington. Moreover, it was an informed guess, not a foregone conclusion, that closing the apparent grassroots-government federal funding gap with community-serving urban ministries would yield measurable and positive civic results.

Least of all did charitable choice and the original Bush plan envision supporting religious nonprofit organizations as an end in itself. Rather, it was to be a way to help Washington help people in need. The needy children, youth, and families came first, not the faith-based programs themselves. Of second importance was ensuring that faith-based programs faced a level federal playing field and that they were not unfairly discriminated against by Washington, as much evidence suggested they had been in the past.

Establishing a level playing field for receiving federal funds was both desirable in its own right and a necessary but insufficient condition for achieving the primary, people-helping civic task. The third priority was to apply neutrality principles to federal public administration, possibly improving the proxy-government system's overall civic performance in the bargain. It would be a nice bonus if, after shaking up the government-by-proxy system with new faith-based grantees, federal programs started solving social problems. If this were to happen on a large scale, it could deepen and widen political support for antipoverty and related civic initiatives.

But neither charitable choice laws nor the original Bush plan were motivated solely by the desire to get more federal money to faith-based organizations. Nor was their purpose to change federal laws so as to conscript government agencies into making religious converts, discriminating against program beneficiaries or employees on religious grounds, or preempting any and all state and local laws to the contrary.

In February 2006 a widely publicized State University of New York (SUNY) at Albany Rockefeller Institute report claimed that the amount of federal funds that went to faith-based groups actually fell between 2002 and 2004. In reply, OFBCI director Towey publicly accused the independent SUNY-Albany researchers of being enemies of the president's faith-based and community initiatives. In March 2006 he released another OFBCI report which claimed that in 2005 about $2.1 billion in federal grants went to faith-based organizations, representing a slight increase over 2004.

The White House's arithmetic was accurate, but so was that of the SUNY-Albany scholars; they were simply counting different things. The math in each case does not really tell us very much. Whichever report one fancies, the big picture has not changed dramatically, either over the period 2001–2006 or since the first charitable choice law was enacted in 1996.

In 2006 as in 1996, even in big cities such as Philadelphia where a large fraction of all nonprofit organizations supplying social services to the needy are faith-based, few faith-based programs received federal financial support or technical assistance. Most also got little or no major philanthropic support. The same story held for faith-based after-school, housing, crime-prevention, welfare-to-work, and other community-serving programs.

Between 1996 and 2006, despite good intentions in both cases, neither the Clinton administration nor the Bush administration had done much to forge partnerships with faith-based groups that measurably helped people in need. The only real difference was that, after the 2000 presidential election, issues like religious hiring rights begat partisan, inside-the-beltway battles in which the charitable choice consensus was often a near-fatal casualty and the needy people whom charitable choice was supposed to help were too often forgotten.

RELIGIOUS VOUCHER VISIONS

Some, however, insist that vouchers are the one true charitable choice promised land. The same December 2002 executive order that resurrected the religious hiring rights issue also contained a provision that revived calls for vouchers. Under this provision, any religious organization that receives federal funding as the result of an individual program beneficiary's "genuine and independent private choice" need not segregate the financed service from its "inherently religious" activities or purposes. "This," one enthusiastic supporter of the provision insisted to me, "is the ultimate charitable choice, and it avoids all the church-state problems with direct aid or grants, too."

Under certain conditions, vouchers for students, prisoners, drug addicts, and others *are* workable and, or so I have long argued, perfectly constitutional and desirable. But they are not government-by-proxy panaceas. Vouchers present many of the same administrative tangles that grant-making programs do and are probably less likely than a charitable choice-reformed grant system to benefit grassroots community-serving religious groups and the people they serve. Nor, finally, do vouchers eliminate constitutional concerns about maintaining government neutrality and avoiding indirect religious establishment.

Most post-*Lemon* Supreme Court decisions, such as *Zelman* (see chapter 2), hold that properly structured voucher programs which are demonstrably predicated on "private choice" by beneficiaries pose few, if any, serious Establishment clause problems. Still, even *Zelman* is crystal clear that neither vouchers nor other indirect funding mechanisms should be presumed to address all possible constitutional concerns or escape due scrutiny in relation to neutrality principles. This is especially true where beneficiary populations like drug addicts, prisoners, or other persons that might be deemed unable to freely exercise true private choice are concerned.

Besides, however much beyond *Zelman* the courts might yet go in support of vouchers (and I do not think they will go much farther), the administrative challenges would be largely the same. By way of illustration, imagine that a parolee exiting prison is required to spend several hours per week in a drug treatment program. Courtesy of a federally funded prisoner reentry program, the individual is given a voucher to pay for drug treatment. Where does he go and how does the drug treatment program that he chooses get reimbursed for the service?

Say he receives a state parole authority–approved list of numerous organizations, including religious ones, that supply drug treatment. Not every organization that claims to have expertise in delivering this service will be on the government-approved list. Even a voucher may not legally amount to "Here's some cash, find some cure, no questions asked." How then, and by what criteria, did the organizations on the government-approved list get there?

Obviously, there must be information gathering, selection protocols, and retention records kept. Thus, we have a government-by-proxy administrative voucher regime that looks suspiciously like the administrative grant regime that we have allegedly sidestepped by supplying government aid to individuals via vouchers. The administrative machinery must also verify that the individuals who receive the vouchers are legally eligible to receive them in the first place.

Next, imagine that the paroled adult freely and knowingly chooses, from the long and diverse government-approved provider list, a drug treatment program with an explicitly religious mission statement. The program's "treatment modality" is none other than learning and practicing a specific religion's "beliefs and tenets," up to becoming a clergy person, or maybe even a missionary.

For the sake of this illustration, just say "amen." Put aside all constitutional conundrums that this would pose. Suppose instead that constitutional theory takes a backseat to practical results. That is, suppose that the only thing we all care about is what measurable results and outcomes the drug treatment program produces.

At one level, this "performance, not process" argument for vouchers and other government reforms is compelling. I have published several books and reports arguing along these lines myself.[19] But how, pray tell, is each voucher-receiving organization's performance to be objectively monitored and measured, by whom, and to what end? Is every organization that is reimbursed by government voucher to keep detailed records and commission evaluation studies? If not, then what?

For instance, what if only half or fewer of all persons in a given program are voucher-holders? What if the same program also serves beneficiaries who pay on their own or have nonprofit sponsors? Must that program also compile and keep all information on all clients, voucher-funded or not? Even far short of scientific rigor, there would be no way to meaningfully measure such an organization's performance without some such systematic data representing (or sampling) all program participants. To get the data that are necessary to validate claims about its performance, the voucher-receiving program must inevitably agree to myriad, detailed, government bookkeeping requirements.

Thus, unless we are prepared to take a voucher-receiving religious nonprofit's performance claims on faith (literally, perhaps), before long government reporting requirements will wrap the faith-based provider in an administrative system that will be virtually identical to—and quite possibly more onerous than—the one that grant-receiving religious and other nonprofits must negotiate now.

Of course, some people are quite willing to take it on faith that non-profits which promote religious conversion or so-called spiritual trans-formation succeed where secular programs fail. Their much-repeated claim is that religious social service organizations are uniquely efficacious when religious faith permeates nearly every action of the staff and vol-unteers. Such sweeping claims are most often made with respect to help-ing people with severe or chronic behavioral problems, ranging from sub-stance abuse to domestic violence to criminal recidivism.

The empirical research on faith-based organizations is discussed in the next chapter. For now, suffice it to say that there is no such clear-cut em-pirical research evidence.

Take Teen Challenge, an enormously interesting and, at least in my view, praiseworthy evangelical Christian program that ministers pri-marily to young adults with substance abuse problems.[20] Claims about Teen Challenge having achieved tremendous results with chronic drug addicts punctuated the 2001 debate over the Bush faith bill. Teen Chal-lenge was, and remains, the poster-child case for religious vouchers. Its success statistics are routinely bandied about by the evangelical Christian media. But a 2001 report, co-funded by two faith-friendly foundations and produced by the Center for Alcohol and Substance Abuse, gener-ously but fairly summarized the actual evidence to date on Teen Chal-lenge's performance as follows:

> When Teen Challenge claims a 70 to 86 percent "cure" rate for graduates, they do not take into account the high percentage of dropouts. For ex-ample, one study of selected individuals seven years after they entered the program found that 65 percent of those who came to the program dropped out. Another study of the Teen Challenge program's effectiveness in re-ducing substance abuse found that 67 percent or more alumni were living a drug-free lifestyle, but the follow-up rate for the study was only 50 per-cent. No rigorous independent evaluation has been conducted.[21]

This does not mean that Teen Challenge is not worthwhile or deserv-ing of support (it is one of the faith-based groups that will share all the au-thor's royalties on this book). But this assessment does remind us that there is as yet no clear-cut empirical evidence that religious nonprofit pro-grams that promote spiritual transformation perform as well or better than comparable faith-based organizations that do not proselytize, or than comparable nonreligious organizations.

Another important point to note is that while many large religious nonprofit organizations—often the same ones that are funded substantially via direct mail campaigns and extensive private donor lists—are set up in ways that would easily enable them to process eligible clients with government vouchers, most grassroots community-serving groups are not. Due in part to their open-to-all, street-level character, the smaller faith-based organizations rarely have either stable budgets or formal intake eligibility criteria that beget stable client lists.

"Vouchers," one Boston inner-city youth outreach minister cautioned me when I was in the White House, "just like the grants all these years, would end up going mainly to the big guys." Or, as one old Louisiana man (a religious leader, I surmised) blurted out to me as I limped into a public town hall meeting with the state's Democratic senator, Mary Landrieu, "Boy, get me some vultures [I gathered he meant vouchers] and we'll faith-heal that back." "Don't," another admonished me, "give all to who has all."

Finally, given that most federal social service dollars flow through state governments and given that most state constitutions that generally prohibit funding for religious organizations make no special provision for permitting funding through indirect aid, religious vouchers would have to clear many of the same intergovernmental high hurdles that federal grants or contracts with faith-based groups must clear.

As is noted in chapter 2, in the 2004 *Locke* case involving Washington State, the Court once again deferred to state constitutional traditions and administrative norms in refusing to require that an individual otherwise eligible for a state-funded scholarship (a virtual voucher) be permitted to use it for expressly religious purposes; and in 2006 the Court refused to hear a challenge to Maine's policy excluding only religious schools from a statewide school voucher program. Whatever one's position on these and kindred cases (I thought the Court was basically right in *Locke* but mostly wrong about Maine), it is sheer folly to think that vouchers make thorny church-state questions and potential challenges disappear. And alas, even if the Court became stridently in favor of religious vouchers, state officials with the political will to do so would still have the constitutional rights and administrative means to limit their use.

HOPE IN THE SEMI-SEEN: AMACHI

Especially in Washington, the Lord does work in mysterious ways. As I have previously mentioned, in the six months after I left the White House, I continued to assist the faith-based and community initiatives effort, and my hopes for renewing the charitable choice consensus and the original Bush plan were born again in February 2002. From 9/11 through mid-2002, the Republicans seemed more genuinely bipartisan on church-state and related issues than the Democrats did. Perhaps for that reason, my lingering frustrations over the saga of the Bush faith bill ran first to certain Democrats who had blocked final progress on the new charitable choice bill and related measures, and who were threatening to roll back existing charitable choice laws and to gut existing religious hiring rights.

I was not wrong, but frustration is a poor moral tutor and a terrible press agent. In public, I unfairly accused Democrats and their leading secular liberal allies of acting against the civil rights and social needs of poor urban citizens.[22]

By fall 2002, however, my frustrations had turned toward certain Republicans, religious purists, and those GOP leaders and staff at each end of Pennsylvania Avenue who had stymied the centrist plans and strayed from neutrality principles in the first place. Secular liberal wrongs did not justify unlimited religious hiring rights or excuse the disregard for presidential compassion promises made but now seemingly forgotten. Private communications fell increasingly on polite but deaf ears. Even a few old friends in high political places suddenly seemed to be engaging in extreme political gamesmanship, with no possible redeeming social payoffs.

From my faraway professor's chair, I scolded them for reinforcing the administration's tendency, notable from the first and denied privately by none, to elevate political rhetoric over policy substance, to ignore inconvenient facts, to avoid complex administrative chores, and to reduce important matters to talking points and "messages." I blamed the least-blameworthy ministers along with the most culpable ones but insisted that all of their actions were a disservice to the president, whose probity and sincerity about helping the needy I refused, then as now, to question.

I began expressing my discontents in public, at first in measured tones; but in December 2002 (during the same week, just coincidentally, that the new executive orders on religious hiring rights were scheduled to be unveiled in Philadelphia), I delivered a public critique in which, as noted above, I mocked the White House staff as Mayberry Machiavellis.[23] Earlier in the year, I had used the same uncharitable phrase, and made the same criticisms about staff, in a personal "tattletale letter" (as one former White House colleague half-jokingly called it) to the president that reached his aide, Harriet Meirs. Even before my criticisms became public, I explained myself, and profusely apologized, to all concerned. At all levels, those who mattered most to me responded with fraternal correction and mutual forgiveness. Nonetheless, I had failed my pre–New Year's 2003 Catholic self-examination of conscience, not to mention my parents, regarding the duty always to be as kind as possible.

As I also noted above, a civic rainbow was produced by this storm, ending in a new pot of federal gold for mentoring the children of prisoners and several other compassion agenda items. Several White House aides joked that I was the Philly Machiavelli, implying that I had engineered the entire affair, from public charges to public retractions, from useful idiots in the press to clued-in friends in the government, to elicit exactly some such semi-panicked substantive responses from the White House. (If I were really that calculating or clever, would I be writing this book?)

Providentially, President Bush and Senator Clinton had both happened upon Amachi. Begun in Philadelphia in 2000, through *buona fortuna*, I had an early hand in conceiving the program and a heavy hand in securing its first private seed-funding.[24] But it was developed by Philadelphia's former two-term mayor, and the first African American in the city's history to hold that high office, Reverend Dr. W. Wilson Goode, Sr. Its apt motto became "People of Faith, Mentoring Children of Promise."

In December 2006 the *Philadelphia Inquirer* selected Reverend Goode as its Citizen of the Year. He had spent the previous five years mobilizing volunteers to mentor the children of prisoners. He worked mainly through a network of inner-city black churches located in communities where there is a heavy concentration of low-income children with incarcerated parents. Goode's main partner in Amachi, both in Philadelphia and the over two dozen cities to which the program has spread, has been Big Brothers Big Sisters of America (BBBSA). The BBBSA-Amachi partnership has received increasing amounts of public and private support, including funds from the MCP program.

Reverend Goode's child-blessing message—as the son of a man who was in prison, a former mayor, and an urban minister—is hard to resist. Amachi mobilizes mentors directly from churches, but all Amachi mentors are subject to the regular BBBSA screening process. As in all BBBSA matches, the child's in-home parent or guardian decides what type of mentor is suitable for his or her son or daughter (religious or secular, white or black, gay or straight, baseball fanatic or library bookworm), and the program is ironclad in identifying and respecting these wishes.

Amachi gathers objective data on all phases of its operations, attracts multiple public and private stakeholders, invites independent research scrutiny, and is otherwise administered in ways that pose no challenges to neutrality principles. While black churches have hitherto been the program's main partners, any religious congregations or other faith-based organizations are free to participate; and secular organizations, like corporations or retirement community associations, that wish to offer mentors to prisoners' children will find non-Amachi BBBSA personnel ready to sign them up and make matches.

All told, by mid-2006 Amachi had made over 20,000 matches between prisoners' children and adult mentors. Roughly a third of all Amachi matches were made in conjunction with government support.

Indeed, through June 20, 2005, the federal MCP program had made 231 grants. Of the 100 most successful grantees, 66 were Amachi-affiliated. These Amachi grantees made 7,049 matches, or about 107 per grant. Had all 231 federal grantees performed at that Amachi average, the MCP program would have made about 25,000 matches by July 2005, or more than twice the actual MCP program's January 2006 tally (barely 14,000).

As one would have thought that the federal response to Hurricane Katrina would have taught for all time, it is best for all concerned to keep the Oval Office as far as possible from Orwellian doublespeak, even on relatively small administrative performance matters like the MCP program. The truth is that the MCP program would be on schedule for achieving the White House's own "ambitious goal" of 100,000 matches had it operated nearer to peak Amachi performance grantee averages.

President Clinton tried to put 100,000 cops in place. Before the next president takes office, Senator Clinton could help President Bush, in partnership with Amachi and other proven faith-based and community initiatives, to reach the milestone of 100,000 mentors for prisoners' children.

More broadly, Senator Clinton and President Bush, together with likehearted and like-minded national leaders, could still get Washington to help religious organizations help people in need, without forsaking the First Amendment or sparking new partisan and ideological battles like the ones that surrounded the Bush faith bill. It is still possible for the federal government, via charitable choice-style faith-based and community initiatives, to make major and measurable progress in obviating the future need for programs like Amachi.

Many Christians embrace the biblical concept of faith as "hope in the unseen." There is civic hope in programs like Amachi, but it takes faith—hope in the unseen—to envision even this model program receiving the support that it needs to reach not only 100,000 mentors, but more.

And it takes a leap of faith to envision other model programs restoring hope in the blighted, low-income, inner-city minority communities that too many American children call home—such as the black males born today, who U.S. Justice Department studies tell us have a one in three lifetime probability of being incarcerated.

Still, I remain convinced that the republic's faith-based future is bright, regardless of what Washington does, or fails to do. With respect to Washington's role, the single most important asset the nation possesses is the core character of the elected and appointed officials to whom we daily entrust the national government of the godly republic.

In late 2006, I was personally asked by then White House deputy chief of staff Karl Rove for some thoughts about how faith-based initiatives might figure in some future George W. Bush presidential library or think tank. As I communicated back, despite all the ups, downs, and twists, President Bush deserves enormous credit for putting "faith-based" permanently on the federal public agenda and into the popular vernacular. Thanks to this president, no matter which candidate or party wins the White House in 2008 and no matter what my former office's fate in the next administration, the next West Wing is more likely than not to display due regard for sacred places that serve civic purposes.

And, as a Baylor University study of Ohio published in January 2007 was only the latest to show, governors' and mayors' offices that have proceeded on faith-based initiatives in the constitutionally sound, bipartisan, and goal-oriented fashion paved by the original Bush plan for the federal role, have succeeded in expanding compassionate, cost-effective services to people in need.

In a Brookings Institution publication in early 2004, I suggested that, if President Bush failed to win reelection, he should consider doing for federal government-by-proxy reform, including faith-based and community initiatives, something akin to what President Herbert Hoover did after leaving office vis-à-vis the famous Hoover Commission reports.[25] Even many among Hoover's worst critics as president (and there were many) came to praise his public service on government administration and reform as an ex-president. Of course, President Bush won reelection, and the administration's record on government administration and reform, both before and after its failed response to Hurricanes Katrina and Rita in 2005, hardly make this work seem like the obvious choice for this soon-to-be ex-president. But it is no less a stretch for our time than was the idea that Hoover, as an ex-president, might preside over studies and projects to retool the executive branch so that it might prove better able to administer large and complex federal policies and programs such as those first begat by President Franklin Delano Roosevelt's New Deal. Although I have as yet gotten no backers (then again, I would need only one), I continue to hope that President Bush might make government-by-proxy reform, with a special focus on leveling the federal playing field for all including religious nonprofit organizations, a particular public service priority in his coming career as a (relatively young and exceptionally healthy) ex-president.

President Bush also deserves credit for frontally challenging the secular state myth. He deserves that credit even though, from the first, some key staff proved at once too cynical and too solicitous toward Christian nation true believers and too prone to substitute political thoughts (regurgitated speeches or campaign pledges, base-rallying executive orders, opposition-research-style public rebuttals) for faith-based deeds. I tried but failed to change that, so I share the blame.

I also remain convinced that President Bush, Senator Clinton, and most of the other top officials in both parties truly want to work together, to do the right thing on church-state issues, and to make decisions that will help millions of people in need.

As I told Amachi-booster Senator Clinton when I met with her in February 2007, given that Democrats regained the Congress in November 2006, and no matter what either 2007 presidential primary politics or the 2008 election bring, she and each party's other most visible national leaders can and should forge a fresh bipartisan coalition on faith-based and community initiatives. But, as I also emphasized, no such coalition can yield substantial civic good works in conjunction with bipartisan public policies if it merely eschews the religious right while embracing the religious left. Indeed, I advised, there are many unmet inner-city social service delivery needs so profound that it takes a village—a "village" that must tap the community-serving resources represented by everyone from public-spirited evangelical Christian conservatives to public-spirited secular liberal elites—to meet them in ways that can predictably, reliably, and measurably improve conditions for America's most truly disadvantaged people. She agreed.

The two final chapters return to an assessment of what faith-based and community initiatives could do to improve life for so many Americans. First, however, chapter 5 lays out the empirical truth about the civic strengths and limits of faith-based organizations and looks for whether there are objective reasons to hope that the nation's faith-based future can bestow greater civic blessings upon all including low-income, inner-city children, youth, families, and neighborhoods.

FIVE

The Nation's Spiritual Capital

FAITH-BASED VOLUNTEER MOBILIZATION, NOT
FAITH-SATURATED SPIRITUAL TRANSFORMATION

Myth 7 Empirical research proves that faith-based programs succeed
where secular programs normally fail.

Myth 8 Empirical research proves that faith-based programs do not succeed where secular programs normally fail.

TRUTH Empirical research proves that many different types of faith-based
programs are highly effective at mobilizing volunteers, that most
help people in need without regard to religion, that a majority
would welcome government support to expand social services, and
that three "faith factors" figure in social well-being.

BOWLING ALONE VERSUS PRAYING TOGETHER

In the mid-1990s, Harvard University social scientist Robert D. Putnam
alerted his academic colleagues to a troubling civic trend. Putnam had
amassed evidence suggesting that fewer and fewer Americans were joining clubs, associations, churches, and other groups that promote civic
trust and cooperation, or what many academics, following the sociologist
James Coleman, called "social capital." As a metaphor for the broader decline of civic participation that concerned him, Putnam highlighted the

fact that, between 1980 and 1994, league bowling had dropped by 40 percent. Americans, once a nation of joiners, were now "bowling alone."[1]

When Putnam speaks social scientists listen. I certainly did. He had been one of my most valued mentors when I was a graduate student at Harvard in the early 1980s. His bowling-alone thesis attracted tremendous media attention. It also drew favorable commentary from many politicians including President Bill Clinton.

Some analysts challenged Putnam's thesis, however. These critics claimed that data supposedly showing a steep decline in social capital were mixed and that other statistics actually bucked the trend.[2] In assorted writings, Putnam answered, and generally bested, his critics. In the late 1990s, he also brought together a diverse panel of academics and experts, including myself, to consult together over several years, consider the evidence, and make recommendations about how best to replenish the nation's social capital.

I was most interested in what Putnam had to say about religion in America. Essentially, he had argued that Americans were now not only bowling alone but also praying alone. Between 1974 and 1999, the fraction of Americans who claimed membership in a church or synagogue remained between 65 and 75 percent, and about 60 percent still attended worship services once a month or more. Still, over the same period, church attendance rates had fallen by about 25 percent. Mainstream Protestant denominations were losing members. Once robust urban Catholic archdioceses had empty pews and were closing Catholic schools.

On the other hand, churchgoing evangelical Christian and black Pentecostal populations were growing. Christian mega-churches claiming (and often seating) 5,000 or more members were springing up in many places. There were hard-to-count but real religious gatherings, including suburban bible study groups, urban "youth chapels" that did not "have church" but did corral teenagers and twenty-something adults, new campus-based student religious fellowship programs, and many others.

Putnam, I think it is fair to say, saw the glass as half empty, or draining.[3] I saw it as half full, and possibly even on the way to overflowing. These contradictory hunches raised certain research questions.

To reclaim the term that I coined in public speeches, interviews with journalists, and writings beginning in 1995, the overarching question was how much of the nation's social capital was actually derived from religious individuals and institutions—that is, how much of America's total stock of social capital was actually *spiritual capital?*

By 2000, this question had proven to be relatively easy to answer, at least in the aggregate: roughly half. All the relevant data revealed that churches, synagogues, mosques, and other religious organizations supplied enormous amounts of social services to their communities and functioned as major civic seedbeds of volunteering and philanthropy. Putnam and his study group summarized the evidence as follows:

> Houses of worship build and sustain more social capital—and social capital of more varied forms—than any other type of institution in America. Churches, synagogues, mosques and other houses of worship provide a vibrant institutional base for civic good works and a training ground for civic entrepreneurs. Roughly speaking, nearly half of America's stock of social capital is religious or religiously affiliated, whether measured by association memberships, philanthropy, or volunteering.[4]

Even this estimate, however, was possibly an underestimate. In the mid-1990s Putnam's bowling-alone thesis made big academic waves and a media splash that still ripples. But with roughly half of the social capital decline question bound up with religious individuals and institutions, my point of emphasis was, and remains, that many faith-driven activities are not picked up, or otherwise duly accounted for, by church attendance trends or by other conventional survey measures of religious life.

Putnam, ever focused upon empirical data, took my point, but ran it through a conceptual wringer that took the edge off its importance. Yes, evangelical Christian and black Pentecostal populations were possibly on the rise. Yes, mega-churches were dotting the landscape. Yes, apart from worship services, there were diverse faith-driven social activities and community-serving civic ventures. And yes, as he emphasized back to me, there was also evidence that religion was associated with greater political participation and "secular" civic engagement. Another Putnam-connected research report, a "Civic Health Index," summarized the evidence as follows:

Belonging to religious congregations and attending religious services comprise an important part of the Index. Affiliation with a religious organization is a strong predictor of secular civic habits (volunteering, giving to secular causes, voting, or giving blood) and an important incubator of social capital.[5]

But all of the best hard data and systematic evidence, Putnam argued, still seemed to spell overall religious decline; and besides, the social capital produced by many religious organizations, especially the orthodox religious ones that were growing the fastest, was probably more "bonding" social capital than "bridging" social capital.

Here was an important conceptual distinction and a provocative, if untested, empirical assertion. Putnam made the bonding versus bridging social capital distinction as follows:

Social capital may be categorized in many ways. One important way is the degree to which the connections reinforce similarities among individuals versus the degree to which the connections span differences. Alliances between people who are more alike than they are different are called "bonding" social capital. Connections between people who are different along some important dimension—such as race, socioeconomic status, or gender—are referred to as "bridging" social capital. [6]

While both forms of social capital are valuable, Putnam and his group agreed that for American society as a whole the more pressing social capital deficit related to bridging, not bonding.

Big academic questions now loomed. America's total stock of social capital badly needed to be replenished. Religious individuals and institutions—spiritual capital—represented about half of the existing stock. But how then might social capital be restored, short of another Great Awakening or a constitutional crisis regarding state support for churches? And was it correct to assume that much religious social capital was more of the bonding type than the bridging type?

Closely linked to such academic questions were other questions with more real-world and public policy bite. As is discussed in chapters 3 and 4, since 1996 federal charitable choice laws and related faith-based and community initiatives had been launched, but, for assorted political and bureaucratic reasons, by 2006 not much had yet been accomplished.

But what if one of the reasons that not much had happened was that many religious nonprofit organizations were not willing to serve people other than their own members or to hire people other than their own co-religionists? What if charitable choice and faith-based and community initiatives were futilely preaching bridging social capital to organizations that specialized in bonding social capital?

Or what if most faith-based nonprofit groups were eager to serve non-members, but to "serve" them only as a means of "saving" them or otherwise turning them into co-believers and members? What if empirical, faith factor research by even the best secular scholars showed that religion's main or sole positive social effects were begat by fostering faith or turning nonbelievers into believers?

In other words, what if most faith-based organizations turned out to be dedicated mainly to religion-specific spiritual transformation, not all-purpose volunteer mobilization? What if, in turn, research showed that programs which gave participants old-time religion were uniquely efficacious and highly cost-effective to boot?

Finally, what would such findings imply about government's necessary and proper role in delivering social services to people in need? Was Senator Hillary Rodham Clinton, Democrat of New York, being realistic when she called for sacred places that serve civic purposes to work through partnerships with other religious groups, with secular organizations, and with public agencies ? Was President Bush right when he repeated that government programs could not be replaced by religious charities? Could they be? Should they be?

BIG PICTURE: BRIDGING BLACKS AND WHITES

Good news. Even most religious congregations and other faith-based organizations committed to the Good News—that is, even community-serving religious nonprofits that are rooted in traditional Christian beliefs and tenets about Jesus Christ as Lord and Savior—serve people in need without regard to their beneficiaries' religion; are willing to work in partnership with other religious groups, secular organizations, or government; and function as volunteer-mobilizing civic powerhouses that daily supply vital social services to millions of people in need.

While Mormons, Muslims, and other faith communities do important civic good works that benefit their members and, in many cases, nonmembers as well, the three religious communities that figure most prominently in serving members and nonmembers alike are Catholics, black Protestants, and white and Latino evangelical Christians. Each of these three religious communities produces social capital by the bucketful, and each showers volunteer hours and money on nonmembers who tend to be unlike members in terms of race, socioeconomic status, or religion.

To generalize, in their respective international aid or relief initiatives, Catholics, black Protestants, and white and Latino evangelical Christians all bridge on race/ethnicity, socioeconomic status, and religion. At home, Catholic community-serving nonprofits, encompassing both religious congregations and other faith-based organizations, also tend to bridge on all three dimensions. Black Protestant churches and faith-based organizations bridge more on religion and socioeconomic status. White evangelical Christian churches and outreach ministries bridge more on race/ethnicity and socioeconomic status. Latino evangelical Christian community-serving organizations, repeating the patterns associated with the early development of America's immigrant European Catholic communities, mainly gather co-religionists and help their own needy members. But they have also begun to develop national religious fellowship and service organizations to help nonmembers.

To help people in need, Catholics, black Protestants, and Latino evangelical Christian nonprofits are generally open to community-serving collaboration, whether ecumenical, interfaith, religious-secular, or public-private. For the most part, white evangelical Christian community-serving organizations are open to ecumenical collaboration but less prone to form other partnerships, especially ones involving secular groups or government agencies.

The vast majority of community-serving religious organizations are headquartered in urban America. Even without any government aid, and with little or no philanthropic or corporate support, these organizations already supply literally scores of vital social services to their needy neighbors, from housing to health care, from child care to job training, from after-school programs to in-prison programs. For instance, as is discussed later in this chapter, despite the failure to fully implement federal charitable choice laws, these urban religious nonprofits have developed a significant, if underappreciated (and underfunded), presence in administering welfare-to-work programs.

As the multi-city data summarized below make plain, most community-serving urban religious nonprofit organizations that administer welfare-to-work and other programs, even those that do not separate sectarian activities from secular activities and that receive no government support at all, do *not* discriminate on religious grounds against beneficiaries, volunteers, or paid employees.

The strongest studies to date demonstrate that there are many different types of community-serving religious nonprofit organizations. Churches, synagogues, mosques, and other houses of worship, functioning as religious congregations with social service arms, supply a tremendous amount of help to people in need. But they are flanked by diverse religious organizations, from well-known national religious mega-charities (Lutheran Social Services, Catholic Charities, and several others) to tiny street-level outreach ministries (sometimes called "blessing stations") that often have no ties to a parent church, no official nonprofit status, and no listing in the local phone book.

The religious congregations' social service delivery arms range from faith-saturated to faith-based. These two categories are defined by the extent to which the nonprofit integrates and subordinates, rather than separates, any sectarian organizational purposes and practices from secular or civic organizational purposes and practices.

Conceptually, at one end of the continuum are prototypical faith-*saturated* organizations that either have no secular or civic purposes, or do not separate secular activities from their sectarian purposes and practices. For example, a religious nonprofit in which spiritual transformation was both the soul mission and the sole method, that made little or no effort to separate its social services from its worship services, and that was otherwise indivisibly conversion-centered, would be a prototypical faith-saturated organization.

One such real-world faith-saturated organization is mentioned in chapter 4: Teen Challenge, a faith-saturated substance abuse program. In mid-2006 the Teen Challenge website described the organization as based "on a literal interpretation of the Protestant Bible." In the website's FAQ section, in reply to questions about whether prospective beneficiaries must be Protestant biblical literalists, the answers were as follows: "conversion is regarded as the greatest hope for breaking addiction"; all beneficiaries are told about the program's religious character in advance; if they choose to be in the program, then "all aspects of the program are mandatory upon entrance" and all are required to "participate in the religious aspects of the program to receive services." In ruminating on why the program works (as is noted in chapter 4, the empirical evaluation research on the program to date remains cloudy at best), the website pointed to behavioral changes begat by born-again Christian beliefs and wrought by divine intervention:

> We believe it is because of something (or someone) we call the "Jesus Factor". . . . New-found life in Christ and learning biblical principles for daily living replace the old lifestyle and the attitudes and behavior underlying them.

Despite being a faith-saturated organization, Teen Challenge has been a proxy-government partner. As its website noted:

> Approximately 15% of our population nationwide is court ordered into our program. However . . . the court is required to give the individual a choice (i.e., do 12 months in a correctional facility or complete the Teen Challenge program). It is important that such a person understand that biblical principles are fully integrated into the program at Teen Challenge.

Such church-state collaboration with faith-saturated organizations, even where it is administered on genuinely voluntary grounds involving true private choice and indirect aid (vouchers or certificates to individuals), raises political temperatures and courts constitutional problems. But this type of church-state collaboration is the extreme exception, not the everyday rule. One very important reason is that faith-saturated organizations are themselves a tiny minority of all community-serving religious nonprofit organizations in America today.

Metaphorically speaking, faith-saturated nonprofits like Teen Challenge are a paper-thin slice of the nation's large and growing spiritual capital pie. Especially in urban America, their role is tiny relative to all community-serving religious congregations and faith-based organizations and tiny relative to the number of people who are actually served. Urban faith-based organizations with substance abuse programs serve more people in a week than the nonetheless laudable Teen Challenge serves in a year. The same can be said for faith-based versus faith-saturated organizations in relation to welfare-to-work programs, after-school programs, and literally scores and scores of other services supplied to people in need.

Thus, the vast majority of religious community-serving nonprofit organizations, most especially those anchored in urban neighborhoods, are potentially suitable proxy-government partners because, even when their social service operations are supported entirely by private means and staffed entirely by volunteers, they are faith-*based*, not faith-saturated: they do not make entering their buildings, receiving their services, or working for their programs conditional upon professing and practicing particular religious beliefs and tenets.

Contrary to what some insist, there is no empirical evidence whatsoever that religious nonprofit organizations only produce real social benefits when their program participants are saturated in a particular religion's purposes and practices. Rather, the best empirical studies to date suggest that the main, and perhaps the sole, proven civic comparative advantage enjoyed by religious congregations and faith-based organizations is their capacity to mobilize demographically diverse volunteers whose faith commitments motivate them to help people in need without regard to religion, race, ethnicity, socioeconomic status, or gender. Empirically, the "Jesus Factor," and other religious inspirations, matter most in getting people to help neighbors in need, no matter who they are.

In sum, this empirical research answers all of our questions about spiritual capital in ways that are perfectly in sync with the founding fathers' hope for an America harboring Madison's multiplicity of sects (see chapter 1); the U.S. Supreme Court's regard for church-state neutrality principles and prohibitions against tax-funded proselytizing (see chapter 2); majority opinions and bipartisan sentiments favoring faith-friendly but constitutionally valid federal laws like charitable choice (see chapter 3); and religious-secular, public-private initiatives for people in need like Amachi (see chapter 4).

For instance, as is discussed in chapter 4, Amachi succeeded in rapidly mobilizing adult mentors for children with an imprisoned parent. First in Philadelphia and then nationally, the program produced volunteers who had been mobilized through churches—mainly urban black churches, but also some suburban churches. Between 2001 and 2006, by appealing to prospective volunteers' spiritual identities and commitments, it accomplished a mentor mobilization effort for a targeted population more extensively and more rapidly than any in the history of its main national secular partner, the century-old Big Brothers Big Sisters of America.

There is highly preliminary empirical evidence that Amachi is having positive effects on beneficiaries; but, like most nonprofit organizations in the nation's vast faith-based sector, the program's clearest success is in mobilizing volunteers who serve people in need without regard to religion. Amachi, like most urban-bred faith-based organizations and programs, is a civic blessing to others in need, no matter what their beliefs, tenets, or backgrounds. It testifies to how most of America's religious individuals and institutions build bridging spiritual capital.

Unfortunately, rather than focus on faith-based programs like Amachi or the good-news empirical research on faith-based organizations more generally, some assert that scientific studies prove instead that faith-based programs—by which they actually mean faith-*saturated* social service programs predicated on spiritual transformation as both method and mission—succeed where secular programs and, by extension, government programs, supposedly fail (Myth #7). Others assert precisely the opposite, namely, that studies reveal that faith-based programs have no proven civic advantages at all, either in delivering social services on their own or in supplying them in collaboration with other partners including government agencies (Myth #8). These myths are prejudicial to the truth about America's broad and beautiful bridging spiritual capital sector.

Indulge me in a rather far-off and fishy analogy. The 1973 big-budget movie *The Day of the Dolphin* was a warm story about a scientist using lovable, super-smart dolphins to foil an assassination plot. It starred the Oscar-winning actor George C. Scott and had other heavyweights in its cast. Still, it totally bombed at the box office. Two years later, however, came the blockbuster movie *Jaws*. It featured a few veteran Hollywood actors but also several virtual unknowns. Of course, the real star was you know who. I say "Jaws," you think "shark," and not just any shark, but the Great White Shark. You think big, sharp teeth and tons of feral flesh eager to attack splashing people on public beaches as lifeguards yell in vain. But, unless you are a marine biologist, you probably do not think "The Great White is one of several hundred species of sharks, it is rare, and rarely attacks ocean bathers" or "People swimming near public beaches are much more likely to see or encounter dolphins, mammals who are known to be intelligent and to help distressed swimmers." Marine biologists explaining what we really know, or do not know, about Great Whites and other sharks do not make for a best-selling book or a big-grossing movie.

Social scientists who study church-state issues have a similar public relations dilemma. Faith-saturated organizations are in no way representative either of the religious organization species or of all the faith-based fish in the nonprofit sea. They rarely swim close to government shores and are not organizationally wired to go hunting for federal grants. The few that do, normally turn and swim away after being spotted by civil servants who watch over grant-making public agencies. Especially in urban waters, the vast majority of community-serving religious congregations and faith-based organizations are prone to be friendly toward all who venture near.

The mere mention of faith-based organizations should not trigger visions of hyper-proselytizing preachers or faith-saturated programs. Rather, a real if romantic image that cuts much closer to capturing the empirical truth about most of America's community-serving religious nonprofits is that of a fairly well-to-do Presbyterian white suburban woman serving as president of an independent Catholic inner-city school that has been generously supported by Jewish philanthropists, attracted teachers and volunteers of many different faiths and of no faith, and successfully educated thousands of African American children—very few Catholic, most Baptist, and some Muslim. As I know from my own decade-plus involvement, and as Washington journalists like Tim Russert and Joe Klein have echoed, this faith-based picture is the reality at inner-city north Philadelphia's Gesu Elementary School (*Gesu* is Italian for "Jesus").[7]

Another faith-based picture worth a thousand studies is the one that appeared in the *Philadelphia Daily News* on March 10, 2006.[8] The local black-and-white photo appeared the same day that national press reports surfaced concerning yet another political tempest regarding faith-based funding between the Bush White House and its critics (the dispute, referenced in chapter 4, involved federal faith czar Jim Towey and State University of New York at Albany scholars). The picture was of Republican Texas governor Rick Perry looking on intently as the Reverend Dr. W. Wilson Goode, Sr., Philadelphia's former two-term Democratic mayor, stood at a podium that had a sign reading "Amachi Texas" on its front. Below the photo, the paper noted that Goode was in Texas with Governor Perry to announce that the Meadows Foundation in Dallas was supporting Amachi's efforts to mobilize mentors for children with an incarcerated parent.[9]

This "Goode news" in black and white eloquently reflects the big picture that emerges from the empirical research on community-serving religious congregations and faith-based organizations in America today. Faith-based, *not* faith-saturated. *Bridging* spiritual capital more plentiful than bonding social capital. Volunteer mobilization, *not* spiritual transformation. Religious-secular and public-private partnerships to help people in need, *not* tax-supported proselytizing or discrimination.

The empirical research reveals that the overwhelming majority of the godly republic's religious individuals and institutions, most particularly in urban America, are ready, willing, and able to partner with other religious people and organizations, with secular individuals and groups, and with government at all levels in helping to serve those fellow citizens who my fellow Christians call "the least of these" in our midst.

FAITHFUL PHILADELPHIA:
SCORES OF SERVICES FOR PEOPLE IN NEED

With Benjamin Franklin as its first citizen-patron of sacred places that serve civic purposes, and with the spirit of James Madison and the godly republic's other framers alive in many historic buildings as well as the National Constitution Center, the City of Philadelphia (a.k.a., the "City of Brotherly Love" or the "City of the Second Great Commandment") is a civic lamplight for the nation's faith-based past, present, and future. Philadelphia's experience with faith-based organizations illustrates the civic contribution that religious nonprofit organizations make across the nation.

I will illustrate by focusing on the three religious communities that, in Philly as in so many other places across the nation, figure most prominently in producing bridging spiritual capital through faith-based and community initiatives: Catholics, white and Latino evangelical Christians, and, most especially, black Protestants. I will expand the geographic location of Philly to encompass nearby places in New Jersey (Camden) and Delaware (Wilmington). And I will risk playing favorites by emphasizing how, in Philly as in most other big cities, black Protestant congregations and faith-based organizations supply a wide variety of services to people in need and, if duly supported by others including the federal government, could contribute in especially vital ways to solving social ills and brightening the republic's faith-based future.

As many scholars have noticed, Catholics tend to identify themselves and their neighborhoods according to their parishes. By custom, Catholics attend church in the parish in which they happen to reside. Until recently, there was no church-shopping (or priest-shopping) Catholic equivalent to the Protestant practice of deciding where to worship. Today some Catholics register, attend Mass, or send their children to school in a parish other than the one that encompasses their home address. But most Catholics, whether or not they are regular churchgoers, are affiliated with the parish where they reside.

Bounded by parishes, Catholic religious congregations are mainly about bonding social capital, not bridging social capital. Increasingly, that bonding social capital is backward-focused. For instance, even after they have moved from the city to the suburbs (no city in America has experienced more out-migration over the last quarter-century than Philly), many ethnic white Catholics still strongly identify themselves, their families, and their friends with the old parish. Whenever I meet other suburban Catholics my age or older who grew up in Philly, the first question we ask each other is "What was your parish?"

Millions of white ethnic Catholics have left the cities where they grew up, and some of the Catholic schools they attended have closed in their wake; but in Philadelphia as in most other cities, the parish map today is not radically different from what it was a quarter-century ago. What *is* radically different is who attends Mass (fewer, grayer people) and who attends the Catholic schools or receives parish-provided social services (fewer whites and Catholics, more nonwhites and non-Catholics).

For example, until recently, Saint Thomas Aquinas, the Catholic parish in a once predominantly Italian American neighborhood of south Philadelphia where I started Catholic school in the early 1960s (and where some scenes in the first two *Rocky* movies were shot in the 1970s), still had an in-residence Italian American priest as pastor. Sadly, he died in 2006, leaving behind flocks that are predominantly African American and Asian American. The old convent where I trembled for my misdeeds is now a shelter for battered women and has Asian lettering over its doors. The faces playing in the schoolyard at recess are almost all black or Asian.

Much the same story holds for many other Philadelphia parishes and for Catholic parishes throughout urban America. For instance, at Saint Frances de Sales in west Philly, two veteran Catholic nuns, both white ethnics, oversee a school that serves a predominantly immigrant population including families from Ethiopia, Eritrea, and other faraway places. The school receives a rising portion of its annual funding from alumni who have not been back to the neighborhood in years, but who still identify as being "from Saint Fran's."

About a decade ago, I attended the twenty-fifth reunion of my eighth-grade class from Saint Barnabas, the Catholic school in once predominantly Irish southwest Philadelphia that I attended after my family moved to a bigger row house a few miles from Saint Thomas parish. Following the reunion, several of us saw to it that "our old parish" got some fresh financial help. During spring break in both 2006 and 2007, the Catholic Church closest to Penn's campus, Saint Agatha-Saint James (a consolidated parish), mobilized Penn's Catholic Newman Center students to go to New Orleans and the Gulf Coast. Joined by dozens of Penn students of other faiths and of no faith, these students did housing rehabilitation and other community service work in the Hurricane Katrina–ravaged communities along the Gulf Coast.

But such parish-based blips of bridging social capital are not the norm. Catholics do reach out to people who differ from themselves by race/ethnicity, socioeconomic status, or religion, but they generally do not do so via their parishes. By the same token, in Philadelphia as in most other cities, Catholics are less likely than Protestants to independently give philanthropic gifts, respond to direct-mail charity drives, or identify and support diverse non-Catholic charities on their own.

Rather, Catholics are more likely to help build spiritual capital bridges through established Catholic nonprofit organizations, both national and local. Thus in Philadelphia in 2005, about 60,000 students were enrolled in Catholic elementary schools, high schools, colleges, or universities; 1,125 patients per day received care in a Catholic long-term care facility; over 26,000 patients were admitted to Catholic hospitals; and nearly $1 billion supported these services, all of which benefited citizens without regard to religion.[10] That is not counting the financial contributions that individual Catholics made to their own parishes, to national organizations like Catholic Charities of America (which receives well over half of its budget from government grants and contracts), or in volunteer hours to street-level Catholic outreach ministries (like the Saint Vincent de Paul ministries).

There is empirical evidence hinting that, compared to most other large religious populations, Catholics are laggards when it comes to building spiritual capital. As Harvard social scientist (and my friend and fellow Catholic) Mary Jo Bane has argued, the best available aggregate data on Catholic philanthropy and volunteering pose a puzzle: America's some 65 million Catholics now rank in socioeconomic terms among the nation's most solidly middle- and upper-class citizens, and they are steeped in religious teachings that frown upon "faith without works" and emphasize helping the poor. Yet, by every measure, Catholics lag behind other large religious groups, and are only just ahead of citizens who profess no faith at all, in their average levels of volunteering and giving.[11]

George Weigel, a conservative Catholic scholar and Pope John Paul II's authorized biographer, would agree with Bane. As Weigel has concluded:

> Catholics are among the worst givers in the country. . . . One-third of the registered members of a parish give constantly and generously, one-third give occasionally, and one-third give essentially nothing. . . . Figures for the mainstay of Catholic fundraising, the archdiocesan appeal, do not paint a much rosier picture. . . . The question of how to instill a greater sense of responsible generosity in U.S. Catholics has thus become a significant issue for the twenty-first century Church, whose vast network of parishes, schools, social welfare and health care institutions can no longer rely on the inexpensive labor of priests, brothers, and sisters.[12]

Do not blame Tony Campolo. He was born into an Italian American Catholic neighborhood in south Philadelphia, but he is not another Philly Catholic guy. Rather, Reverend Campolo, an evangelical Christian, is a sociologist and theologian at Eastern University, located just outside of Philly. He came to national attention when he personally ministered to President Clinton immediately after the president admitted his relationship with then–White House intern Monica Lewinsky. Even before those fifteen minutes of fame, Campolo was famous in evangelical circles. He was known mainly for his decades spent advocating for the poor and the dispossessed, and was a white evangelical Christian preacher much beloved by many black and Latino church leaders.

Campolo taught sociology at Penn before settling for good at Eastern University. His best-known colleague at Eastern, the Reverend Ronald J. Sider, is a public policy analyst and theologian. Decades before any other evangelical Christian in America had done so, Sider brought the Bible's admonitions to honor and serve the poor into popular and public policy-relevant focus. He made the case in his big-selling 1977 book *Rich Christians in an Age of Hunger*. Sider, a "lifestyle evangelist" with a Mennonite conscience (and wife), does not live like a successful author; he resides in one of the poorest sections of Philly's Germantown neighborhood.

Campolo and Sider are Philly's white evangelical Christian faith-based dynamic duo. Among other initiatives, Campolo founded Urban Promise, a multifaceted urban outreach ministry and one of the few faith-based organizations that has stuck it out in Camden, New Jersey. Camden, a small city just south across the bridge from Philadelphia, is wracked by homicidal street violence and has been America's murder capital. For many years, Camden did not have so much as a single supermarket, but the city was teeming with malt liquor to-go outlets and open-air illegal drug markets. But in schools, in after-school programs, in local business development initiatives, and more, Campolo and his faith-based minions have made a commitment to Camden—and made good on promises to do what they could to help its needy residents.

Campolo is a principled evangelical Christian political progressive, while Sider is a principled evangelical Christian political centrist. Because of Sider's pro-life, pro-family, and pro-poor stands, he is an urban evangelical leader who is taken seriously by Catholics as well as by more conservative evangelical leaders like Charles W. Colson. Colson and I coauthored the foreword to Sider's 1999 book on antipoverty initiatives, *Just Generosity*. (I say much more about good Brother Colson in chapter 6.) In 2005 Sider was the driving force behind public statements on environmental issues and other policy matters that were endorsed by a broad spectrum of evangelical Christian organizations.[13]

But Sider's local and national credibility within and beyond evangelical Christian circles is derived from his decades-long, suites-to-streets efforts to support community-serving religious congregations and faith-based organizations that help people in need. For instance, Sider, together with Campolo, was an early advocate of philanthropic and public support for the Latino evangelical Christian groups that have become important social service providers in Philadelphia and many other cities all across America.

As Villanova University political scientist Catherine Wilson has chronicled, Philadelphia's Nueva Esperanza is a dynamic Latino evangelical Christian faith-based organization that, like Latino faith-based organizations in many other cities, is growing in size and civic impact.[14] Wilson, who got her Ph.D. at Penn, has found that such Latino community-serving religious nonprofit organizations have cropped up all across the country. Philly's Nueva Esperanza was simply a decade or so ahead of its time.

Since its founding in 1987 by the Reverend Luis Cortés, Jr., Nueva Esperanza has not only served the city's Hispanic citizens but also been a launch pad for a new national Hispanic religious movement, Esperanza USA. *Esperanza* is Spanish for "hope." In January 2005, *Time* magazine rightly ranked Reverend Cortés, still in his 40s, among the twenty-five most influential evangelical Christians in America. In Philadelphia, Nueva Esperanza operates a charter high school, a junior college, and myriad homebuilding and employment training programs. Its nearly $30 million Latino Corridor community redevelopment project is replacing vacant lots in north Philly with new and renovated homes and local businesses.

Begun by Reverend Cortés in July 2004, Esperanza USA is a national network of about 10,000 Hispanic faith-based organizations. Among its many community-serving projects is Esperanza Trabajando ("Hope Is Working"), an $11 million, nine-city, three-year project focused on Latino youth who have gotten into serious trouble with the law.

These Latino evangelical Christian faith-based initiatives, and many others in Philadelphia and other cities, have involved collaboration with federal, state, and local government agencies. For instance, the aforementioned program for at-risk Latino youth has received money from the U.S. Department of Labor. The ever-plainspoken Reverend Cortés has occasionally raised eyebrows by stating that he and other Latino evangelical Christian leaders were willing to put their political faith in whichever elected officials helped them and their nonprofit organizations to help Latinos and other people in need.

For at least three reasons Reverend Cortés's point should guide, not shock. First, there is nothing wrong with community-serving people of faith favoring elected leaders who favor their civic cause. Second, historically, large but still-assimilating immigrant populations have gone through their religious leaders and organizations to get government aid; this practice is as American as Anglo apple pie, Irish potatoes, and now, Mexican tacos. Third, collaboration between religious leaders and sympathetic government officials is precisely how progress was made in the 1950s and 1960s, when African Americans began to achieve full civil rights and launched their still-ongoing march into America's middle class.

Today, in Philadelphia and all across America, black churches and faith-based organizations continue to be especially vital and promising providers of social services to people in need. Penn's Ram A. Cnaan, an Israeli-born social work scholar and self-described agnostic, is among the empirical research scholars who, over the last decade, have produced a rich literature documenting the enormous extent to which black churches and other faith-based organizations mobilize volunteers and deliver vital social services.

I first encountered Cnaan in the mid-1990s before I joined him on Penn's faculty. I was so impressed that I steered him to significant private funding I had obtained for my own research (no greater love has any academic). With help from my friends Democratic U.S. senator Joseph Lieberman and Republican former U.S. secretary of education and drug czar William Bennett, I assisted in preparing and disseminating a report by Cnaan that was commissioned by another great Philly-based nonprofit, Partners for Sacred Places. I wrote about him and his work in both academic and popular venues, and in 1999 I decided to leave Princeton for Penn on the bet that we could work together. I was right, and Cnaan even puts up with my jokes—like the one about a "Jewish agnostic" being a person who knows precisely what the God he is not sure exists expects of him.

Since the mid-1990s, numerous major multi-site studies by Cnaan and others have carefully counted the diverse social benefits begat by community-serving religious congregations, most especially African American churches located in the urban neighborhoods that many low-income children, youth, and families call home.[15]

For example, in *The Other Philadelphia Story: How Local Congregations Support Quality of Life in Urban America* (2006), Cnaan and his Penn research team report on the final results of their census of community-serving congregations in Philadelphia.[16] The research involved hours on site at each of over 1,000 churches, synagogues, mosques, and other religious properties, plus an extensive questionnaire. Based on this work and related research in other cities, Cnaan concluded that, whether or not Americans were bowling alone, religiously motivated Americans were not only praying together but serving together.[17]

As Cnaan and his research teams have documented in great depth, in Philly and other cities, urban religious congregations and faith-based organizations supply scores of social services: food pantries, summer day camps, recreational programs for children and teenagers, clothing closets, drug and alcohol prevention, neighborhood cleanup, blood drives, job counseling and placement, street outreach to the homeless, computer training, mentoring for children and youth, health screening, crime watch, day care, prison ministry, after-school programs, anti-gang violence programs, international relief funds, welfare-to-work programs, and literally scores upon scores of other programs.

As I read it, four policy-relevant sets of facts have consistently emerged from this line of empirical research, and from similarly in-depth studies of urban faith-based organizations.

First, virtually all urban faith-based organizations and programs that deliver social services rely almost entirely on volunteers. They have few, if any, paid service-delivery staff. Only a negligible fraction receive any public funds whatsoever. Each urban congregation's social services "replacement value"—what it would cost, on average, to supply the services they supply even at below-market rates for labor and building space— easily exceeds over $140,000, or as Cnaan has estimated, a grand total of nearly $250,000,000 a year in Philadelphia alone.

Second, as huge as the faith-based social service sector turns out upon close inspection to be, President Bush's repeated caution that "government cannot be replaced by charities" is absolutely right, and so is his claim that America's community-serving religious armies of compassion receive little or no philanthropic or public support and make bricks without straw. Cnaan has taken pains to emphasize that, as big and vital as it is, the country's community-serving religious nonprofit sector remains a distant second to government when it comes to aiding low-income children, youth, families, and other citizens in need.[18] Even if every religious congregation in America, over 350,000 strong, gave every penny it collected each year to health and human services for people in need (forget keeping heat on in the church or fixing the organ), the total would still be billions of dollars short of what the federal government alone spends each year on these services.

Third, despite being its least well-funded segment, black churches and faith-based organizations lead the urban community-serving religious nonprofit sector in at least four ways: average levels of service provision, propensity to locate among and serve the most acutely needy people and at-risk youth populations, bridging spiritual capital outreach to non-members, and willingness to partner with other religious groups, secular organizations, and government agencies.

Fourth, in every systematic study to date that has examined interracial differences in what faith-based organizations do for people in need, black religious congregations are found to outperform white and other non-black religious congregations, not only relative to each group's resources but often in absolute terms, too. For example, disaggregating the data in the aforementioned Cnaan Philadelphia census reveals that black community-serving religious nonprofits provided a statistically significant higher level of many services including, but not limited to, the following:[19]

- Education (e.g., tutoring for adults and computer training for youth)
- Health (e.g., education and substance abuse counseling)
- Economic development (e.g., business incubation and investment clubs)
- Child care (e.g., summer camps and safe corridor programs)

The same picture holds for the broader Philadelphia, defined in metropolitan terms as encompassing its Delaware Valley and tri-state region (southeastern Pennsylvania, south and central New Jersey, and Delaware). In a report for the Annie E. Casey Foundation, Hara Wright-Smith, a former Penn doctoral student in city planning and expert on church-related community economic development programs, examined how black faith-based organizations served people in east Wilmington, Delaware. After gathering and analyzing detailed data on every black congregation and faith-based organization in the area, Wright-Smith found that all, including inner-city black churches that have predominantly commuter congregations (members who live outside the low-income neighborhoods where they attend church), supplied an incredible range of social services to both members and nonmembers alike.[20]

When it comes to black community-serving nonprofits, metropolitan Philadelphia's story is America's story. For example, as summarized by Stephanie Boddie, a social work professor at the University of Washington at Saint Louis who did her doctoral studies in social work at Penn, a survey of 251 congregations in seven cities found that, compared to interracial and white congregations, black religious groups "were more involved . . . in providing social services across a wide array of areas," a statistical finding reinforced by several in-depth, city-specific comparative case studies.[21]

It is heartening, but not surprising, that African Americans, the American citizens who by many measures are most inclined toward praying together, are also most successful, despite economic and other disadvantages, at serving together. The black church has long been a main institutional engine of black progress in America.[22] Most black Americans (82 percent) believe that the church "has helped the condition of black people in America."[23] Multigenerational surveys have found that "compared with whites, blacks demonstrate higher levels of religious involvement, publicly (e.g., religious attendance), privately (e.g., reading religious materials), and subjectively (e.g., personal importance of religion, religious comfort)."[24]

In almost every study of the subject, the greater religiosity/spirituality of blacks persists "despite controls for demographic and religious factors that are differentially distributed within black and white populations and are known to be of consequence for religious involvement."[25] For instance, other things equal, black Catholic congregations are significantly more likely than white Catholic congregations to engage in social action and deliver social services in their communities.[26]

There is also an empirical research literature relating blacks' greater religiosity/spirituality to success in reducing the incidence of serious social problems. For example, in 1986 Harvard University economist Richard

Freeman stumbled upon multi-city evidence that young black low-income urban males who attended church were significantly more likely to avoid unemployment than otherwise comparable males who did not attend church. Since Freeman's studies, other social scientists have produced a steady stream of similar findings, including data indicating that church attendance has significant inverse effects on illegal drug use and crime.[27]

Perhaps higher levels of spirituality, faith-based services, and positive social effects among blacks, as measured by such studies, are behind the fact that black religious nonprofit organizations are generally more likely to locate and stay in needy neighborhoods, rather than follow socioeconomic success to the suburbs. The tale I told in the introduction about Philly's black Pentecostal pastor Benjamin "Pops" Smith was dramatic, but as many studies would suggest, Pops's "stay and serve" ethos was not dramatically different from urban black church attitudinal and behavioral norms.

Nisha D. Botchwey, a social scientist at the University of Virginia who did her doctoral studies in Penn's city planning program, systematically examined how both religious and secular nonprofit organizations served the poor in a predominantly black low-income section of north Philadelphia. Compared to secular social service organizations, the faith-based groups were far less likely to be located along business thoroughfares and far more likely to dispense myriad services right in the area where most low-income blacks lived. For both social and practical reasons (including, among the latter, no transportation problems), blacks benefited most from faith-based nonprofits that were "tightly integrated into communities."[28]

Black urban congregations and faith-based organizations produce bridging spiritual capital by serving people who differ from members in socioeconomic status and religious affiliation—beneficiaries tend to be poorer and, whatever their beliefs, they are not typically members of the church that serves them. The aforementioned Wright-Smith study found that even black "commuter" congregations with predominantly non-neighborhood memberships supplied many services to indigenous inner-city people in need. The Cnaan surveys in Philadelphia and other cities consistently found that the black religious nonprofits' primary beneficiaries were needy children and youth from surrounding neighborhoods who were not church members.

Finally, abundant systematic and anecdotal evidence shows that urban black religious nonprofit organizations are especially likely to partner with other religious groups, secular organizations, and government agencies. Based on a nationally representative survey of 1,236 religious congregations, a careful statistical analysis that controlled for congregation size and other variables found that, compared to other religious groups, "predominantly African-American congregations" were "particularly likely" to "seek government support for social service delivery."[29] In Philadelphia, more black (65 percent) than nonblack (55 percent) congregations were interested in applying for federal charitable choice grants.[30]

PUTTING FAITH IN CIVIC PARTNERSHIPS

Unfortunately, most urban black congregations, like most community-serving religious nonprofit organizations generally, have little knowledge about federal charitable choice laws or related opportunities for public-private partnerships involving faith-based groups. For instance, in 2000, four years after the first charitable choice law was enacted, the only congregation in Philadelphia to apply for and receive federal government funding under charitable choice was Cookman United Methodist, a black church in north Philadelphia.

Cookman received its federal grant to administer a welfare-to-work program for women. It was a bumpy church-state learning process.[31] The church's welfare-to-work program had an unambiguously Christ-centered mission statement. But it was open to all women regardless of religion. Some Muslim women chose the program, as did many women with no other ties to the church. As time progressed, the church's charismatic and dedicated pastor, Donna Jones, navigated the choppy and uncharted charitable choice waters fairly well. Participants who wanted to pray together were able to find a spot in the daily schedule to do so, but no prayer or any other religious practice was required. Funds for sectarian activities were kept separate from funds for civic purposes. Volunteers and paid staff of all faiths and of no faith were welcome to help train the participants and find jobs for them.

After a few years, the Cookman welfare-to-work program ran its course, used up its funding, and quietly folded. Its significance was not its efficacy—nothing approaching an impact study was ever even contemplated. Rather, as Pastor Jones testified before Congress and other bodies in 2001, its greatest significance was in being first. The Cookman experience prompted people on both sides of church-state issues to wonder aloud whether, for good or for ill, there were more "Cookmans" to be found and funded in Philadelphia and other cities.

As discussed in chapter 3, the 1996 charitable choice provision was part of a large federal welfare reform legislative package that mainly featured new grants to states, conditional upon their meeting certain welfare-to-work mandates.[32] In 1999 and 2000, just as the Bush-Gore charitable choice consensus started to get noticed by the press, healthy skeptics (and even unhealthy cynics) began asking legitimate empirical and policy questions. Just how much of an active presence were religious congregations and faith-based organizations in supplying welfare-to-work services to their own needy neighbors? Could their proxy-government role, whatever its present state, be expanded? Should it be? Why or why not?

Cnaan and other scholars had documented that community-serving religious nonprofits all across the country supplied scores and scores of social services. But exactly how deep or wide were such faith-based and community initiatives? To employ the concepts introduced earlier in this chapter, to what extent and in what ways were most welfare-to-work programs faith-based rather than faith-saturated? Even if most proved to be faith-based, would this category include any grassroots groups with orthodox religious views? In particular, would any orthodox Christian organizations be found to have forged religious-secular or public-private partnerships? Would they be a significant presence among the faith-based organizations that mobilize volunteers to help welfare recipients find work, without regard to religion?

Calvin College in Michigan is not the first place one might think to look for the best empirical answers to these questions, but that is precisely where you will find them. Calvin political scientist Stephen V. Monsma is the dean of political scientists who study religious individuals and institutions. As I frequently noted when introducing him to other faculty during his stint at Penn as a senior fellow in the religion research program that I directed, Monsma was studying "faith-based" community-serving programs before anybody called them that, and before "religion was cool—or a fundable empirical research topic."

For example, Monsma has studied welfare-to-work programs in Chicago, Dallas, Los Angeles, and Philadelphia.[33] During the period covered by his research, these cities had a grand total of about 1,500 organizations supplying welfare-to-work services. They came in six varieties: government agencies alone, for-profit organizations, large secular nonprofit organizations with professional staff, grassroots secular nonprofit organizations with volunteer staff, faith-based programs that kept their religious elements separate from their social service delivery (which Monsma termed "faith-segmented"), and both faith-based and faith-saturated organizations that integrated at least some religious elements into their social service delivery practices (which he termed "faith-integrated)."

Most welfare-to-work programs are faith-segmented, not faith-integrated. For example, virtually all serve beneficiaries without regard to religion, and the vast majority hire staff largely without regard to religion. Overall, only 2.9 percent of these programs hired only co-religionists, and only another 6.9 percent gave them preference in the hiring process. Four in ten faith-integrated programs had no religiously based hiring restrictions *whatsoever*, and none reported dissatisfaction with how government managed its end of the service-delivery contracts.

Among those faith-based welfare-to-work programs with government contracts, nearly 40 percent complained about the paperwork (amen), but none reported that government support or terms made them less effective, displaced private donations, or reduced volunteer manpower in favor of paid, full-time help (amen again).

Rather, two-thirds of the faith-based programs reported that public funds permitted them to expand their services to more people in need, and only 8 percent reported that the partnership with government "cut down" on their religious emphases and practices. In 2005, Dan Treglia, a stellar Penn undergraduate who went on to graduate study in public policy at Harvard, did an independent study course with me in which he followed up with Monsma at Calvin and double-checked some of Monsma's data that were specific to Philadelphia. It was all sound.

Among the most prominent of the Philly faith-based welfare-to-work providers, and one of its most prominent religious organizations period, is People for People, the nonprofit led by the Reverend Dr. Herbert H. Lusk III, pastor of Greater Exodus Baptist Church. As noted at the start of chapter 2, that church, with Lusk preaching and presiding, was the site of the Justice Sunday III event that brought together some of America's most high-profile conservative evangelical Christian leaders. As I have overheard said about him in certain black churches, when it comes to his religious convictions and how they apply to controversial political matters, the proudly Republican Lusk (Herbert's middle name is Hoover) is somebody who will "pray but won't play, won't blink, and won't wink."

But neither, however, do Lusk and his community-serving religious nonprofit organization serve only people who share particular conservative Christian beliefs and tenets, work only with others who ascribe with equal fervor to orthodox Protestant views, or do anything other than try to play by the neutrality rules that come with the federal, state, and local proxy-government grants they have sought and received.

Founded in 1989 as the community economic development arm of Greater Exodus Baptist Church, People for People displays faith-based civic teamwork that comes almost as naturally to Lusk as football teamwork once did. In the 1970s Lusk played pro football for the Philadelphia Eagles. Kneeling down in the end zone after every touchdown, and leading teammates in prayers before and after games, he became known as the National Football League's praying halfback. Today he serves as a team chaplain-advisor to the Eagles (who, dare I say, have needed divine help since they lost the Super Bowl following the 2004 season). The team's practicing Mormon head coach, Andy Reid, is a frequent People for People fund-raising celebrity-speaker.

But Lusk left the Eagles as a player decades ago while still in his prime.

With miles still to go on his football career, he left money, fame, and the then Super Bowl–bound Eagles (they went but lost) to revive a historic but dilapidated church in a poor north Philly neighborhood. Greater Exodus Baptist Church was collapsing. The roof was leaking. The big old building's heating system was shot. The neighborhood had thriving illegal drug markets and failing public schools. But Reverend Herb had faith that he could return the church to its former glory and in the bargain, help rebuild the church's impoverished, crime-torn community.

For nearly two decades now, the good north Philly orthodox Christian pastor and his faith-based organization People for People have provided job skills training, education, and other social services to thousands of low-income people in Philly without regard to religion. Carp though Pastor Lusk sometimes does about judicial tyranny, he is a prototypical urban faith-based leader. His sacred place has served civic purposes via ecumenical, interfaith, religious-secular, and public-private partnerships. The partners have included nearby Catholic congregations, well-to-do white Protestant churches on Philadelphia's suburban Main Line, other local and national black churches (for example, Greater Exodus Baptist Church is part of the Amachi network), and others including, in 2005, the national and international ministries led by California's Pastor Rick Warren, author of the mega–best seller *The Purpose-Driven Life*.

ESPERANZA OBJECTIVO: THE THREE FAITH FACTORS

By the time I was directing the White House Office of Faith-Based and Community Initiatives, Philadelphia's faith-based People for People and Nueva Esperanza were each over a decade old. In April 2001, flanked by People's founder, Pastor Lusk, and Nueva's founder, Reverend Cortés, I made my umpteenth try to get the inside-the-beltway press and the national media to understand church-state issues through the lens of charitable choice and to stop obsessing on faith-saturated organizations. I figured that maybe if I could show, not just tell (or, as sometimes happened, yell), they might relent long enough to learn, find a fresh angle, and do something more like fact-based, civic-spirited reporting.

Right. At age 40-something and with a physique like an overstuffed human meatball, I might as well have tried out for Lusk's old job running the ball for the Eagles. There were literally hundreds of news reports that bird-dogged my White House entry, tenure, and exit.[34] But the single entry that said the most appeared in *Christianity Today* shortly after my Lusk-Cortés press briefing.

The magazine's editor-at-large, John Wilson, captured the event and its broader lessons under the heading "DiIulio Keeps Explaining, But Is Anyone Listening?" Describing me as "Fat, rumpled, plainspoken, funny, and seemingly possessing total recall of hundreds of public policy studies," he welcomed me as "an immensely refreshing presence," then added:

> On his right was Herb Lusk, the pastor of Philadelphia's Greater Exodus Baptist Church; on his left, Luis Cortes of Nueva Esperanza, also from Philadelphia. The two represent the sort of faith-based community services that DiIulio hopes to encourage. Since World War II, DiIulio reminded us . . . [we have had] "government by proxy," whereby federal funds are disbursed to non-governmental organizations. . . . Nevertheless, in the Q&A session that followed—cut short, alas, because DiIulio had to leave for an appointment to brief the president—many of the media queries proceeded as if DiIulio had said nothing, as if the most obvious church-state issues hadn't already been addressed. . . . [He was asked] "what would happen if a church said we will help you, but you have to accept Jesus as your savior." Well, DiIulio said pleasantly, as if this were a perfectly reasonable question, churches can't do that in the context of federally funded programs. And so it went.[35]

And so it has gone pretty much ever since. One reason is the politics of the issue as outlined in chapter 4. By means that are recommended in chapters 6 and 7, those politics, however, can be brought back into line with the majority opinion, bipartisan sentiment, and court doctrine that all favor a level proxy-government playing field for community-serving faith-based organizations.

For now, it would be a double pity if, having temporarily thrown the faith-based baby out with the faith-saturated bathwater, empirical research dealing with broader questions about religion's social consequences continued to be similarly miscast or ignored. Whatever one's views on church-state issues, charitable choice, or faith-based and community initiatives, it would be good to know what the best science now has to say about how religion matters to health, happiness, and social well-being.

My own interest in faith-based phenomena actually began with questions only loosely related to religion and government. In the early 1990s, I had researched the effect of liquor outlets on urban crime and violence. I discovered that, other things being equal, crime and violence rates were higher where booze stores were more concentrated (surprise, surprise).[36] Former drug czar, ex–U.S. education secretary, and best-selling author William J. Bennett agreed to help me in letting the world know about the finding, but teased me (mercifully as usual) about the social science gymnastics that produced it—"the elaborate demonstration of the obvious by methods that are obscure," he cleverly called such. Little did he know that I was next to discover and try to demonstrate that (stop the presses!) religion had many pro-social effects.

By the mid-1990s, I had found that merely by living in places with a high density of liquor outlets, even young people who did not drink or hang out in or near these places were at higher risk of becoming either a victim or a perpetrator. Economists call such effects, like living downwind from a nearby smokestack, "negative externalities." Geo-mapping analysis techniques were still in their infancy, as I had first learned in 1988 when a Princeton University colleague (Mark Alan Hughes) and I did a geo-mapping analysis of where New Jersey prisoners had lived and worked before their latest conviction. But that primitive technology meant having to notice other "dots" on the street grids. I noticed that far more common than dots for liquor outlets (or, for that matter, gas stations) were dots that represented churches.

The obvious questions followed: If liquor outlets produced negative externalities, did churches produce *positive* externalities? If neon-lit windows with beer signs spelled social toxins, did stained-glass windows with religious icons spell social tonics? Specifically, if, independent of other factors, liquor outlets and bars increased crime and violence, did churches and street ministries restrain crime and violence? Nobody had a clue, except for the street ministers I began meeting all over the country. They needed no proof.

My next discovery was that, while most social scientists had been asleep at the wheel when it came to scientifically examining religion's neighborhood and behavioral effects, academic researchers who specialized in medicine and public health had been wide awake. I became close friends with Dr. David B. Larson, the medical research scientist who had pioneered that field's faith-factor studies and who was the single most significant force in getting serious empirical researchers in all fields to take religion seriously.

As you may have noticed, this book is dedicated to him. Larson died at age 54 in 2002, but he left behind a monumental scientific legacy encompassing over 270 professional publications. He developed an objective, quantitative research methodology to help eliminate knotty data problems (known as selection bias) that often plague or confound empirical research on human subjects, and he inspired literally dozens of major medical schools to create "spirituality and health" courses and training programs. To wit: in 1992 only three medical schools in America had such programs, but by 2006, 141 had them, almost all that growth due largely to Dave's catalytic research and careful advocacy.

Larson's body of work proved that there were links between religion and a variety of physical and mental health outcomes, including prevention, recovery, and coping with chronic and serious illness.[37] For the most part, through the mid-1990s religion remained what Larson had termed "the forgotten factor" in the social sciences. But the years since 1995 have witnessed the publication of well over 500 empirical studies that link religious influences and institutions with a dozen-plus positive health and social welfare outcomes, including lower rates of depression, hypertension, suicide, delinquency, street crime, recidivism, educational failure, and nonmarital teenage child-bearing.[38] Almost none of these studies are experimental, and most raise almost as many questions as they answer. But it would take more than a Doubting Thomas to deny that the best studies tend to confirm that religion has multiple positive health and social effects.

Likewise, careful case studies suggest that in cities from coast to coast faith-based programs achieve impressive success in mobilizing volunteers, most especially in relation to programs that serve low-income urban youth and young adults who are at risk of experiencing multiple social ills that diminish their life prospects.[39]

Still, for all of the excellent quasi-experimental and ethnographic research to date, for all the superb statistical analyses and multi-site surveys, and for all of the positive preliminary findings that have flowed from this significant and growing body of empirical research, there has yet to be a single experimental evaluation study of any major faith-based program. For instance, there is as yet no research on the faith-based programs to match the experimental impact research on secular mentoring organizations done over a decade ago by Penn's Joseph P. Tierney.[40]

One of America's leading experts on effective urban community program development, Tierney has pioneered inner-city programs, both secular and faith-based, that have achieved well-documented successes on literacy and violence reduction. He played a leading role in designing the Amachi mentoring program, and he has spearheaded a Penn-Harvard project examining how Catholic nonprofits provide social services.

Nobody is more dedicated than Tierney is to helping urban community-serving programs, religious or secular, Catholic or other, succeed. And yet nobody is more faithful than Tierney is when it comes to advocating the need for objective information about these same community-serving programs, or pressing the point that even the finest quasi-experimental or comparison-group studies have severe limitations.[41]

The fact that we need more, and more systematic, research on community-serving religious nonprofits and programs is hardly surprising, or the least bit damning. Despite decades of tax-supported funding and expenditures of literally hundreds of billions of public and private dollars, only a trivial number of experimental evaluation studies of major secular social-service-delivery programs have been conducted, and there are practically no performance studies that meet even the government's own research evaluation protocols and criteria.

Still, the fact that secular nonprofits that receive significant public money have gotten a de facto pass on having to document rigorously their cost-effectiveness or prove their efficacy is no excuse for not holding religious nonprofits of whatever type to the proper evidentiary standards. And it furnishes no excuse for exaggerating their success.

Unfortunately, while religious boosters of faith-saturated programs too often make sweeping success claims that have only weak or pseudo-scientific studies behind them, their secular detractors too often deny the substantial evidence that faith-based programs are effective at providing vital social services and mobilizing volunteers. More generally, the latter are too quick to deny the empirical data that religious beliefs and behaviors tend to be associated with myriad positive social and health consequences.

Greater conceptual clarity might help all around. There are at least three different types of religious influences, and keeping them straight is no mere academic imperative. Much controversy and confusion on church-state issues might be avoided if people were to separate these three different faith factors: organic religion, programmatic religion, and ecological religion.[42]

Organic religion is defined mainly as belief in God and regular attendance of religious services in a church or other traditional place of worship. *Programmatic religion* refers to purposeful individual participation in social programs with a religious affiliation.

Finally, even if one does not believe in God or attend religiously affiliated social programs, one may yet be influenced by religious ecologies. Essentially, ecology is the science concerned with the totality of interrelationships between organisms and their environments. *Ecological religion* is present in everything from the church, synagogue, or mosque that you drive by every day but never enter, to the community-serving ministry that unbeknownst to you serves your next-door neighbor or cleaned up the playground across the street, to the football idol whom you watched pray in the end zone after every touchdown.

Larson, the late, great pioneering medical faith-factor researcher, often joked that "if you think going to church makes you religious, you must think sitting in your garage makes you a car." His serious point was that measuring organic religion as a dichotomous variable, such as in "churched or unchurched," probably misses as much as it reveals. His basic point applies with even greater force to programmatic religion and ecological religion.

Without getting deeply into the relevant conceptual and methodological challenges, consider the hypothetical case of a low-income young adult living in an economically depressed urban neighborhood. This young person could be a one-, two-, three-factor individual, right?

Does he or she believe in God or have other regular exposure or engagement with organic religion? Does he or she participate in a local social service delivery or other program administered by a religious or religiously affiliated organization? Does he or she happen to live on the side of the neighborhood where the only outdoor symbols more ubiquitous than neon beer lights are stained-glass windows, and the city's department of family services contracts mainly with ministers?

Do the simple arithmetic. There are over a half-dozen possibilities. How would you know or find out whether a given individual was high, low, or average on one, two, or all three faith factors? How do you suppose such information ought to matter or be "factored into," say, an empirical analysis assessing a given faith-based program's behavioral impact or other measurable outcomes? Even the most sophisticated statistical analysts in the world (and I have discussed the subject with numerous scholars who would meet that qualification) are not really sure how to gather, analyze, and interpret diverse empirical faith-factor data in ways that yield results that are general, meaningful, and true.

Alas, it is a multivariate world. Empirical analysis has three main rules: disaggregate, disaggregate, and disaggregate. These rules are especially hard to follow when it comes to ecological religion. For example, most nonbelievers will tell you that their lives have been affected by living in a society where most fellow citizens are, or may reasonably be presumed to be, believers. But affected how, under what conditions, and with what positive or negative consequences?

Analytically, one big problem in studying faith-saturated programs that promote spiritual transformation is selection bias: the people who are most likely to opt into such programs are, in effect, people who are religious believers and are already likely to practice what the program preaches. To use our new vocabulary, they are more likely than an otherwise comparable group to be high on organic religion before they are exposed to the influence of this particular program.

Obviously, experimental research is out: people cannot be randomly assigned to believe and practice a given religion; there cannot be placebos;

and both researchers and participants would know who was and was not getting the "treatment."

In 2006, at my suggestion, the outstanding young Rutgers University economist Anne Morrison Piehl was asked by the National Academy of Sciences (NAS) to assess these faith-factor research dilemmas in relation to certain criminal justice programs. The NAS is to scientific research what NASCAR is to speed racing. She focused on prisoner reentry programs.

Piehl is a former Harvard professor of public policy who had been a graduate student of mine at Princeton. Back in the 1990s, we had done and published together several prisoner surveys and cost-benefit analyses of imprisonment (for *The Brookings Review*), and she held her old mentor's hand in analyzing the aforementioned data regarding how liquor outlets affect crime rates. Several years ago I had encouraged her to begin thinking about the methodological challenges, both generic and unique, posed by religious influences. She did her usual spectacular job. Her observations about the analytical knots associated with faith-factor research were right on target. Her conclusions about the state of empirical research on faith-based prisoner reentry programs could apply equally well to faith-based welfare-to-work, substance abuse, and myriad other faith-based programs. After explaining and employing my three faith-factor framework, she wrapped up her NAS report as follows:

> Which of these factors can be studied, and how? . . . [P]rogrammatic religion is the most straightforward to study . . . [but it] is harder to imagine how to collect or use information on the organic religious influence. Government-sponsored randomization is not appropriate, and influence [of organic religion] is confounded in the same way that many individual-level influences are. . . . The ecological influence of religion is perhaps the most interesting in general, as it likely functions throughout a community, with ripple effects and interactions with other community characteristics and institutions. Such an aggregate impact is hard to identify, but important for understanding communities and for questions of the appropriate level of government support for religious institutions. . . . For many reasons, faith-based re-entry programs appear to be well-positioned to make unique contributions to prisoner re-entry. In fact, a great variety of programs and partnerships have been developed in which faith-based institutions play many different roles. But there is little reliable statistical evi-

dence about the specific contributions of faith-based organizations to successful reintegration. The opportunities for adding to the knowledge base are enormous.[43]

The opportunities for adding to our knowledge base about faith-based programs are enormous, but we will be likely to miss these opportunities if we become unduly focused on faith-*saturated* programs that, as we have seen, represent only a small portion of the nation's spiritual capital. It is certainly worthwhile to study programs that try to build spiritual capital by effecting spiritual transformation. But trying to understand the community-serving religious nonprofit sector as a whole by understanding faith-saturated programs only would be like trying to understand national fast-food hamburger franchises by studying a few small regional chains that specialized in deep-fried fare for meat lovers only while ignoring McDonald's, Burger King, and Wendy's.

Also, when it comes to objectively studying faith-saturated programs, philosophical difficulties compound analytical ones: people who run and believe in faith-saturated programs generally insist that only those who complete or graduate from the program and "get religion" should count as having received the program's services or "treatment." Accordingly, they often keep reliable records only on program graduates; but nearly all social scientists who do program evaluation work (not to mention the federal government's own assorted research evaluation protocols) strictly reject that preference and are trained to start the clock with all who enter a program.

In the end, the social scientists and the federal government are right, but faith-saturated program providers are not as dogmatic or as wholly unsophisticated about this difficulty as some academic experts suppose them to be.

Essentially, their argument is that, unlike many faith-based programs and most secular programs, their faith-saturated programs do not purport to have a universal cure or treatment that is assumed to work on any person who has the particular behavioral problem in question. Rather, they see themselves as primarily engaged in identifying and attracting that subset of persons for whom their particular approach might work, especially where other religious or secular approaches have not helped or have helped but little. (Let me save social science cynics the trouble and beat them to the academic insiders' point: people who believe in serving by saving souls also thereby believe in selecting on the dependent variable.)

For example, it is well established that, whatever the intervention or treatment, most people with multiyear substance abuse problems do not succeed on their first try. Many do not succeed even after multiple tries. There is possibly a subset of addicts for whom an intervention that takes shape as a spiritual transformation process or a conversion ritual might prove to be an effective bulwark against a propensity to abuse alcohol or drugs, or both.

Anecdotally, there is no shortage of testimonies proclaiming that this or that faith-saturated program succeeded in getting addicts to resist the temptations of drugs and alcohol. There are plenty of colorful and dramatic stories about people who, having tried everything else, tried a program that promoted spiritual transformation, got better, and stayed better. Especially in and around prisons, which I studied for over a decade back in the 1980s and early 1990s, I myself have heard dozens of such stories.

But, as Berkeley political scientist Raymond Wolfinger has quipped, "the plural of anecdote is not data." There are as yet no credible quasi-experimental studies to support claims that faith-saturated programs routinely succeed where either faith-based or wholly secular programs supposedly almost always fail. Such claims, however, often are asserted by those who wish to challenge one or more neutrality principles governing public law and administration in this area.

This is *not* to say either that we know that faith-saturated programs do not work, or to suggest that they do not embody best practices, or to imply that they do not deserve the benefit of doubts about their cost-effectiveness or efficacy. At least in my view, they do.

But it is important that future research focus more on faith-based organizations. They are not only far and away the dominant category of community-serving religious nonprofit organizations but also far more capable of being described, analyzed, and evaluated in ways that take no leaps of faith to comprehend.

So, what can we say without making any leaps of faith? We can say that all the best empirical research to date indicates that the nation's bridging spiritual capital reserves are vast and quite possibly growing.

We can say that America's faith-based volunteer-mobilizing nonprofit organizations, especially in urban America and most especially from within black religious communities, bless needy people with myriad social services in cities from coast to coast.

We can say, with the late, great faith-factor research pioneer Dr. David B. Larson, that religion, till recently the forgotten factor in scientific research, is generally associated with many positive social and health outcomes.

And we can say with Professor Piehl of Rutgers that the three faith factors are important, hard to study, but well worth exploring in greater depth and with greater rigor in the years ahead.

In sum, based on all the latest and best empirical research, even a civic-spirited skeptic has good reasons for objective hope (or, as Reverend Cortés might prefer, *esperanza objectivo*) about faith-based organizations.

In the end, however, the honest-to-goodness facts about the nation's spiritual capital, uplifting though they are, can inform church-state debates but cannot resolve them. Those debates are, at bottom, more about competing values than they are about competing facts. People who take extreme positions in these debates also take liberties with the facts when it suits their cause.

The godly republic's faith-based future depends more on whether orthodox sectarians and orthodox secularists can learn to disagree without undermining the civic consensus on religion and government; and it depends ultimately on whether the rest of us, including leaders in Washington, practice effective compassion toward the "least of these." But how? The next two chapters provide some answers.

SIX

The Republic's Faith-Based Future

CIVIC ECUMENISM, NOT SECTARIAN
TRIUMPHALISM OR SECULAR EXTREMISM

Myth 9   Political common ground on church-state issues and other controversial policy matters has been shrinking, and the fault belongs to
orthodox sectarians, mainly religious conservative Republicans.

Myth 10   Political common ground on church-state issues and other controversial policy matters has been shrinking, and the fault belongs to
orthodox secularists, mainly secular liberal Democrats.

TRUTH   Political divides are natural in a healthy representative democracy,
but religion in a republic can and should do more to moderate than
to metastasize such differences. Faith-based leaders and organizations can help government to solve persistent social problems and
spread civic trust. That future is ours to choose.

TAKE PRISONERS: EVANGELICAL CHRISTIANS
VERSUS SECULAR LIBERALS

Charles W. Colson is not the first name that most Americans associate
with helping vulnerable citizens or advocating just treatment for convicted criminals. Colson is remembered instead as the crew cut with horn-
rimmed glasses who was President Richard M. Nixon's political hatchet

man. Trained as a lawyer, Colson went to federal prison after being convicted for crimes associated with the Watergate scandal.

That was over a quarter-century ago. Colson left prison a changed man. Even before his stint behind bars, he had become a born-again Christian. He left prison promising the men with whom he had served that he would never forget them. He dedicated the rest of his life to helping prisoners and ex-prisoners.

In 1976, Colson formed Prison Fellowship Ministries (PFM). He became a best-selling author and popular Christian radio host. With Colson as its pitchman, PFM has raised tens of millions of dollars a year from donors and direct mail. Colson himself has given millions of dollars to the ministry. As I witnessed in the late 1990s as a PFM board member, Colson is even more persuasive when speaking to life-term felons inside a maximum-security prison than when he is walking into a corporate boardroom or working a Washington political crowd.

In the 1980s I had studied prisons and visited scores of them all across the country. Never had I seen inmates respond to a VIP visitor the way they responded to Colson. One Easter Sunday, I joined him for a visit to Trenton State, a maximum-security prison in New Jersey where I had been many times before. Colson shared his personal power-to-prison story. He preached redemption and rehabilitation. As he spoke, hundreds of prisoners, all but a few of them black men, rose to their feet clapping and cheering. As usual, he stayed longer than his schedule allowed and was clearly reluctant to leave. As he finally made his way to the gates, the prisoners crowded around like teenagers at a rock concert. Typical exclamations were "You're for real, man!" and "Love you back, brother!"

William F. Buckley, Jr., who many consider to be the intellectual godfather of America's post-1950 conservative movement, once quipped to me that anyone who doubts that Colson is truly religious must also doubt that *Playboy*'s founder Hugh Hefner is truly lascivious. Amen.

I first got to know Colson in the early 1990s. We met—or more precisely, collided—at a private dinner with a dozen or so conservative leaders. After dinner, he and I were to debate prison policy, with me as the young get-tough hawk and him as the old pro-reform dove. He went first. He led with a moving moral argument but then embroidered his case by selectively citing statistics from a government-sponsored report that, unbeknownst to him, I had virtually authored.

I gave Colson no quarter. I turned his every moral point back on him (a trick mastered during my days at Harvard) and then matter-of-factly directed him to "please open the report" in his lap to pages featuring statistics (which I cited in detail) that devastated his case. "It was," said one Colson friend and confidante who was present, "like watching a rising boxer destroy an aging champion in the first round of a fifteen-round heavyweight prize fight."

But Colson himself was more amused than embarrassed or upset. He was also concerned, not for himself, but about me. Pulling me aside as the meeting broke up, he put his hand on my shoulder. He looked me straight in the eye. ("My God, " I remember thinking as he leaned closer, "this *is* the 'Watergate guy' from my high school textbook!") With avuncular warmth, he told me that he had admired my writing on government reform and social policy for many years. But then he dropped a bomb: "I know you, John. You remind me very much of me at about your age." Yikes.

In the years that followed, this gentle evangelical Christian giant joined black Pentecostal leaders and others who had begun encouraging my deepening interest in how my own Catholic identity ought to inform my roles as academic analyst, public intellectual, and Philly-based civic dogooder. By the late 1990s, with fresh empirical data and a renewed Catholic heart, I had joined Colson's pro-reform, "restorative justice" chorus. I started writing op-ed pieces with titles like "Stop Crime Before It Starts" (for the *New York Times*) and "Two Million Prisoners Are Enough" (for the *Wall Street Journal*), essays against mandatory-minimum drug laws (for *National Review* magazine), book chapters like one calling for a moratorium on federal funding for state prisons (for the Brookings Institution), reports on the need to increase federal funding for prevention and treatment programs (for the National District Attorneys Association, among others), and even an article entitled "Zero Prison Growth" (for a University of Notre Dame journal). And that is just a small post-1996 sample. "Only you," one dear old secular liberal pal teased me, "could have become a soft-on-crime liberal by meeting an old right-wing Republican hack like Colson."

I became and am no such thing, least of all by elite secular university standards. (Neither is Chuck a right-wing Republican hack—he is no hack.) But there is no doubt that, in the mid- to late 1990s, Colson's influence, together with what my inner-city urban ministry friends were preaching and with what I was learning about my own policy-relevant Catholic beliefs and tenets (another op-ed piece, in the *Wall Street Journal,* put me on record against capital sentencing), changed my heart even as new studies were changing my mind. And, quite obviously, their influence was wind beneath my wings in developing faith-based ideas and proposals that most academic colleagues (even fairly conservative ones) and many journalistic pals (notable exceptions being Joe Klein and E. J. Dionne) repeatedly told me to ditch or risk losing my reputation. As the same friend who teased me about Colson half-kidded after I left the White House, "Told you so!"

In the late 1990s, Colson took to introducing me to PFM board members. My standard shtick was to say how impressed I was that old Chuck had learned so much about prison reform since I first met him. It became a favorite joke between Colson and me. I repeated it to him as he stood among the diverse religious leaders who attended President Bush's January 29, 2001 announcement of the new White House Office of Faith-Based and Community Initiatives.

Although we have had more than a few disagreements over the years (he is, after all, a staunch Republican, an all-out Evangelical, and a nonacademic and I am . . . not), my personal affection and civic regard for Colson, and for many other evangelical Christian leaders and their organizations, is real and abiding.

Over the years, however, I have learned that even my fellow faith-friendly centrist Democrats and open-minded secular liberal friends prefer that I keep such affection and regard to myself. They draw the line, not only on church-state collaboration but on church-state dialogue, at evangelical Christians like Colson and organizations like PFM. Even though many evangelical Christians reach beyond their own leaders, supporters, and volunteers to serve people without regard to race, ethnicity, socioeconomic status, or for that matter, criminal record, any favorable mention of them often moves secular liberals to express contempt and centrist Democrats (including many urban Catholics) to feel suspicion.

For instance, in April 2006 I gave lectures on religion and government at the University of California at Berkeley. I did so in conjunction with the twelfth annual Aaron Wildavsky Forum for Public Policy. Wildavsky, who died in 1993, was a political scientist whose penetrating research on many topics (budgeting, the presidency, federalism, the environment, and others) was always original and often iconoclastic. He was partial to Moses as a model leader and to the biblical injunction about "speaking truth to power" as a moniker for the art and craft of policy analysis. Despite the university's reputation as a bastion of liberal and radical thinking, Berkeley's annual Wildavsky lectures are meant, in his spirit, to do more than justify politically correct conclusions favored by secular academic elites. Mine certainly did, and I was generally well and warmly received.

On one point, however, my Berkeley interlocutors were politely up in arms. I had concluded my lecture by arguing that Democrats and secular liberals needed to do more than embrace what the Constitution's framers, the contemporary federal courts, the present-day public majority, and most political leaders in both parties had to say about religion and government in America. They also needed, I insisted, to put their partisan, ideological, and religious differences with Republican conservative evangelical Christians far enough aside to start meaningful civic dialogues with them. These civic dialogues, I preached, should start with church-state issues and faith-based and community initiatives. In addition to turning down the viscerally negative volume on both sides, the purpose would be to discover shared civic goals that probably could not be achieved without greater mutual forbearance.

For instance, if faith-friendly Democrats and secular liberals truly want to address acute social challenges, such as how to ensure literacy among inner-city children, or how to raise high school graduation rates among low-income urban minority teenagers, or how to help find jobs for the over five million men who will exit the nation's prisons over the next ten years, then they would do well to find Republican conservatives and evangelical Christians who share these civic goals.

One Berkeley audience member summarized the audience's reaction to my call for a civic truce as "To hell with Republicans and their religious fanatics." Another admitted to recoiling at the mention of "somebody like Colson" and argued, essentially, that centrist Democrats and secular liberals do not really need to build broad coalitions, either to achieve traditional antipoverty objectives or to meet related social challenges on the civic horizon. "They stole God," said another (who found me the next day after simmering all night about my talk) "and now they want to steal the poor."

My official Berkeley faculty respondents were all very thoughtful and offered many different comments and criticisms. But they, too, were fairly united in pushing back my call for civic dialogue and joint action with evangelical Christians. I had, as one faculty respondent rightly stated, "unconvincingly" used Benjamin Franklin's religious toleration and dying words (no less) to make my appeal for both sides to "all just get along." Even among political scientists with smartly progressive views, the prevailing wisdom is that the time has come to beat conservative Republicans and "the Christian Right" at their own game by copying their "off-center" strategies and hardball tactics. Almost nobody at Berkeley, or in the many other university and "unchurched" audiences before which I had previously voiced the idea, seemed sincerely interested in reaching out to find common ground, or initiating joint community-serving programs, with evangelical Christians like Colson and organizations like PFM.

Unfortunately, the negative feelings are mutual. Even the most openminded and big-hearted evangelical Christians and Republican social conservatives tend to believe that starting a civic dialogue with people with whom they have such deep partisan, ideological, and religious differences is a waste of time. Sadly, each side has learned that persistently attacking the other side (when not simply ignoring its existence), exaggerating differences, and even virtually making up outrages is what works to create or reinforce in-group camaraderie, stir latent supporters into becoming activists, and raise more money.

As many studies have suggested, one-sided negative emotional appeals are now standard in national campaigns and elections. Less widely noticed but no less consequential is that they are equally common now in everyday politically charged "nonprofit campaigns." One fund-raising professional I know has generated donations for evangelical Christian and pro-life groups as well as for one liberal ethnic advocacy group. As he once confided to me, "Both sides do it. . . . Direct mail appeals directly or indirectly damn the other guys and their views. . . . On the religious right, it's damn the secular liberals who took God out of schools. Or damn the federal judges who support them. Always damn the liberal Democrats . . . [and the secular media] for helping to destroy the culture. . . . On the left, it's damn them all on the right. . . . The ethnic and religious groups [on both sides], but especially the conservatives, do it, too. . . . Then [the appeal letter] says 'Oh, and praise God for your contribution.'"

This mutual take-no-prisoners civic mistrust does not define American politics, freeze America into a red state–blue state nation, or otherwise fatally threaten the godly republic's future. It does, however, diminish Americans as a people, restrict what civic good gets done, and stymie citizens on both sides who sincerely want to help others in need.

There is a better way, and Americans have a civic genius for finding it even when Washington keeps burying it. The better way is to search for common ground, a search that boosts civic trust even if, in the end, none is found. The better way is to stick to your principles, whatever they may be, but give the other "extreme" a chance to explain its principles. The better way is to give "them" the benefit of the doubt that you wish they would just once give "us." The better way is not to be high-handed or arrogant in using any power advantages that you may have today but that "they" may have tomorrow (or after the next media frenzies, court decisions, or elections—a lesson that some Republicans learned the hard way after the 2006 elections).

Predictably, evangelical Christians and secular liberals were sharply polarized in their reactions to a June 2006 federal court decision that came down like a ton of bricks against Colson's PFM. This court case, or the bifurcated reaction to it, illustrates the dilemma, but it may also light a single candle by which a wider search for common ground might begin. There is no easy solution, but there is a better way.

DO UNTO OTHERS: PRATT VERSUS PRATT

On June 2, 2006, Iowa federal district court judge Robert W. Pratt declared that the relationship between Iowa's Newton Correctional Facility and a particular PFM program, the InnerChange Freedom Initiative (IFI), was unconstitutional. Writing for the U.S. District Court of the Southern District of Iowa, Judge Pratt issued this decision in *Americans United for Separation of Church and State v. Prison Fellowship Ministries*.

Judge Pratt ordered that the IFI program be closed within 60 days and that IFI refund the state of Iowa a total of $1.5 million that it received over six years in program grants. These orders do not take effect until after the appeals process is completed.

Before the ink dried on Judge Pratt's opinion, PFM declared that it would appeal. On the PFM website, the organization's president, former state of Virginia attorney general Mark Earley, promised that the decision would be appealed "all the way to the Supreme Court if we must."

Instead of paving the way for a protracted court battle, the Iowa IFI case could help to pave a path to greater mutual understanding. It might even lead to mutual action on such shared civic goals as helping ex-prisoners, their families, and the low-income urban communities that most call home.

Dream on? Maybe, but there is nothing inevitable about heated church-state controversies that divert attention and steal support from ecumenical, interfaith, religious-secular, and public-private partnerships that help people in need. As examples in chapters 3 and 4 show, this has happened in the recent past. But precisely because we know that it has, the past need not be prologue. Besides, neither religious conservative Republicans (Myth #9) nor secular liberal Democrats (Myth #10) have been solely to blame for deep church-state civic divides or for serious political differences over other controversial issues.

Rather, persistent public policy failures to help religious organizations meet social needs—like most such civic failures—have reflected, and continue to reflect, much wider failures of moral and political will. The civic center cannot always hold, but it can coach, coax, and court compromises. If factions led by orthodox sectarians or orthodox secularists dominate public church-state discourse and decision-making and if, in turn, the nation's faith-based future produces more ideological and partisan heat than social light, we will have only ourselves to blame.

The godly republic's faith-based future is ours to choose. Iowa, which is the first state to host presidential caucuses every four years, is as good a place as any to begin a search for common ground and model mutual civic forbearance.

When I first heard about the Iowa federal judge's decision against PFM, there was a funny misunderstanding that I have since taken as a sign. A message relayed to me from an old IFI insider was phrased as "Pratt came down against PF." ("PF" is preferred to "PFM" by many of the Colson organization's veteran supporters, volunteers, and watchers.)

Pratt? Against Colson and the ministry? Over what? Impossible, I thought. I knew *Tom* Pratt, PFM's former president, as the man who in the mid-1990s had guided IFI's introduction into the ministry's already multifaceted behind-bars operations. The first major IFI operation was in Texas, followed by Kansas, Minnesota, Iowa, and Arkansas. The Wheaton College–educated Pratt was an ex-businessman and former wrestling coach with a "real heart" for prison ministry, as my evangelical pals like to say. He could never do enough, work enough hours, or sacrifice enough to help this cause. He felt called by God to help mend lives that had been broken by crime.

Obviously, I had the wrong late-middle-aged Pratt. IFI is one of former PFM president Tom Pratt's legacies, though hardly the only one worth noting. IFI is also likely to be among Judge Robert W. Pratt's legacies. Since he graduated from Creighton Law School in 1972 and was appointed to the federal bench in 1997, Judge Pratt, judging only by his professional record as summarized in various public sources, has done some interesting things. Nothing, however, is more likely to define his career than what he wrote about IFI, what happens as PFM appeals his decision, and what transpires as future church-state activists on each side characterize, caricature, and publicize his 140-page opinion.

Before explaining precisely what Judge Pratt decided, where he was half-right, where he went all wrong, and what ought to happen in response to his ruling, we need to learn more about the Pratt who founded the IFI program.

During Tom Pratt's presidency, PFM radically expanded its programs for the children, youth, and families of prisoners and recent parolees. With Colson's blessings, Pratt put PFM at the disposal of several national secular organizations to assist in the early development of what became the Amachi program. PFM invested substantial time and money in the effort. Pratt and PFM leaders viewed the religious-secular initiative as an extension of the ministry's well-known Angel Tree program, which delivers hundreds of thousands of gifts each Christmas season to children on behalf of their incarcerated parents. I once watched a prisoner cry with joy as he showed me a crayon-written letter from his young son thanking his dad for the gift. By putting a mentor into such a child's life year round, Angel Tree was to give rise to a new program to be known as Evergreen.

However, the secular Evergreen partners and their circumspection about religion were an uneasy match with PFM's evangelical mission and methods. Communication, fiscal, and data-sharing problems that commonly crop up in multiorganizational nonprofit undertakings were amplified by the underlying evangelical-secular differences. I was the go-between; but as usual, even when I did not intend to be, I was better at sharpening or even exacerbating differences than I was at smoothing them over or sidestepping disagreements.

PFM's Pratt compared the situation in relation to a shakedown cruise, a Navy term for a first voyage intended to work out any operational, mechanical, or organizational bugs. "Only this shakedown cruise," he joked when he visited me in the White House in 2001, "never quite left the dock." To stick with Pratt's metaphor, each crew agreed to set sail on its own. Led by Philly's former mayor the Reverend Dr. W. Wilson Goode, Sr., a man uniquely qualified to navigate uncharted religious-secular and public-private waters, the non-PFM partners rowed together as Amachi, while PFM cruised toward new summer camps for prisoners' children.

PFM's Pratt was no stranger to organizational innovation. He had launched IFI in 1997. Two years later, IFI became a separate 501(c)3 nonprofit organization. Many such separate (or "satellite") nonprofits, including ones established in conjunction with universities or by private foundations, remain very closely tied to the bodies that created them.

IFI is a prisoner reentry program. It begins behind bars for inmates who are eighteen to twenty-four months from their official release dates. The program then follows its participants into the community for an additional six months' to a year's worth of counseling and aftercare. The IFI program has three phases: first, prisoners get a biblically derived "values-based" education that includes work and interpersonal skills-building; second, prisoners are put to the test through real-life conflict resolution situations and in off-site work environments; and, third, the ex-prisoner reenters the community and receives job placement help, housing in a "halfway house" facility, and other transitional services.

The IFI apple did not fall very far from the PFM tree, but the PFM tree has a religious root system more complex than that of many other evangelical Christian organizations. For instance, unlike Teen Challenge, PFM is not predicated completely on "a literal interpretation of the Protestant Bible." Per its official charters, PFM is unmistakably and unapologetically anchored in a belief in "the power and truth of Jesus Christ," but its mission is to "apply biblical thinking to all of life" and thereby "to seek the transformation of prisoners and their reconciliation to God, family, and community." Its vision statement includes "enabling the Church to influence every arena of life, advancing truth, justice, mercy, love, goodness, and beauty." Its board-certified core values range from "centered in Jesus Christ" to such secular values as "loving others by treating all people with grace, trust, and respect" and "seeking excellence by demonstrating integrity and wise stewardship."

The Iowa IFI program began when PFM filed a typical proxy-government "request for proposal" application put out by the state government. In March 1999, PFM won the contract for Iowa's Newton Correctional Facility through a competitive bidding process. In the ensuing years, the IFI program delivered the services called for in the proposal application and complied with related reporting requirements in the manner that its successful proposal had indicated it would.

While Judge Pratt ordered PFM to reimburse the state $1.5 million, the Newton facility's IFI program had also been supported by over $1.5 million in private investment, not to mention over 4,000 hours each year in help from ministry-mobilized volunteers.

The group that filed the suit against PFM's Iowa IFI program, Americans United for Separation of Church and State, is led by the Reverend Barry Lynn. Over the years, the organization has made some reasonable attacks on church-state policies that strain neutrality principles. I so respected its former legislative counsel, Julie Segal, that I invited her to consider joining my White House staff (an offer she declined). I chose the articulate Reverend Lynn to be a dissenting voice on the PBS-aired documentary *God and the Inner City* that I helped to produce several years ago.

Americans United for Separation of Church and State is an important civic check and balance group on church-state issues, and it ought not to be demonized by anyone. But make no mistake. Reverend Lynn and his organization reflect the strict, no-aid church-state separation doctrine favored by many who have funded their legislative and court campaigns over the years. They were opposed to the original federal charitable choice laws, and they have opposed every charitable choice law proposal since. Their website has also boasted of having "a significant impact on President Bush's Faith-Based Initiative generally." Theirs is the First Amendment religion-clauses jurisprudence of Justice Hugo Black's *Everson* opinion, scrubbed of its anti-Catholic antecedents, but born again to sever even incidental government support for religious ideas, icons, or institutions.

During my first weeks as the so-called faith czar, I took to publicly begging strict church-state separation advocates to stop talking and start suing over charitable choice laws. I even repeatedly sang the offer to the tune of the "sue me, sue me" song popularized by the 1950s musical *Guys and Dolls,* a performance that left many Washington journalists momentarily nonplussed.

I was not being reckless or rude (though I was being what the British call "cheeky," and what a few in the Washington press corps called "crazy"). Rather, I was making the point that there was absolutely no way that any faith-based program that operated between the double-yellow constitutional lines painted by charitable choice could ever be successfully sued on church-state grounds. Through early 2007, none has been.

I was also thereby inviting everyone to take a closer look at how the vast majority of community-serving religious nonprofits, especially those in urban America, actually do what they do, and for whom. As these terms were defined in chapter 5, I was saying, in effect, "They're mostly all faith-based, not even close to faith-saturated; but, if you want to start suing inner-city day care centers that operate in church basements, or urban welfare-to-work ministries that are getting jobs for poor women, or religious but medically certified neighborhood health screening and immunization programs, then be my guest, for you will eventually lose in courts of law, and you will lose immediately in the court of public opinion."

Of course, an organization such as PFM makes for a fatter and far easier target, especially if you light up the bull's eye by denying everything around it that is *non*sectarian in purpose and in practice. That is what you would do if your true aim was not to fire warning shots or change specific neutrality-violating features but to bring down the program, deter others from pursuing similar projects, and splatter as much collateral damage as possible on kindred organizations. Sadly, that is how many who cheered Judge Pratt's decision against Tom Pratt's ministry sounded.

By the same token, an organization like PFM can respond aggressively to its critics and their real or perceived ill will, or it can recognize, as it were, that some things are true even though our least fair-minded detractors say they are. It can either respond to specific charges and make changes where appropriate or it can spare its worst critics the trouble by overgeneralizing the adverse federal court judgment into an all-out attack on itself, on all other orthodox Christian nonprofit groups, and on all evangelical co-believers.

As a national political leader with close ties to evangelical Christian organizations taught me in 2002, "*Engel* [the 1962 Court decision prohibiting state-sponsored public school prayers, discussed in chapter 2] was the biggest boon to the [religious conservative political movement]. The next big burst was *Roe* [the 1973 Court decision that legalized abortion at all stages]. . . . Now we've got [*Newdow*, the 2002 federal district court opinion ruling that students should not be required to recite "under God" in the Pledge of Allegiance, discussed in chapter 1]. You couldn't pay the kook federal judges in Frisco enough for that. . . . [The nuances of such decisions] matter only to law professors. Every court ruling like that against religion just means more passion and support on both sides. . . . You can't lose. If you win the case, you win. And if you lose, you still win, because now the threat has never been greater. Now everybody has to do more or die."

In response to Judge Pratt's decision, Tom Pratt's worthy successor,

PFM's President Earley, went beyond his aforementioned promise to appeal, if necessary, all the way to the Supreme Court. On PFM's website, he pushed the *Engel* button:

> We can only hope that what has happened with God being taken out of the classrooms of America thirty years ago does not repeat itself in America's prisons as a result of the federal courts. . . . [Prisoners should be free] to take part in a program—yes, even a Christ-centered one—that will help them change their lives for the better if they so desire.

Actually, as Virginia's former attorney general has got to know, the federal courts did no such thing, either several decades ago or since, regarding religion and education.

And Judge Pratt's opinion, fatally flawed and deeply offensive though it is in key parts, is not quite the antireligious diatribe that some PFM and IFI supporters have interpreted it to be, perhaps out of pardonable regard for Brothers Colson and Pratt and their well-meaning organizations.[1]

The easy part is to agree with Judge Pratt where I have no doubt that Tom Pratt would agree with him as well: PFM is a "pervasively sectarian" organization committed to a particular religious faith and dedicated to spreading that faith by word and deed—and so, by extension and association, is its IFI offshoot.

Judge Pratt, however, needlessly trivialized IFI's IRS-approved independent nonprofit status. He almost made it seem that the program's ties to its parent body were somehow sinister when, in fact, such ties are closer to being the national nonprofit industry norm for all organization spin-offs, including secular ones. As one old PFM supporter lamented to me, "When you were in Washington the liberals and the Democrats kept whining 'Just get a 501(c)3!' PF did that for [IFI], but the judge just goes and disrespects it and says 'So what? You're still all a bunch of Christians.'"

While Judge Pratt cited *Lemon* and reviewed other key precedents, he vacillated in grasping the central and abiding Establishment clause neutrality point regarding "pervasively sectarian" nonprofits. Namely, even a completely, totally, and unambiguously sectarian organization, subject to the terms of any particular federal, state, or local government proposal application, is free to compete for government grants or contracts on a level playing field with all other prospective proxy-government providers.

Arguably, one innocent reason for Judge Pratt's extraordinarily broad interpretation of "establishment" relates to his blanket invocation of a 1988 precedent regarding "public function doctrine."[2] This latter doctrine requires that, if typical government beneficiaries cannot distinguish between the public authority exercised by government workers (say state corrections officers) and proxy-government workers (say on-site contractors who work right alongside state corrections officers), or if the government and proxy-government administrative functions are otherwise highly intertwined, then any proxy-government agents' "public function" is such that they, no less than government civil servants themselves, must, when on the job and thus representing the state, be devoid of any particular religious identities and refrain from even indirect or symbolic religious endorsements.

If you do not understand all that, then get this: quick, somebody tell Washington that virtually every intergovernmental program on the books, including giant health, human services, and environmental ones that spend hundreds of billions of dollars each year, has to close within 60 days! Almost all of these programs have had at least one or more religious proxy-government contractors that, although far less "pervasively sectarian" than PFM, would nonetheless fail the public function doctrine test as Judge Pratt misapplies it in relation to his misunderstanding of neutrality doctrine.

A less innocent take on Judge Pratt's decision might focus on his unfortunate attempts, following a doth-protest-too-much disclaimer about not questioning the validity of anyone's religion or theology, to summarize what evangelical Christians really believe. Even worse are the inferences he then draws about their fundamental fitness—or, as he concludes, fundamental lack of fitness—to function as proxy-government partners. He implies that, given what they all supposedly think about creationism and other matters, evangelical Christians cannot be trusted not to proselytize no matter what they actually say, no matter how fairly they actually compete, and no matter how completely they actually comply with all specific grant-related government reporting requirements and other administrative program protocols.[3]

Just try to imagine how it would be received if a federal judge wrote a superficial summary about what all Catholics or all Jews supposedly believe, followed by sweeping inferences about what they cannot be trusted to touch if it relates to government in any way. Just imagine how it would be received if a federal judge described any other major religious tradition as if it were, beneath it all, a strange cult and a civic danger. Undoubtedly, these rambling *obiter dicta* passages of Judge Pratt's opinion will rankle so badly as to keep many evangelical Christians from taking seriously his more cogent questions about the constitutionality of the IFI program.

As a Catholic, these passages smell all too familiar to me. To his credit, Judge Pratt is no Hugo Black—he even notes in passing the "irony" that faith-friendly Jefferson is invoked as the early republic's authority on strict separation. Still, these passages are Black's bigoted *Everson* opinion as applied to today's evangelical Christians rather than the immigrant Catholics of yesteryear. Little in the opinion, including the good judge's not-so-good religion-clauses analysis, renders these passages inoffensive.

Even after heavily discounting most testimony that emphasized the nonsectarian aspects of the IFI program's mission and methods, Judge Pratt could not claim that prisoners need to profess Christianity, or any particular type of Christianity, before being accepted into the IFI program. Neither could he claim that participants need to profess Christianity, or any particular type of Christianity, to complete the IFI program. As close as he could come was to object that the state of Iowa has not created IFI-like programs predicated on other faiths (he cited Islam and Lubavitch-sect Judaism).[4]

By the same token, Judge Pratt invoked *Zelman*'s "true private choice" standard against IFI, even though he admitted that prospective prisoner-beneficiaries are fully informed about all aspects of the program and may choose to participate in it or not, or to remain in it or not, on a purely voluntary basis. He even admitted that some inmates who have complained about the program's religious character wanted to return to it after they had quit it. He asserted that the IFI program unfairly induces prisoners to participate because it is housed in a nicer physical plant and is associated with food, recreation, and other amenities that are not available to eligible prisoners who choose not to participate in it. He solemnly declared that it is "not permissible to use otherwise neutral benefits to encourage participation in a religious program."[5]

I do not know how well Judge Pratt knows prisons, but he might as well have included among "otherwise neutral benefits" things like not having to worry as much about violence, being treated less like a number and more like a human being, and having a sense that the people responsible for your custody really care about whether you make it once you are released. He might also have avoided legal logic that renders in-prison religious programs constitutional shoo-ins if they prove popular despite having less decent digs or colder chow.

Judge Pratt noted that most of the program's official goals do not mention Jesus Christ. He did not claim that PFM did anything misleading, let alone illegal, in how it responded to the state's program protocols or how it competed for and won its contract. He did not identify a single major administrative compliance conundrum or noncompliance issue—a minor miracle for any proxy-government program scrutinized so closely after five years of service. He recognized that PFM itself paid for most of what went into administering the program and mobilized many volunteers as well. He even acknowledged that IFI "volunteers caught . . . disparaging non-evangelical Christians appear to be disciplined or even expelled from the program."[6]

In the end, Judge Pratt's semi-just but wholly unmerciful decision—to close the program in 60 days, pay the state $1.5 million for sincerely serving for almost six years, box up your Bibles, and do not let the prison gates hit you on the way out—is based on empirical suppositions rather than on any constitutional doctrine or legal findings.

The judge's main supposition is that IFI's "nonsectarian aspects are substantially subsumed within its religious nature," so much so that "separation of InnerChange's sectarian and secular aspects" is impossible.[7] He may be right that, in our terms, IFI, for all its nonsectarian elements, is presently a faith-saturated program, not a faith-based program. But that is a supposition that could and should be empirically tested rather than imperiously asserted. It is also a supposition that begs the question of whether the program, if it is faith-saturated, can be made faith-based in a way that satisfies all concerned except, perhaps, church-state extremists on both sides.

The cardinal constitutional question concerns operational character, not program efficacy; besides, no evidence on the program's impact on recidivism was presented by PFM at the Iowa trial.[8] As I myself have argued many times before, in fidelity to neutrality doctrine, even if a given faith-based intervention were proven to be 100 percent effective, and even if it cost next to nothing to administer, it would still be wrong to have government promote or fund it if the intervention involved either tax-funded proselytizing or involuntary adherence to or acceptance of a given religious orientation or tradition, or both.

Still, per the judge's dictum, putting all efficacy or impact questions to one side, is the program irredeemably faith-saturated? Essentially, Judge Pratt foreclosed remedial action options by supposing that because PFM is pervasively sectarian, its IFI program model is irredeemably faith-saturated.

Maybe, but not if it is more like the Texas IFI program than not. The Texas IFI program was the subject of a baseline statistical study by the Texas Department of Criminal Justice (TDCJ). Before PFM filed for IFI to become a freestanding nonprofit in 1999, it commissioned Vanderbilt University sociologist Byron Johnson to follow up on the TDCJ study (or bird-dog it, as they say in Texas) and independently track the Texas IFI program's administration and implementation.

When Johnson, for several years now a tenured full professor at Baylor University, moved from Vanderbilt to Penn as a nonfaculty fellow of a now defunct religion research center, he brought several research grants and projects with him, including his PFM Texas IFI project. Over roughly a six-year period stretching back into the 1990s, he and research teams that he empanelled studied the Texas IFI program. They gathered secondhand statistics (most courtesy of TDCJ) and, more germane to Judge Pratt's decision, made firsthand ethnographic observations.

In 2003 Johnson wrote a preliminary evaluation report that summarized what he and his independent research teams had learned to that point about the Texas IFI program.[9] They had reanalyzed statistics on recidivism that had previously been analyzed by TDCJ, gotten the same results, and reported them in the same fashion: the program's graduates recidivated at lower rates than an otherwise comparable group of prisoners, but there was no statistically significant difference between the average recidivism rate for all program participants versus that for the comparison group. The report, which was reviewed and commented on favorably prior to its release by independent scholars including Harvard economist Anne Morrison Piehl, also contained an explicit discussion of selection bias and related problems associated with empirical research on spiritual transformation.

Despite its caveats and qualifications as a preliminary report, the publication triggered fair and foul criticisms of the findings, the researchers, IFI, PFM, and Colson. The fact that the report had rehashed the TDCJ finding regarding program graduates, the fact that PFM emphasized that particular finding in its public communications (and still does), the fact that Johnson (himself an evangelical Christian) appeared with Colson at a White House photo-op gathering featuring President Bush, and the fact that some newspapers editorialized about the study under such headings as "Jesus Saves," all contributed to the controversy.

But the resulting church-state research tempest in a teapot obscured the report's only policy-relevant and only empirically original sections: its richly detailed ethnographic accounts concerning how the Texas IFI program had actually evolved administratively and actually worked on a day-to-day basis.

Basically, Johnson and the researchers reported that the Texas IFI program's daily spiritual transformation dynamics were observationally similar to what one often finds in holistic residential treatment settings, including secular ones. For instance, certain positive-psychology themes emerged: "I'm not who I used to be," "Positive outlook on life," "Need to give back to society," etc. So, too, did the importance of mentoring relationships, and how difficult they are to effect and sustain—another close parallel to other total life commitment programs, whether religious or secular.

The report suggested that, during its first few years, the Texas IFI program unfolded in ways that practiced spiritual transformation mainly as "a developmental process marked by key turning points or events." The inmates were up to their ears in biblical values learning and such, but their main complaints had nothing to do with being indoctrinated and everything to do with being awakened early, saddled with a packed daily work schedule, and kept extremely busy.

Most Texas IFI participants, it seems, loved the "hug a thug" program culture, as one inmate quoted in the report called it. Even prisoners from non-Protestant backgrounds who voluntarily attended revival services featuring outside religious speakers felt respected. A typical comment was as follows:

> The InnerChange staff really seem to care about us. I'm Catholic and they haven't tried to force me to become a Protestant. If people want to get something out of the program they will.[10]

Of course, Texas is not Iowa; that was then, this is now; and the Texas IFI program, as characterized in the Johnson report, arguably had enough sectarian aspects to qualify as faith-saturated, rather than faith-based.

At the same time, however, Judge Pratt should have acknowledged that Tom Pratt's program model was designed so as to be flexible, that there are many strictly nonsectarian purposes and practices running through the program, and that the Iowa IFI program met all its administrative obligations under law as a proxy-government provider. Furthermore, Judge Pratt should have recognized that the time, money, and effort that PFM's supporters, leaders, staff, and volunteers dedicated over a six-year period to the civic cause of successful prisoner reentry in Iowa dwarfed the $1.5 million in grants that he ordered PFM to repay.

Judge Pratt's decision is history, but until the appeals process is exhausted the IFI program continues to operate in Iowa, and PFM need not "pay back" the $1.5 million. On September 21, 2006, an appeal joined by attorneys general and other counsel representing nine states was filed with the U.S. Court of Appeals for the Eighth Circuit. Over the next few years, each side can either show good faith or prepare for a multiyear, legal, legislative, and communications Armageddon.

Each can either model how to search for church-state common ground or leave behind more political scorched earth. If fight they must, each can choose to fight in ways that keep faith-based noncombatants, like the vast majority of urban community-serving religious nonprofits, out of the legal, political, and communications lines of fire.

Or, as happened in 2001 over the Bush faith bill, each side can instead drag faith-based organizations into the conflict and make virtual hostages of the needy people those organizations could otherwise be serving through expanded ecumenical, interfaith, religious-secular, and public-private partnerships. In sum, each can either beat swords into plowshares or attack each other in ways that cloud the church-state consensus regarding how sacred places can and should serve civic purposes.

It takes two to fight to the finish or negotiate in good faith. The plaintiffs and their supporters should want to get at the whole truth about the IFI program, help ex-prisoners, and enforce neutrality principles—which would almost certainly mean making some changes to public partnerships with IFI. They should not be content to score a short-term court-ordered hit against religious conservatives. They should not, in the end, succeed mainly in giving anti–God squad and judicial tyranny myth-makers something new to carp about.

Were a good-faith negotiation or arbitration plan ever offered, PFM and its supporters should think twice (or should that be seventy times seven?) before refusing. They should refrain from escalating the matter by linking it to "Godless schools" or the like. They should resist the temptation to use the conflict in direct-mail appeals and other fund-raising ventures. By behaving as godly people, they can refuse to be defined by ideological, partisan, or even religious differences with detractors.

Unfortunately, the *New York Times* helped to sour any chance that religious conservatives who support ministries like PFM would want to come reason together, let alone consider doing civic good together, with their secular liberal detractors. In a December 10, 2006 story about the case, about the only news that the paper saw fit to print were points that parroted the IFI program's worst critics.[11] It was as if the counterarguments and counterexamples that appeared in the September 2006 appeals brief did not merit the slightest serious notice.

As I would be the first to freely admit, PFM's self-defense leaves much room for fair criticism. For instance, the empirical claims made in the appeals brief regarding the program's efficacy are exaggerated; and its closing arguments, implying that religious programs require no greater constitutional scrutiny than nonreligious ones, are unfounded. As the Court reminded us in *Locke* (2004), and as the framers themselves agreed, religion in the godly republic is of a "different ilk."

Needlessly, the *New York Times* story on the case traveled the orthodox sectarian low road. Only a few months earlier, the paper had paved that road in a four-part, page-one series, "In God's Name: Favors for the Faithful," which warned that "pervasively sectarian" religious nonprofit organizations were now awash in government money and regulatory waivers.

I had lambasted the lopsided series in print.[12] By analogy to campaign finance reform, the logic behind the newspaper's series on religion ran as follows: because so many federal, state, and local campaign finance laws are now on the books, campaign spending is therefore restrained, which can be proven by cataloguing the laws, citing anecdotes about selected races where spending is down, and quoting experts who are pleased as punch that it is (plus a few who doubt it or are not so pleased). Never mind that the laws, old and new, national and other, are not all enforced; or that many new laws were passed precisely because the existing ones were not, in fact, working; or that, all exceptions to the rule and expert surmises aside, most relevant empirical datasets and studies suggest that the laws have done nothing to restrain record spending.

After taking the *New York Times* to task, I discovered that its background analysis was even more superficial than I had initially supposed; and I heard from legal experts and community-serving ministers, some claiming knowledge concerning certain examples spotlighted in the series, who wanted me to further expose its biases. But personal outreach by the series' lead author, who seemed thoughtful and sincere, stayed my pen. I even offered to have the newspaper run a rebuttal with no reply from me, which happened; and I offered to meet in person, debate in public, or (the reporter's idea) be interviewed for its next story (focus: PFM), none of which happened.

THINK CATHOLIC: CHURCH, STATE, AND LARGER COMMUNITIES

Of course, the godly republic will survive, and most white, black, Latino, and other community-serving religious congregations and faith-based organizations will, too, regardless of whether secular liberals and evangelical Christians can learn to play fair or reach more suitable civic accommodations with one another.

I believe that the desire to serve the common good is universal and, save under totalitarian rule or the like (and sometimes even then), almost irrepressible. But the common good as a strong human impulse only comes to practical fruition in societies where it is also woven into prevailing political theory and reflected by living constitutional norms.

In order to get people to cooperate with this civic ideal and selflessly serve citizens in need, it helps to have an overarching and widely shared conception of why such good works are good and may even sometimes be morally required. It helps to establish who will be considered responsible for providing help to whom, when, and how. It helps to define the conditions, if any, under which wider groups of citizens, including those who have no desire to help, may be required to do so—for example, by paying taxes to support public human services programs to which they strongly object. Finally, it helps to define the parameters within which the federal government—the national political community in the person of its democratically elected national government representatives—can and should act, and exercise all necessary and proper authority, to help people in need.

In other words, it helps to have a working conception of the common good that relates individual rights to social duties. It helps to have some generally accepted concept concerning the conditions under which individuals, social institutions, and governments are expected to work alone or work together to provide help to people in need.

The godly republic's first leaders talked about the common good a great deal but never quite got around to fleshing out the concept in this way. James Madison and other framers of the Constitution frequently used the term. The concept also crops up in their writings even when they do not explicitly use it; for example, as is quoted in chapter 1, Madison in the Federalist Paper No. 10 defined "factions" in opposition to "the permanent and aggregate interests of the community."

If "the permanent and aggregate interests of the community" sounds a bit religious, it is. Conceptually, the idea of the common good has deep religious roots in the Judeo-Christian tradition and in the Natural Rights–Natural Law doctrine ("endowed by Nature," "inalienable rights," etc.) that was inscribed by Thomas Jefferson into the Declaration of Independence. It is also present but implicit in the Preamble to the Constitution's organic conception of "We the People" as encompassing "ourselves and our Posterity."

Madison and many of the other founding fathers were essentially conventional Christian believers in the Protestant or Reformed tradition. With the exception of the only clergyman to sign both the Declaration and the Constitution, Madison's Princeton tutor Reverend John Witherspoon, Madison and the other great minds of the early republic pretty much, as it were, took their Protestant theology off the rack. They brilliantly borrowed much of their political theory (separation of powers, checks and balances, and limited government itself) from ideas once current in Tudor England, and they smartly lifted much of their underlying moral theory about individual rights and social duties directly from Anglo-Protestant tracts like the *Westminster Confessions* and quasi-Christian Enlightenment treatises on the social contract (most famously the writings of John Locke).

As if I am not already in enough trouble (Judge Pratt's offensive discourse on who believes what may soon seem slight by comparison), let me simply observe that the godly republic's' faithful Anglo-Protestant founders therefore largely ignored (and often compounded) the profound philosophical disconnect between their conceptions of the common good and limited government in relation to *individual rights,* on the one side, and *social duties,* on the other side.

That philosophical disconnect has intellectually limited Anglo-Protestant moral, social, and political theory for centuries. It is arguably related to the theological self-contradictions and hypocritical social practices attacked by many American writers both before and after the Civil War, most notably by the ex-slave Frederick Douglass after Irish Catholic immigrants taught him how to read. What evangelical Christian writer Mark Noll has lamented as the modern-day "scandal of the Evangelical mind" has its roots in this profound philosophical failure.

As I joked to Vice President Al Gore in May 1999 during a public meeting in Nashville, Tennessee, citing the Catechism of the Catholic Church: "Don't leave home, or Rome, without it!" He laughed, and joined the audience in laughing even harder when I pulled the tome out from behind my chair and "Catechism-thumped" it. I had done much the same act in the preceding years at conservative Protestant gatherings. For instance, at a Pepperdine University forum, in answer to a question about how Protestant groups might do more social service work in poor communities, I joked, "Well, would you like to become Catholic?"

But I was only half-joking. When it comes to defining the common good in a theologically anchored and intellectually coherent yet practical fashion, there is, I believe, no one source better or truer than my beloved Catechism, especially the parts that deal with "human community."

As I argued in 1998 before the Pontifical Academy of Social Sciences at the Vatican, modern Catholics have a time-tested way, made consistent in the twentieth century with representative democratic ideals, of thinking about individual rights in relation to social duties. Essentially, to "think Catholic" here means to understand core Catholic theological precepts as they relate to traditional Catholic social teachings—universal social teachings that can be embraced even by citizens who totally reject some or all of the Catholic theological precepts from which they are derived.[13] As is noted in chapter 1, Thomas Jefferson personally edited the Protestant Bible's Gospels into a booklet entitled *The Life and Morals of Jesus of Nazareth*. For civic purposes, he wanted to introduce Protestant social teachings to Native Americans. By analogy, let me now briefly sketch certain civic-minded social teachings that happen to have a Catholic pedigree but that citizens of all faiths or of no faith can follow or not without regard to religion.

Theologically, Catholics believe in the God of Abraham and in the divinity of Jesus Christ. Catholic theology animates a social teaching about family, community, and government that can be accepted or rejected without accepting Catholicism or any other particular religious belief system: *subsidiarity*. The Catechism defines the family as "the original cell of social life," the "community in which" we first "learn to care and take responsibility for the young, the old, the sick, the handicapped, and the poor." Following the subsidiarity principle, we must "take care not to usurp the family's prerogatives or interfere in its life." Following the exact same principle, however, when families cannot fulfill their responsibilities, "larger communities" have "the duty of helping them."

But which larger communities are to help distressed families, how, and under what conditions? "Excessive intervention by the state," the Catechism cautions, "can threaten personal freedom and initiative. . . . The principle of subsidiarity . . . sets limits for state intervention." That, however, is only half of the principle.

The other half is that larger communities, up to and including national political communities of citizens acting through their democratic governments, must support the family "in case of need and help co-ordinate its activity with the activities of the rest of society, always with a view to the common good."

Fidelity to the common good requires that each of us work to bring about a condition of social well-being in which we "make accessible to each what is needed to lead a truly human life: food, clothing, health . . . and so on." As former Vice President Dan Quayle argued, and as his successor, Vice President Al Gore, heartily agreed, when families are happy and healthy, communities thrive. Or, as I have heard many conservatives quip (the celebrated American Enterprise Institute scholar, and my fellow Catholic, Michael Novak, was the first), "The family is our best department of health, education and welfare."

Granted. But how should a subsidiarity-minded citizen respond to the plight of the roughly two million children in America whose fathers or mothers are imprisoned, whose families are often broken and impoverished, and whose own life prospects, as all the research shows, are thereby badly diminished? How should he or she respond to the plight of millions of children and families in poor neighborhoods from north central Philadelphia to south central Los Angeles? How should we all manifest effective civic compassion for the innocent inner-city toddlers and teenagers who this very night could lift their eyes to heaven and with complete justification cry, "My God, my God, why have you forsaken me?"

Subsidiarity says that in all such cases one should respond by giving at least some time and money to family-supporting organizations—national and local, public and private, religious and secular, in the suites and on the streets. I am talking about national secular nonprofit organizations like Big Brothers Big Sisters of America and Amachi; national religious nonprofit organizations like Prison Fellowship Ministries (Angel Tree, IFI, and other PFM programs); charity dollars for grassroots volunteers who know the low-income inner-city children whom they serve; tax dollars for government employees who, without knowing these same children, serve them by faithfully implementing federal-state programs like Medicaid or the State Children's Health Insurance Program (S-CHIP); and many more.

Metaphorically speaking, subsidiarity teaches that the first call for help should always be a local call, starting with a house call. Charity begins at home, and so does compassion. We should do our utmost to honor our social obligations through families, voluntary associations, churches, and charities. We should prefer social cooperation to social engineering, the veneration of subsidiarity norms to the proliferation of bureaucratic rules, and the cultivation of civic virtue to the exercise of public authority.

However, as happened massively during the Great Depression, private initiatives and civil institutions are sometimes unable to help the needy and neglected in our midst. We should then call on ourselves as members of a larger community. As necessary, we must enlist to the cause of effective social compassion our representative political institutions and the federal, state, and local government bureaucracies that translate legislative decisions into administrative actions on behalf of people in need.

Political communities, like all human communities, are morally required to serve the common good. Local government is always preferred to state government, and state government is always preferred to national government, but these preferences are to be tempered by due consideration of which levels of government are necessary to serve the common good. As many Catholics who marched into the Democratic Party during the New Deal believed, the national government can be a legitimate and effective means of promoting a humane social order within which ordinary men, women, and children can lead peaceful and productive, if not uniformly prosperous, lives.

While we are not to be allergic to national government, we must be ever wary about becoming addicted to national government, and ever mindful that government action can enervate families and smaller communities. This weakening effect can occur regardless of whether the public laws are malintentioned or well intentioned. For example, through malintentioned Jim Crow laws, state and local governments weakened the black family and stifled its socioeconomic progress. After new federal civil rights laws were enacted, Washington's well-intentioned welfare laws undermined another generation of poor black families from coast to coast. We must be vigilant about pruning government policies that enervate civil institutions and planting ones that make it easier for government at all levels to bolster these institutions, including grassroots, family-supporting, community-serving religious ministries.

In sum, as a rule, we should prefer civil society action to local government action, local government action to state government action, and state government action to federal government action. But theoretical guidelines are the easy part. We need to apply our subsidiarity principle to an America that is today a demographically diverse society of over three hundred million souls, living in fifty states and tens of thousands of local jurisdictions. It is a sprawling society with millions of people in need and numerous pockets of concentrated poverty.

NO POST-POVERTY NATION: MATTHEW 25

In 1996, when President Clinton declared that the era of so-called big government was over, he was right but only because, in the godly republic, that era never actually began.

Instead, after the Second World War, as Washington's taxing and spending exploded, America developed the government-by-proxy system described in chapter 3. What American government does to help our society's distressed families, our deserving poor, our disabled, our infirm elderly, our abused and neglected children, it does through all manner of intergovernmental, public-private, and religious-secular partnerships. This uniquely American hybrid of public administration and public finance puzzles our civic cousins in European democracies and miffs or mystifies Americans themselves; but for all its many flaws and foibles, it is in theory at least fully compatible with subsidiarity doctrine. And, sometimes at least, the system even works effectively.

For instance, wearing subsidiarity doctrine on my sleeve and sitting in Philadelphia, I was heartened when not just local charities and local governments but also federal disaster relief agencies responded to the plight of fellow citizens in Oklahoma City who in April 1995 suffered a terrible bombing. I was likewise pleased when, in the mid-1990s, a Republican-led Congress and a Democratic White House enacted a new federal law that extended federal-state Medicaid coverage to all needy persons aged nineteen or younger, including low-income kids who live in Philadelphia, Mississippi. And, in the late 1990s, I was gratified when partnerships between inner-city preachers and local law enforcement officials, in conjunction with intergovernmental social welfare and public health programs, helped to reduce youth violence in many cities.

But to preach subsidiarity without practicing it is to forsake the common good. For literally millions of Americans, subsidiarity doctrine is a false gospel, social compassion is a polite fiction, and social policy is a cruel hoax. A toddler living in a blighted inner-city neighborhood; a middle-school student who has never had adequate food, money, or medicine; an illiterate teenage high school dropout who has not been protected from street violence or sexual predators or consistently cared for by at least one socially responsible adult; a nonviolent young adult who sold a small amount of illegal drugs and will be behind bars until middle age—these Americans and millions like them have been failed by our society. They have been failed by family members, neighbors, religious believers, fellow citizens, and government officials.

There is no shortage of arguments, all appealing to enlightened civic self-interest, which contend that unless we help needy children, youth, and young adults, their problems will eventually become ours. Americans have repeatedly been warned that inner-city social ills will spread, "spill over," or otherwise cost us all dearly. Even when made with a straight face, a sincere heart, and a post-1968 copyright, such claims create only minor civic stirs and are, in any case, empirically unconvincing. America is an extremely prosperous country and an international economic colossus with an expanding college-educated middle class. This is so, even though Americans and their political leaders in both parties have spent the last half-century perfecting a devilishly self-serving "urban" policy: mass suburbanization and mass incarceration.

As a result, low-income people with extreme risks of suffering from multiple social ills have become ever more highly concentrated in inner-city neighborhoods. Their plight is a social, moral, and civic disgrace, but most Americans are not, in fact, adversely affected by it in any way that truly moves them—other than moving them to the suburbs. For the last several decades, when they feel threatened by crime and other social problems, Americans have been more interested in investing in gated communities than in rallying larger communities.

As the nation's top social scientists have documented and documented, socioeconomic inequalities in America, especially ones linked strongly to formal educational attainments, have grown since the 1970s. The 2005 Hurricane Katrina disaster reminded us that America is home to many citizens who live in extreme poverty, in places like the lower ninth ward of New Orleans. Before long, this problem disappeared from daily news headlines.

The failure to fix, or even to consistently and compassionately focus on, what in 1962 the Catholic-educated democratic socialist Michael Harrington termed "the other America" has left a moral stain.[14] But alas, it has not been either an economic drain or a social strain sufficient to get most Americans to act as if they really cared about achieving the common good in our "one nation, under God, with liberty and justice for all."

Thus, "think Catholic" must, in the end, mean to dig down to the deepest moral roots of the subsidiarity doctrine. Personally, I have no idea whether Jesus would have supported passing a capital gains tax cut or repealing the estate tax, but I am certain that He would not want us to ignore needy children or to deny what He called "the least" of His "family": "I was hungry and you gave me food, thirsty and you gave me drink . . . in prison and you visited me. . . . Amen I say to you, whatever you did for one of these least . . . you did for me" (Matthew 25:35, 40).[15] As the Bible also admonishes us, God has "chosen the poor in the world to be rich in faith and to be heirs of the kingdom that He has promised to those who love Him," but we have too often "dishonored the poor" (James 2:5–6).

Liberal cynics can be forgiven for concluding that conservatives start preaching compassion only when they think there is no one left who actually needs it. Because America's poor are so much better housed and better fed than the poor of any previous generation, because poverty often results from an individual's own bad choices (for example, dropping out of school, using illegal drugs, committing street crimes, having children outside of marriage), and because post-1996 federal and state welfare-to-work policies have had considerable successes (though by no means the unqualified successes that they have often claimed), many conservatives now openly doubt that America still has a serious domestic poverty problem.

They are empirically wrong, and they are morally at risk. Anyone who thinks that America is a post-poverty nation should try living with their family on under $17,000 a year (roughly the federal poverty-line measure in 2000), as one in five African American children still do. They should plan their next summer vacation in one of the inner-city public housing complexes where, legend has it, everyone maxes out on government benefits and air conditioners buzz in every window. They should stop by an inner-city social services agency that is placing formerly welfare-dependent adults into jobs all right, but also coping with a rising tide of abandoned children and child-only welfare cases.

They should next visit a state maximum-security prison and read the pre-sentencing investigation reports, summarizing not only the felons' crimes but also the poverty, abuse, and neglect that most long-term prisoners have suffered. These early life scars do not exonerate these felons, but they do explain why so many Americans behind bars are young males from low-income urban neighborhoods. They should talk to former Philadelphia mayor and Amachi leader Reverend Goode, who can tell them that incarcerated black men in prison have confided to him that they met their own fathers and grandfathers for the first time in prison.

There is far less grinding poverty in America today than there was during the Great Depression and as little as two decades ago. Still, millions of America's "least of these" still need help—up-close volunteer hours, private donations, public support—from the rest of us and our larger communities, including the national government. "If someone who has worldly means sees a brother in need and refuses him compassion, how can the love of God remain in him: Children, let us love not in word or speech but in deed and truth" (I John 3:17–18).

The godly republic's faith-based future can be defined mainly by civic compassion in truth and action or it can be defined mainly by ideological, partisan, and religious strife. Which will it be?

SEVEN

The Faith-Based Future's Blessings

In the preceding chapter I described three principles that ought to guide our journey into the republic's faith-based future: take prisoners, do unto others, and think Catholic. It is more than coincidence that religious concepts are embedded in each of these principles. To summarize:

- *Take prisoners:* Reflect honor and respect for other people with whom you may disagree fundamentally. Neither seek nor exploit any power advantages that may enable you to misrepresent them, to treat them less than fairly, or to have others misrepresent or mistreat them in accordance with your least generous impulses. Evangelical Christians and secular liberals have much work to do in building mutual understanding and civic forbearance. The relevant religious principle here goes by various names, but the "take prisoners" disposition would be familiar to many Catholics as "fraternal correction," to some other Christians as "seeking fellowship," and to Jews as the generous spirit of *tikkum olam*—"repair the world."

- *Do unto others:* This widely invoked religious precept is sometimes styled "treat others as you would wish to be treated," but that is not really correct. The theologically correct rendering, at least in the Catholic tradition, is closer to "love others as all-loving Almighty God loves you" or "as Christ loved all humankind." To wit: with love and compassion "do unto" even your enemies and those who have done you harm or wish you harm.

- *Think Catholic:* Not be, but think Catholic, at least in relation to seeking the common good by all civil and governmental means necessary. Strive to address human needs and social problems through individual initiatives, families, churches, and other civil bodies, but rally larger communities to the cause, including the national political community via the federal government, when necessary. Religious-secular, public-private, and intergovernmental partnerships working to achieve the common good are a proxy-government reality. They also can effect civic cooperation in ways that are consistent with what Catholics call subsidiarity doctrine.

But a moral way is nothing without a moral will. Persistent failures to address the needs of the "least of these" reflect persistent failures of moral will. Appeals to address these issues through the lens of enlightened self-interest in America fall increasingly on deaf ears and are empirically suspect at best. "Their" problems have not really become "our" problems to the extent required to trigger or sustain effective civic action. In the end, one is forced back to biblical moral injunctions, not quasi-religious social doctrines, for an appeal that connects individual rights to social duties and commands compassion in truth and action.

Now, suppose that you have agreed with virtually everything that I have argued in this book, with the exception of chapter 6. For instance, suppose that you rejected my three principles for a better faith-based future—take prisoners, do unto others, and think Catholic—perhaps because you deemed them too religious or too Christian or too Catholic or just plain too idiosyncratic. (If you have actually liked and agreed with everything that you have read in this book, pray for greater wisdom for yourself and for me, too.)

The race is almost run, but I have three more principles to offer. Each is as faith-free as I can muster. Like the first trinity, these three principles, if followed, could also brighten the godly republic's faith-based future: invest wisely, target blessings, and honor thy Franklin.

- *Invest wisely:* Analyze faith-based organizations (hereafter FBOs) as if they were companies trading on a civic stock exchange and your only purpose was to reap sizable civic dividends. Which FBOs should you invest in yourself? Why should government invest more in them, too?

- *Target blessings:* Identify major social problems that FBOs would be particularly well-suited to target and address, given adequate public and private investments of resources. What civic responses to major social needs can be most effectively transacted by FBOs? On which particular urban problems should FBOs be empowered to take the lead?

- *Honor thy Franklin:* Memorize (in Latin!) what the least conventionally religious of the founding fathers, Benjamin Franklin (another Penn guy from Philly), had to say about how essential religious individuals, institutions, and ideals were to civic life. Marvel at how he personally practiced what Madison preached about the multiplicity of sects. And memorialize him and the other framers by going back, as it were, to their faith-based future—back to the vision of a great republic at once predicated on belief in the God of Abraham yet dedicated in full to achieving religious pluralism and full citizenship rights for all.

INVEST WISELY: FBOS AS CIVIC VALUE STOCKS

After over a decade of studying and assisting FBOs in cities all across the country, I view FBOs as the nonprofit sector's "civic value stocks."[1] Let me briefly elaborate upon the analogy, which was first suggested to me in the late 1990s by the Manhattan Institute's brilliant board chairman, and one of America's leading financial experts, Roger Hertog.

Basically, value investing is predicated on the view that a company does not need to be outstanding for its stock to outperform the market or to yield big profits; it only needs to be better than investors think it is. Any stock that is viewed with undue pessimism or rejected irrationally by investors is a likely bargain. Value investors buy stocks of sound, if not sensational, companies that research reveals to be undervalued for a number of reasons: because they represent an industry that has long been out of favor, because they once experienced management or other problems to which investors overreacted, because they have an erratic history of earnings, etc.

Value investors buy stocks that are priced low in relation to company assets, sales, earning power, management ability, changes in commercial environments, and other factors that matter economically. Value investors thus profit by paying close attention to economic fundamentals and trading against the economically unwarranted emotions of others. So, rather than picking or riding high-priced hot stocks, they make lots and lots of small bets on cheap stocks. Rather than courting sudden growth in hot sectors, they court steady growth in cheap sectors. Value investing is often more successful than the opposite approach, so-called growth investing.

By analogy, FBOs are the value stocks of the nonprofit sector. From the 1960s until quite recently, they were out of favor, not only because of the irrational exuberance that the policy elite expressed in strictly secular, government-centered solutions to social problems, but also because of widespread doubts about their future assets. Religion was supposedly on the wane throughout the world and in the United States. Domestic religious organizations, then as now, most often made headlines mainly in relation to corruption scandals, charges of politicization, and dramatic if innocent instances of fiscal mismanagement or administrative incompetence. The FBO sector's volatile hot stocks were big-name ministries that promised much but delivered little.

Today's FBO "industry," however, has begun to regain public and "consumer" trust and confidence in a country that turns out to be stubbornly religious. Many of its new "CEOs" are willing to open themselves and their organizations to outside scrutiny by skeptical secular researchers and professional foundation auditors, and they are quite eager to engage in interdenominational and interfaith partnerships and program "mergers."

There are many kinds of community-serving FBOs, and only recently have we begun to identify the common characteristics and best practices of those FBOs that seem to be especially effective in achieving various civic purposes among the disadvantaged residents of poor urban neighborhoods. My experience suggests that people of quite different faiths, traditions, partisan leanings, and ideological orientations have developed strikingly similar lists of these characteristics and practices. I would refer to them as "best features."

One best feature is that the community-serving FBO is *community-*

based, not just in rhetoric but in reality. The ministers and religious volunteers have the same zip code as the people they serve, and they subject themselves to many of the same hardships that neighborhood residents suffer. They do not "live large," either within the neighborhood or outside of it. In inner-city neighborhoods, their leaders, staff, and volunteers walk the same blighted, crime-torn streets as do most of their program beneficiaries.

Another best feature is that the FBO came into existence before it was ever offered financial support from anyone—government agencies, foundations, or parent churches. Once an FBO was established, its leaders might file a government or foundation "request for proposal" application, *but only to strengthen an effort that already was part of their core mission, or to expand a program that they already offered.* Said a veteran community-serving minister in Washington, "Anybody that's got time or staff enough to mess with all them government forms or fill out thirty, forty pages of what the foundation wants you to say, they ain't got no real heart for [these children] and they ain't about doing no real work . . . on those ugly streets."

Another FBO best feature that follows naturally from the two I just mentioned might be labeled "keeping the 'faith' in faith-based, but not by faith alone." The 2005 speech by Senator Hillary Rodham Clinton referenced in chapter 3 was given before inner-city clergy in Boston, many associated with the National Ten Point Leadership Foundation (NTLF). Harvard sociologist Christopher Winship and others have documented how, in the 1990s, the city's NTLF ministers partnered with probation officers and succeeded in improving police-community relations in ways that helped to cut the homicide rate (to zero for nearly two years during one stretch). The partnerships worked largely because the ministers, though unmistakably motivated by religious ideas and ideals, were faithful about working with law enforcement, within the law, and without proselytizing. Senator Clinton's talk included much well-deserved praise for these youth outreach ministries and their police-probation partnerships. They started on shoestring budgets and in one case were sustained even after local drug dealers twice fired shots into a leading minister's home (once just over the head of his sleeping young son). The Reverend Mark Scott, who had served in the White House as my office's associate director, was among the Boston ministers who made a civic difference. As he recounted, the effort was inspired by a local drug dealer who schooled the ministers about why "thuggers and muggers" attract so many inner-city youth: "I'm there, you're not; I win, you lose." As Senator Clinton duly noted, thank God that the ministers chose to be there, and to work in partnerships to reduce human suffering and achieve a vital civic goal.

Reverend Scott was unfailingly business-like when it came to documenting the civic advantages of grassroots ministries. As he liked to stress, to be worthwhile to government, business, and nonprofit "investors," civic value investing in FBOs does not need to produce daily miracles of individual or social transformation. It needs only to outperform its nonprofit market competition over time, even if only by producing the same civic results at a smaller human and financial cost.

Much research suggests that Scott was right. For instance, the four-city welfare-to-work study by Stephen V. Monsma summarized in chapter 5 also yielded this provocative if hardly definitive cost-effectiveness finding. On average, welfare-to-work FBOs served about 200 clients a year on $90,000 annual budgets that included little or no public money, while secular counterpart nonprofits served about 400 clients a year on $900,000 annual budgets that often included substantial government grant dollars. The FBOs served clients with more checkered job histories, and also served more minority citizens, than the secular programs served.

Given the well-documented gaps in urban social-service delivery, the point is *not* that FBOs outperform secular nonprofits. The point is that, whether or not they do, they are already vital if heavily undercapitalized social service providers who produce plenty even though they often choose to serve the hardest cases in the toughest places. In particular, the studies by Ram Cnaan, Stephanie Boddie, Nisha Botchwey, Hara Wright-Smith, and others (discussed in chapter 5) suggest that community-serving black churches and other black-led FBOs are among the nation's most vital but undercapitalized civic value stocks.

Of course, nobody can say with certainty that the biggest bang for the civic purpose buck is to be had by investing in black churches or, more generally, in small religious congregations and grassroots inner-city outreach ministries. Still, many small grassroots FBOs are widely credited with yielding tremendous social profits, seemingly overnight. In the late 1990s, that seemed to be the story of Washington's Alliance of Concerned Men. Led by Tyrone Parker, an ex-prisoner who had been convicted for violent crimes, the Alliance's five principals, all of whom had had serious troubles with the law in the past, brokered a truce among rival gangs in a low-income Washington neighborhood that had witnessed more than fifty murders in five square blocks within two years. The murders suddenly ceased, and the Washington press noticed.

But even though, as Parker told me at the time, the Alliance had unquestionably helped to stop the noise in its neighborhood and even though its crime-reduction "stock" was "advertised" through stories in the local and national media, this tiny FBO remained radically undersupported. Funds to help monitor, mentor, and minister to ex-delinquents and their younger siblings remained scarce, and no one supplied any civic venture capital to determine whether the Alliance could cut gang violence in other neighborhoods. "If we were McDonald's," said one of Parker's do-good ex-convict compatriots, "we'd already be franchised."

As my former Princeton students Jeremy White and Mary DeMarcellus discovered for themselves, much the same story held for other small inner-city FBOs led by people without either college degrees or professional credentials, whose raw faith and rough real-life experiences had led them into frontline service for urban residents in dire need.

In the course of their research, White and DeMarcellus came across a former Washington police officer named Tom Lewis. An elder in his local African American church, Lewis mortgaged his own house to start his modest open-door street ministry. It began as part after-school program, part safe haven, part homeless shelter. Lewis brought himself and others (including me) to tears with his preaching about how Jesus wept before he raised His friend Lazarus from the dead. He used the story as an analogy to describe how street ministries like his were desperately trying to "raise up" inner-city children and "roll back the stones of indifference, apathy, and racism" that "are their social tombs," to help the "innocent but unloved, without hope, in hunger, in fear, walking dead among us every day."

On my second day in the White House in 2001, I brought President

Bush and Senator Joe Lieberman to visit Elder Lewis and his all-purpose youth ministry, by then called the Fishing School. It was still located in one of the capital city's very poorest, crime-torn sections. "The body was dead for three days," said Lewis as he preached his truth to the two good men with power, "and when I was a policeman I came across dead bodies that old. The smell was awful."

The president and the senator were both clearly impressed by Elder Lewis. But the media were more interested in my apparent gaffe in brushing by the president when we arrived at the site, to hug my old friend the senator. It was only another photo-op. A year later, Lewis had something else to cry about. With a few press clippings from the VIP visit taped over the Fishing School's semi-functional radiator, private funding for his ministry had fallen (some supporters did not like the fact that Bush had visited), and no federal charitable choice grants or public support was forthcoming, either. In 2004, Lewis was struck with a life-threatening illness. I still pray for his ministry and wonder what might have been in his community had his civic value stock risen like Lazarus did.

Civic value investing in FBOs should be relatively easy for corporations, philanthropists, other private institutions, and individuals. After all, they can find or pick their favorite sacred places by religious affiliation, location, civic purpose focus, or just about any other organizational characteristics and performance criteria that they choose. They can provide selected FBOs with money, technical assistance, or both. They can identify themselves closely with an FBO's religious mission and character, or remain detached from everything except the FBO's secular dealings and achievements. And they can increase or decrease funding and other support to FBOs as their resources and preferences dictate.

As chapters 3 through 5 suggest, even with federal charitable choice laws on the books for a decade, civic value investing in FBOs by government is a taller and trickier order. There are all of the usual church-state issues and all of the resulting red tape. But that is a good thing. Yale and Brookings political scientist Herbert Kaufman is often credited with the insightful quip that "one person's government red tape is another person's treasured procedural safeguard."

Nobody, religious or secular, likes paperwork. Few organizations, including research universities, are eager for independent and objective evaluations of their performance. But if widespread trust and confidence is to be maintained, government grants or other public investments in FBOs should be duly regulated and monitored. Even though politically well-connected national secular nonprofit organizations and religious charities may have benefited over the decades from the proxy-government grant-making equivalent of "insider trading" and, even though they have escaped systematic performance evaluations, local FBOs should compete fairly and prove their civic value.

Of course, even if every community-serving religious nonprofit in the United States were ready, willing, and able to work with government agencies and even if nobody ever sued or countersued anybody, would government be good at civic value investing in FBOs? Even without the constitutional, political, and bureaucratic barriers that have hitherto obstructed public-private partnerships involving religious organizations, the remaining challenge would be to pick the right civic investment portfolio.

TARGET BLESSINGS: YOUNG BLACK LOW-INCOME URBAN MALES

My bet is that the republic's faith-based future will be brightest in all ways that ought to matter most if we target the civic blessings of FBOs on America's toughest unresolved urban social problems and the nation's most needy children, youth, and families.

Many recent studies document the plight of young low-income urban black men. On March 20, 2006, the *New York Times* ran a front-page story headed "The Plight Deepens for Black Men, Studies Warn." The article proclaimed that "a flurry of new research" showed that "black men are becoming ever more disconnected from mainstream society." It cited these statistics:

- *High school dropouts:* Among inner-city black males, over half.
- *Joblessness:* Among black male high school dropouts in their twenties, 72 percent.

- *Incarceration (prison plus jail):* Among black men in their twenties who did not attend college, 21 percent.

- *Incarceration-to-employment ratio:* Among black male dropouts in their twenties, more are behind bars (34 percent) than are working (30 percent).

The *New York Times* characterized the expert consensus about the deepening plight as follows: "Terrible schools, absent parents, racism, the decline in blue collar jobs and a subculture that glorifies swagger over work."[2] It also quoted several black male ex-offenders "from the airless neighborhoods of Baltimore," who echoed the experts.

Since this article appeared, copycat news stories and op-ed articles have circulated other ostensibly novel statistics concerning black males. A small sample:[3]

- *Special education:* A third of all students in special education are black, and 80 percent of blacks in special education are black males.

- *School discipline:* Among black males in school, 17 percent are expelled or suspended each year.

- *Lifetime imprisonment probability:* Among black men, 32 percent.

Employment among young black male high school dropouts did fall between 1982 and 1996, partly due to this cohort's increased incarceration. But the study documenting that relationship was almost six years old.[4] A March 2006 study of high school dropouts that I co-authored led to a *Time* magazine cover story and other mass media coverage.[5] It reported new data from surveys and focus groups with high school dropouts. But it correctly treated as old news the fact that the black male graduation rate in many inner-city districts was only about 50 percent. Nor were analyses about how poorly black male dropouts fared later in life anything new. Harvard's president James B. Conant called the dropout problem among urban minority males "social dynamite"—in 1961.[6]

Similarly, the following criminal justice statistics appeared in a paper published in an academic journal in 2006, based on a lecture that I had prepared several years earlier:[7]

- *Lifetime imprisonment probability:* 1 in 3 for black males, with some evidence that it may be higher for black male children with a father or sibling incarcerated.

- *Prison sentences:* 40 percent of the 1.4 million inmates sentenced to one year or more are black males.

- *Past or current prison terms:* 16.6 percent of black males are current or former prison inmates.

There is, however, much good news. For instance, black male incarceration rates have steadied from previous decades' spikes as black criminal victimization rates have dropped. A September 2004 U.S. Bureau of Justice statistics report showed that from 1993 to 2003 the violent victimization rate for blacks fell by more than 50 percent. The 2003 rate for blacks (29.1 percent) was 39.2 percent below the comparable 1993 rate (47.9 percent) for whites.

In 1996, Boston's aforementioned National Ten Point Leadership Foundation established a program called "Operation 2006." The program began in response to worries expressed in the mid-1990s by several analysts, myself included, that even with expanded prevention and enforcement efforts, the post-1993 dip in violent crime could hit a wall by 2006 as teenage and young adult male populations expanded. Over the last few years in Boston, Philadelphia, and many smaller cities, murders and other serious crimes have risen, and youth gangs have resurfaced as a national law enforcement concern. But the worries proved to be way overblown, and faith-based and other efforts seem to have made some positive difference.

America's roughly 40 million African Americans, including most black males, are doing well by many socioeconomic measures. In a 1997 book, the Manhattan Institute's Abigail Thernstrom and Stephen Thernstrom were among the first to comprehensively document blacks' mixed but steady socioeconomic progress.[8] Today, most black men do complete school, get jobs, avoid serious trouble with the law, and lead peaceful and productive lives. The black male incarceration and unemployment rates remain calamitous, but over 90 percent of black males are not incarcerated, and most adult black males do work. As former National Urban League president Hugh Price has stated:

The country is filled with successful black men who are leading balanced, stable, and productive lives. . . . They're stringing fiber-optic cable for Verizon or working the floor at Home Depot. . . . It's a somewhat invisible story.[9]

Not invisible, however, to most black men themselves. While reflecting concerns about lingering racism, a survey released in June 2006 by the *Washington Post*, the Kaiser Foundation, and Harvard also reported the following results for black men ages eighteen to twenty-nine:[10]

- Nearly 9 in 10 said they were either working or in school, and considered career success to be important.
- About 8 in 10 said they were satisfied with their lives, and 6 in 10 said that now was a "good time" to be a black man in America.
- About 9 in 10 said they would tell their sons that they can become anything they want in America.

But the March 20, 2006 *New York Times* story was hardly alarmist, or all wrong. In 2006, University of Pennsylvania sociologist Elijah Anderson organized a conference at Penn under the heading "Poor, Young, Black, & Male: A Case for National Action?" The participants made up a diverse who's who among academics who have studied the subject. Most agreed that the "plight deepens" thesis was truer than not. I participated on the concluding panel, but an earlier panel featuring Georgetown economist Harry Holzer stole the show, even as it depressed the crowd.

Released in 2006, Holzer's Urban Institute study, "Reconnecting Disadvantaged Young Men: Improving Schooling and Employment Outcomes," added to earlier evidence indicating that black women made big economic gains during the boom labor market of the 1990s, while black men not only made no such gains but experienced increased unemployment rates. Holzer speculated that the resulting gap had several sources: educational differences (black women have been outdistancing black men in school performance); work-based welfare incentives (family-detached black men in the underground economy were largely unaffected by welfare reform); child-support enforcement (which further discouraged black men from getting regular jobs); and increased black male incarceration.

Even this finding, however, had a famous if unacknowledged antecedent. It fell from research done by a then-38-year-old assistant secretary in the U.S. Department of Labor who authored a 1965 government report entitled *The Negro Family: The Case for National Action*.

Daniel Patrick Moynihan's 78-page document contained 48 pages of text and 30 pages of footnote references and appendix tables. The Moynihan Report, as it became known, featured a figure derived from the employment and Aid to Families with Dependent Children (AFDC) statistics in its last table. Moynihan's friend and fellow Harvard social scientist James Q. Wilson called the figure's 1963–1964 crossed lines "Moynihan's Scissors." For the first time, the black unemployment rate was going down, but the black welfare dependency rate was going up.

On the 50-pound empirical hook nailed by the employment-AFDC data, young Moynihan hung a 500-pound theory about the "Negro family." He speculated that ever more "lower class" black men were impregnating and then deserting "lower class" black women. Hard data were "few and uncertain," but all the numbers Moynihan mustered indicated that "family disorganization" was increasing among blacks: the ratio of illegitimate births to all births, female-headed households, children on AFDC with absent fathers, unemployment rates, juvenile crime and delinquency, narcotics addictions, rejection rates for military service, and more. He estimated that about half of all families in the "Negro community" were no longer "living according to patterns of American society in general."[11]

Where numbers were wanting, Moynihan used narratives. For instance, he cited an ethnography suggesting that ever more "Negro youth" in Elmira, New York were "growing up with little knowledge of their fathers" and were thereby more likely to "flounder—and fail."[12] He noted reports that "large numbers of Negro youth" were experiencing social "alienation."[13] He cited unnamed "observers" attesting that black males' "contacts with middle-class whites" and with "the Negro churches" were down.[14]

According to Moynihan, these numbers and narratives suggested that the "Negro family" was becoming trapped in a "tangle of pathology."[15] Under the subheading "Matriarchy," he anticipated that black women would do better than black men in future labor markets. After besting "Negro males" in school, he predicted that "Negro females" would increasingly function as the their family's sole breadwinners. Relative to black men, black women had "established a strong position for themselves in white collar and professional employment, precisely the areas of the economy which are growing most rapidly."[16]

The plainest symptom of this "pathology," Moynihan maintained, was the "steady expansion" in the fraction of blacks who were receiving federal welfare payments or relying on "public assistance programs in general."[17] But its main future victims, he prophesied, would be young black low-income urban males. Raised in homes without fathers and in neighborhoods with few working males, they would suffer "a disastrous delinquency and crime rate."[18] Already "a majority of crimes against the person" (murder, rape, aggravated assault) were being "committed by Negroes."[19] Most "offenses committed by Negroes" were against "other Negroes: the cost of crime to the Negro community is a combination of that to the criminal and to the victim."[20]

"In a word," warned Moynihan in 1965, "the tangle of pathology is tightening."[21] He called for "a national effort designed to resolve this problem."[22] At the same time, he tacitly doubted that much could really be done. A "cycle is at work," he concluded, in which poor unmarried young blacks have "too many children too early," fail or quit school, and "produce low income levels," leading ever more girls onto welfare and ever more boys into crime.[23]

When I met with Moynihan in 2001, he enjoyed hearing me repeat how, as a graduating Penn senior in 1980, I hotly debated protesters who opposed his selection as that year's commencement speaker. The critics succeeded in getting the Penn administration to cave and Moynihan to withdraw. That was 1980, four years into Moynihan's first of four terms as a Democratic senator representing New York (Senator Clinton succeeded him and inherited his neat Capitol Hill office), and fifteen years after many predictions in the Moynihan Report had already come to pass.

By the late 1980s, politically progressive black scholars like University of Chicago (later Harvard) sociologist William Julius Wilson would pretty much permanently discredit such reactions by agreeing, with due caveats and qualifications, that a black inner-city "underclass" culture exists and is implicated to some degree in unemployment and many other problems that disproportionately afflict inner-city black males.[24]

On crime, it was not until the mid-1990s that Moynihan's focus on black-on-black male violence became widely accepted. That happened, however, less through academic arguments and more because the raw statistics had become so irrefutably sad. For example, in 1994 black males aged fourteen to twenty-four made up 1 percent of the nation's population, but 17 percent of all homicide victims and 30 percent of all homicide perpetrators. In the country's seventy-five largest counties, black males accounted for 7 in 10 violent juvenile defendants in criminal courts and about 65 percent of juvenile murder defendants.[25] In Philadelphia alone, between 1996 and 1999, over 1,000 black males were murdered and 95 percent were killed by another black male.[26] Black males aged eighteen to twenty-four were 2 percent of the city's population, 24 percent of its murder victims, and 40 percent of its alleged murderers.[27]

Today nobody who wishes to be taken seriously can seriously doubt that the low-income black family has long since undergone the wrenching changes that Moynihan saw coming four decades ago. A 1995 study by Robert G. Wood summarized the data as follows:

> The proportion of young black Americans who have married has decreased dramatically in recent decades. In 1960, 80 percent of black women and 66 percent of black men 20 to 34 had married at least once; in 1990 these figures were 46 percent and 38 percent. . . . The result has been an increase in the proportion of black births to unmarried women, from 38 percent in 1970, to 55 percent in 1980, and then to 61 percent in 1988.[28]

Moynihan's social policy prescriptions, however, were never up to his social analysis diagnostics. In 1965, later as a Nixon White House aide, and several more times before he ran for the Senate in 1976, Moynihan recommended that the national government enact policies that "guaranteed employment for men" and provided a "regular program of income maintenance" for families with children.[29] In his December 1966 Senate testimony, the Harvard professor explained his position as follows:

> [E]ven full employment will no longer produce a family income in the United States at a level necessary to maintain social stability in the slums. . . . You can't raise a family in New York on $80 a week.[30]

Thirty years later, in 1996, Moynihan led the Democratic charge in the Senate against the work-based welfare reform compromise bill. By then, he was convinced that the "tangle of pathology" had become so profound that welfare-dependent inner-city black women with children, even amidst favorable labor-market conditions, would not find and keep living-wage jobs.

As noted above, the Moynihan Report highlighted the educational and employment advantages that black women had over black men. In 1996, however, Moynihan seemed certain that second- or third-generation welfare-dependent black females had become as captive to poverty-culture norms as jobless black men. Logic compelled his view that enforcing time limits on welfare would inevitably force black women and children by the millions into abject squalor. Never one to mince words, he called the reform bill "brutal" and predicted that it would go down as the worst social policy since Reconstruction.

I did not share Moynihan's grim predictions about massive "welfare displacement"—the economy was simply too robust. But I still worried that, maybe not millions, but perhaps hundreds of thousands of women and children risked being tossed into extreme poverty by the new federal law. I said so in *Commentary* and *The Public Interest*, among other venues.[31] It was then that I first got to know my favorite fellow working-class, urban, Roman Catholic, Democrat, Ivy league public intellectual.

Moynihan was right (and so was I) in arguing that both federal and state welfare reform provisions intended to reduce nonmarital births would have little impact. The nonmarital birthrate began dropping in 1991, stabilized for women of all ages in 1994, and has decreased only slightly among black women since. Nor has the percentage of children living with single mothers plummeted, as was predicted by many pro–welfare reform analysts.[32]

But reducing nonmarital births was not the first order of business of these reforms. Post-1980 federal and state welfare-to-work policies were mainly intended to reduce welfare dependency and move low-income women with children into the workforce. There are endless debates about whether policy changes or the economy were the biggest motivator, about how many women traded welfare dependency for working-poor misery, and about which state programs worked best. But one thing is beyond reasonable doubt: after the federal welfare reform was enacted in 1996, neither unmarried, welfare-dependent black women with children nor others experienced anything like the disaster that Moynihan had forecast. Rather, as Brookings analyst Ron Haskins has cogently summarized it, the main result was a simultaneous drop in dependency and a rise in net incomes:

> Before 1996, never-married mothers were precisely the ones most likely to drop out of school, go on welfare, and have long welfare spells of over a decade or more. Yet their employment . . . grew by almost 50 percent. . . . [By 2000] earnings in dollars leaped while welfare income fell. . . . In total, overall income of these families increased by more than 22 percent . . . despite a large drop in welfare income. Rising earnings and falling welfare are the precise goal of welfare reform. Changes in income of this magnitude over such a short period for low-income families . . . are unprecedented. [33]

Moynihan knew better than anyone that welfare had perverse and unintended consequences, starting with its tendency to encourage black male desertion. Yet he never quite considered AFDC itself to be a major pathogen in the tangle of pathology. Instead, from 1965 on, the only "one general strategy" that he consistently favored was tinkering with AFDC or turning it into a virtual ghetto-to-grave federal financial guarantee.

Behind this persistent mistake was a New Deal child's pardonable delusion. For all his enormous wit and wisdom, Moynihan never liberated himself from the assumption that Washington was *the* place from which to formulate, fund, and direct programs that could predictably and reliably improve life for whichever huddled masses now suffered in America's most blighted urban places. He would sometimes recount (as he first did at book length in 1969) how federal programs designed to encourage "maximum feasible participation" in antipoverty programs by grassroots groups had gone awry.

But assuming that Washington could effectively channel local problem-solving action by faith-based and community groups or that the policy was poorly executed rather than wrong at its core, was the same mistake in another guise. As I teased Moynihan and myself when we met not far from my White House office in 2001, how could anyone be so mistaken?

Moynihan liked to quip, "Everyone is entitled to their own opinions, but they are not entitled to their own facts." In the Moynihan Report, he had noted in passing that the growing "alienation" of black males seemed to be associated with their falling away from black churches. But he never saw black churches as more than incidental players in possible solutions to the growing dilemma.

Moynihan was not alone. From 1965 through the mid-1990s, when it came to social problem-solving and associated proxy-government funding and technical assistance, Washington treated black churches and other black community-serving religious nonprofits as either wholly irrelevant or (whenever early faith-based ideas were floated) highly radioactive. Rather than partner with local black churches to expand social services, the government virtually created and lavishly funded national secular nonprofit organizations and community development corporations to deliver social services that indigenous black religious leaders and volunteers were already struggling to provide.

The fact is that, over four decades after the Moynihan Report, young urban low-income black men are still the single most severely at-risk population in America. Sad statistics old and new tell that truth, including statistics that receive little press attention; for instance, since 1980 there has been a young black male suicide spiral. From 1980 to 1995, among males age fifteen to nineteen, the suicide rate rose by 146 percent for blacks and by 22 percent for whites.[34]

Just as when Moynihan wrote his report in 1965, the single most ubiquitous institution in the neighborhoods where these needy young citizens live, and the only one with both a demonstrated moral interest and the potential organizational capacity to serve and save them for real, is the black church. There are approximately 55,000 black churches in the nation, plus thousands more community-serving black religious nonprofit groups.

At the aforementioned Penn conference in April 2006, Columbia's Ronald Mincy lamented that there are hardly any public policies expressly dedicated to helping poor urban young black men to overcome their decades-old plight. I concurred but added the caveat that such de facto policies as we do have are perverse and make things worse—for instance, mandatory-minimum drug sentencing policies.

The time is at hand for a significant federal push to empower national and local black faith-based organizations, if they are willing, to take the lead in providing effective civic compassion to these young fellow citizens.

The Census Bureau tells us that there are about 17 million black males in America, roughly 3 million of whom are under ten years old. It is time to put 17 million men and 55,000-plus churches together. It is once again time to have a big, faith-inspired, civic-minded dream.

Start with the Amachi mentoring program for the children of prisoners. As is mentioned in previous chapters, Amachi is led by Philly's Reverend Goode and supported mainly by networks of volunteers mobilized via black churches. Now, what if every low-income young black male child under ten in America, with or without a parent or sibling behind bars, was guaranteed a mentor if his parent or guardian requested one?

It costs about $1,000 per year per child to effect a high-quality, well-managed mentoring relationship. Thus, at the absolute outside (for every black male child under ten), the financial cost would be $3 billion a year—*less than a tenth* of what is expended each year (about $40 billion) on state prisons alone. To guarantee a mentor for every black male child or teenager under eighteen (just under 6 million), the outside annual cost would still be under $6 billion—*less than a sixth* of what is expended each year on state prisons alone.

Or, if you prefer, build a dream about education. Conservatives are typically big fans of school choice and school vouchers. Conservative rhetoric about school choice is often linked to the claim that private or religious schools, including Catholic schools, are more cost-effective than public schools and do better by poor inner-city minority children and youth. I believe in vouchers, but I have long since stopped asking my conservative friends why they do not zero in on the main educational problem that these truly disadvantaged youngsters face: illiteracy.[35] School choice initiatives have been voted down in most states. Waging rhetorical or research battles with liberal elites gains no real educational ground for inner-city children, least of all for poor young black urban males.

But it would help to provide private vouchers or scholarships at scale. The late John Walton helped to bankroll the Children's Scholarship Fund. In recent years, the Fund's Philadelphia operation alone has received 65,000 applications from poor parents, mostly blacks, but has had only enough money to support 3,250 scholarships. The scholarships are destination-neutral, but most parents choose to use them at local Catholic or other religious schools.

Were a Walton-like program targeted on scholarships for the most economically disadvantaged fifth of black males age fourteen or younger, then at $4,000 per year per scholarship, the total cost of such a program would be approximately $4 billion—just twice as much to help educate young black males *nationally* as the annual $2 billion budget for the Philadelphia public school system.

So, for $10 billion a year, we could have a mentor for every young black male under the age of eighteen whose parent or guardian requested one, plus a private school scholarship for every extremely low-income black male under high school age.

And by "we," I do not mean just the national government. As noted in chapter 3, President Bush's original compassion fund plan envisioned the national government putting a quarter to a half-a-buck in the mentoring dollar, provided that another quarter or fifty cents came from local governments, myriad private individuals, and nonprofit partners.

The at-scale school scholarship funds could all be raised locally and privately. Rather than engage in additional high-impact problem-mongering or pretend that building high-performance high-tech schools is a realistic near-term answer, the Gates Foundation, which supported the aforementioned high school dropout report I co-authored, could sneeze and fund a national children's scholarship fund for poor young black urban males.

The controversy over the Moynihan Report's thesis about black family breakdown is increasingly of antiquarian interest. Black faith-based leaders, volunteers, and organizations are no less vital when it comes to addressing this hard reality: many black males grow up without fathers in the home, themselves father children whom they do not come to know as fathers, and end up as ex-prisoners before reaching their thirty-fifth birthdays. For well over a decade now, major black leaders, writers, and cultural experts have argued, preached, or written under such headings as "Healthy Marriages in Low-Income African-American Communities: Expanding the Dialogue with Faith Leaders" or "God's Gifts: A Christian Vision of Marriage and the Black Family." This group includes the Columbia scholar Ronald Mincy, Amachi leader Reverend Dr. W. Wilson Goode, Sr., the Annie E. Casey Foundation's Ralph Smith, Emory University's Robert M. Franklin, the National Urban League's president Marc H. Morial, the syndicated columnist Clarence Page, and literally dozens more who I could list just off the top of my head.

In 2004, for instance, following a series of meetings on the black family sponsored by the Annie E. Casey Foundation, black leaders issued a report that concluded with "An urgent call to African-American churches."[36] Their recommendations were:

- Intensify and expand efforts to prevent out-of-wedlock pregnancies
- Seek training in the broad field of marriage and family resources
- Engage in dialogue with young people, other churches, hip-hop artists, entertainment industry power-brokers, etc. on the negative influence of popular culture
- Seek opportunities to collaborate with other churches, religious communities, and secular entities to ensure the quality of services and avoid duplication and poor stewardship of precious resources

In 2005, the Seymour Institute for Advanced Christian Studies released a report on the black family that was discussed and debated everywhere including Black Entertainment Television. It began: "There is a crisis of unprecedented magnitude in the Black community. . . . The Black family is failing. This crisis has been long in the making, as was memorably noted by Daniel Patrick Moynihan as early as 1965."[37]

Over 600,000 men will be released from prison this year and in each of the next five years. Roughly 40 percent of these parolees will be black males. They will return home to low-income neighborhoods like north central Philly and south central Los Angeles. Public/Private Ventures has conducted preliminary research on one federally funded faith-based prisoner reentry program.[38]

The Public/Private Ventures analysis suggests that the program's recidivism rate is half the national average, but that finding means less than meets the eye. The program's participants are not representative of all parolees nationally; if anything, they are a somewhat "better class" of ex-criminals, whose predicted recidivism rates, absent any intervention, would be below the national average for all parolees.

Still, the preliminary findings are somewhat encouraging, especially as they relate to employment's role in keeping ex-offenders out of trouble. The results to date suggest that job mentors and local institutional supports are possibly essential to keeping these men from returning to crime and helping them go on to lead decent and productive lives: "Enrollees who took part in one-to-one mentoring were more than twice as likely to find jobs as participants who had never been mentored. . . . [But] these findings must be interpreted cautiously since mentoring and employment are both related to motivation and possibly to other factors as well."[39]

The Reverend Samuel Atchison has a unique perspective on such academic research. For over a dozen years he was the prison minister inside Trenton State, the New Jersey maximum-security prison mentioned in chapter 6 in relation to an Easter visit by Charles Colson. Reverend Sam, as he likes to be called, is an African American clergyman who has been doing faith-based outreach both behind bars and among inner-city youth since he first (in his words) "tightened up my pastor's collar." He was another mind behind the mentoring program for children with incarcerated parents that began as Evergreen and succeeded as Amachi. With his own social science bona fides to go with his practitioner's knowledge, he helped Public/Private Ventures design its studies. But, as he stresses: "No way these guys make it without a J-O-B, period; and no way to get them that, for real, without some one-on-one job mentoring and other one-on-one help, end of story."

Like Reverend Sam, Emory's Robert Franklin dreams about cutting by half the number of black men who are in prison:

The men who are tonight sitting in prison are not available to become husbands, and are not available to rear their kids. Churches, colleges, and nonprofit organizations should develop a coordinated plan to ensure that every prisoner scheduled for release will be received into the community with lots of supports. . . . What might happen if at your next church meeting, you introduced a resolution to make this a priority?[40]

Also like Reverend Sam, Franklin wonders whether today's black churches, even with all necessary support, would accept the challenge:

Black churches are asset-rich institutions. They have talented leaders, armies of potential volunteers, a weekly cash flow, available meeting space, track records of service, trust, and credibility in most communities. . . . Without . . . these churches, the civil rights movement would not have occurred. . . . [It was] a revolution led by preachers, church women and Sunday School children. . . . [But black churches today] are torn between serving the needs of the poorest . . . and being user-friendly institutions for their upwardly mobile, "paying customers." Most . . . do not appeal to people on the economic margins, a tragic irony given the teachings of Jesus of Nazareth.[41]

HONOR THY FRANKLIN: BACK TO AMERICA'S FAITH-BASED FUTURE

The plea by Reverend Sam, Robert Franklin, and others to support urban black churches that tackle prisoner reentry and other social problems would have found a sympathetic ear and secured a generous check from Benjamin Franklin. When it came to respecting and supporting diverse sacred places that serve civic purposes, Father Ben never told anybody to go fly a kite. Nor, I want to argue by way of conclusion, should we.

In 1749, Franklin founded the Academy of Philadelphia, the school that decades later begat the nonsectarian University of Pennsylvania. Penn proudly claims to have been strictly nonsectarian even though its early leaders were mostly ministers and even though its modern-day mascot is "the Quaker." In any case, there is no disputing that its founding father liked Philly taverns on Saturday nights more than he liked

Philly churches on Sunday mornings. He once even claimed that beer was proof that God exists and loves mankind.

As Jerry Weinberger's 2005 biography makes plain, Franklin wore many public and private masks. It is not at all clear whether he believed, even provisionally, in any spiritual concept or reality, Christian or other.[42] It is, however, crystal clear what Franklin believed regarding religion in the American public square.

In his award-winning biography, former Cable News Network executive Walter Isaacson aptly describes Franklin as an "apostle of tolerance" who "contributed to the building funds of each and every sect in Philadelphia" and "opposed religious oaths and tests in both the Pennsylvania and the federal constitutions."[43] Ben's religious beliefs "were driven by pragmatism."[44]

Or, as Franklin himself put it, under certain conditions, religion can "serve as a powerful regulator of our actions, give us peace and tranquility in our minds, and render us benevolent, useful and beneficial to others."[45] The month before he died, Franklin opined that if there is indeed "one God" per the Judeo-Christian tradition, then "the most acceptable service we render to him is doing good to his other children."[46]

Communiter Bona profounder Deum est.

Memorize that. It is Latin for "To pour forth benefits for the common good is divine." Thus goes the motto of the Library Company of Philadelphia, founded by Franklin in 1731.

Communiter Bona profounder Deum est.

Amen. In chapters 1 through 5, I claimed to find a faith-friendly but pluralistic perspective on religion and government everywhere I looked: in the Constitution's framers, starting with Madison and his multiplicity of sects; in Supreme Court opinions and church-state doctrine (neutrality); in present-day mass public opinion on religion and faith-based programs; in best-practices public administration (with a charitable choice proxy-government fix); in bipartisan elite political sentiment; and in the latest and best religion-relevant empirical research on faith-based (versus faith-saturated) organizations and the three faith factors.

In chapter 6, and up to this point in this chapter, I have pointed back to the founders' faithful consensus by means of six principles or precepts:

three quasi-religious (take prisoners, do unto others, think Catholic) and three less so (invest wisely, target blessings, and now, get right again with Ben).

Having unapologetically worked in a little Catholic apologetics on the common good and other concepts, I also have claimed that our best bet for a brighter faith-based future might be to focus in common on how black faith-based organizations can address a major social challenge—how to help poor young black urban males.

But perhaps Franklin's most important and timely guidance concerns how we ought to relate to others with whom we have profound disagreements about religion and public life. On his deathbed, Ben penned the following words:

> I have ever let others enjoy their religious Sentiments, without reflecting on them for those that appeared to me unsupportable and even absurd. All Sects here, and we have a great Variety, have experienced my good will in assisting them with Subscriptions for building their new Places of Worship; and, as I have never opposed any of their Doctrines, I hope to go out of the World in Peace with them all.[47]

Before, during, and since my time as the nation's first faith czar, I have struggled, often unsuccessfully, to be "in Peace with them all." I find it difficult to be totally at peace with those who are on either church-state extreme or to be diplomatic when I find what they advocate to be "unsupportable and even absurd." Even after all that I have written in these pages, I am still not quite there.

Virtually every time that I have found myself nearing a comfortable distance from policy positions taken, or complaints espoused, by my friends on the religious right, my friends on the secular left have said or done things that . . . remind me why I also have friends who are religious conservatives, and vice versa.

For instance, in late 2005, I felt that I had heard just about all I could stand from orthodox secularists who opposed faith-friendly federal legislation providing funding to Catholic and other religious schools that had selflessly opened their doors to elementary and secondary school students displaced by Hurricane Katrina (the legislation passed anyway).

They also opposed the original charitable choice provisions as retained in the reauthorization of the 1996 welfare reform law (it passed anyway), and they opposed other measures (including some related to the Head Start preschool program) by which Washington could help religious organizations to help people in need without violating the Constitution.

But then the orthodox sectarians said and did equally off-center things, like pushing (albeit unsuccessfully) a new federal job training ("work investment") bill that contained a blanket "religious hiring rights" provision. They also ratcheted up the polarizing rhetoric and repeated old canards (like the "judicial tyranny" and "Godless schools" tales cited in chapter 2). Unfortunately, too often they found facile echo chambers and champions in the Bush administration.

For example, in May 2007, the White House rejected a bipartisan House bill, passed by a 365–48 margin, that increased funding for Head Start, a program that benefits millions of low-income preschoolers. Among the main reasons the administration gave for opposing the bill was its failure to include a provision giving religious nonprofit groups that receive grants to administer the program an absolute right to discriminate on religious grounds in hiring. But the responsible officials knew that such a provision would have disrespected neutrality doctrine and violated existing civil rights and charitable choice laws. They also knew that the vast majority of faith-based organizations that deliver social services in the low-income urban communities where the program is most popular do not insist on an absolute right to discriminate on religious grounds in hiring program staff who are to be paid with tax dollars. And they knew that a bipartisan, centrist coalition in the House had even passed an amendment to the bill reinforcing the rights of religious nonprofits to participate in the program on the same basis as all other nongovernmental organizations.

What would Franklin do? At a minimum, he would try to keep his balance even as others lost theirs. He would be quick, I have little doubt, to point out that most Americans, in his time as in ours, have kept theirs. He might even indulge himself and us in taking a gentle poke at the Europeans and their increasingly faith-free democracies.

Over the last several decades, the percentage of people who rarely or never attend church rose in most European countries. As Europeans have retreated from religion (and Catholic Europeans have embraced contraception), birthrates have fallen all across the continent. Once the envy of American progressives and socialists, Europe's cradle-to-grave welfare programs are becoming massive unfunded public liabilities as fewer cradles get filled and fewer people enter the workforce and pay taxes.

Still, the mid-2006 headline of a *U.S. News & World Report* story about religion in present-day Europe exaggerated a bit: "European, Not Christian: An Aggressive Secularism Sweeps the Continent."[48] Rather than becoming aggressively secular, Europe, others claim, is becoming Islamic; but even as Muslim populations have increased from France to Scotland, it is still too soon to know whether Europe is undergoing an immigration-related religious realignment and becoming "Eurabia." I doubt it.

The better evidence, for now at least, suggests that Europe is in the final phases of a religious de-alignment from mass Christianity to mass secularism. This de-alignment is taking shape differently in different Old World republics. For instance, once solidly Roman Catholic European countries like Italy and Ireland remain culturally Catholic, but their peoples manifest ever weaker formal attachments to the Church of Rome. Europe is secularizing even as many regions all around the globe undergo a religious resurgence, and even as European-bred Christianity, in both its Catholic and Protestant forms, is *the* growth religion in the southern hemisphere (for instance, Africa is on the way to having 200 million Catholics).

Franklin would have considered the European retreat from religion to be the latest in a string of world-historic mistakes that began when King George III and the Parliament could not quite figure out their American colonists or imagine ever surrendering to a praying George Washington. Even the enlightened and cosmopolitan Franklin, together with other key godly republic patriots, saved some of his most impassioned denunciations of England for Sunday worship services at Philadelphia's Christ's Church (still standing and still functioning jolly well).

Religion, above all, made Americans different from Europeans in Franklin's day. Religion, above all, makes Americans different from Europeans now. With the forgivably Francophile Franklin, let us all say *vive la différence.*

That said, in a world in which religion matters more, not less, to peoples almost everywhere except old Europe, Americans, not Europeans, have every reason to lead, not follow, in international affairs. Average Americans get religion, because they have got religion. Now, the Council on Foreign Relations and other elite idea shops are finally taking global religions and religious movements seriously too, and not a moment to soon. The need to do so goes well beyond America's troubles with radical Islam in a post–9/11 world. The Pew Forum on Religion and Public Life, led by the Cuban-born Catholic political scientist Luis Lugo, has been instrumental in making the case. Writing in Pew's *Trust* magazine in 2006, Sue Rardin said it best: "It's as imprudent to ignore the role of religion in foreign policy as it is to pretend that the elephant is in some other room, rather than right here."[49]

Franklin would second that motion. His intellectual and civic cosmopolitanism was not a globe-trotting secularism in disguise. He would instantly understand that, precisely because America has been, and continues to be, a godly republic that has struggled with religious orthodoxy, diversity, and pluralism, twenty-first century Americans and their leaders are naturally much better positioned than their secular French cousins to navigate potentially faith-polarized geopolitics in our time.

Back home, Franklin would also be quick to fall in love with the Williamsburg Charter. It sounds old, but it was published on June 25, 1988. A group of religious leaders and First Amendment thinkers composed it together in Williamsburg, Virginia, one of America's most historic "colonial towns." They gave it the subtitle: "A National Celebration and Reaffirmation of the First Amendment Religious Liberty Clauses."

Franklin might nitpick at this document; I would too. But it is arguably the single soundest statement on the subject that has been crafted since, well, young Madison marveled at how old Ben managed to sweat it out with him in Philly in the summer of 1787.

Unfortunately, the Williamsburg Charter is hard to find. I had heard about it, but it was not until I had already been struggling for years to craft some such statement on my own that I was handed a copy in 2005 while visiting Calvin College in Michigan. "This," my gift-giver said, "is pretty much like what you seem to want to say." How right he was.

The Williamsburg Charter appears in full as the one and only appendix to this book. If you do not like the book, then at least learn to like Franklin, study Madison, and, regardless, love the Charter. Its penultimate section is aptly headed "A Time for Reconstitution." Let me bid farewell by quoting directly from that section's final two points concerning "conducting public debates regarding religion in a manner that is democratic and civil."

> Third, those who claim the right to influence should accept the responsibility not to inflame: Too often in recent disputes over religion and public affairs, some have insisted that any evidence of religious influence on public policy represents an establishment of religion and is therefore precluded as an improper "imposition." Such exclusion of religion from public life is historically unwarranted, philosophically inconsistent and profoundly undemocratic. . . . Religious liberty and democratic civility are also threatened, however, from another quarter. Overreacting to an improper veto on religion in public life, many have used religious language and images not for the legitimate influencing of policies but to inflame politics. . . . As a result, they bring to politics a misplaced absolutism that idolizes politics, "Satanizes" their enemies and politicizes their own faith.

> Fourth, those who claim the right to participate should accept the responsibility to persuade: . . . Arguments for public policy should be more than private convictions shouted out loud. For persuasion to be principled, private convictions should be translated into publicly accessible claims. Such claims should be made publicly accessible for two reasons: first, because they must engage those who do not share the same private convictions, and second, because they should be directed toward the common good.

Directed toward the common good.
Communiter Bona profounder Deum est.
To pour forth benefits for the common good is divine.
Benefits for the least, the last, and the lost of our society.
Ecumenical, interfaith, religious-secular, and public-private partnerships that, as necessary, include the national political community acting through its duly elected and appointed public servants in Washington.

Faith-based benefits that become ever greater civic blessings received by America's most truly disadvantaged children, youth, and families.

During the Constitutional Convention, Franklin often wondered silently whether the half-sun carved into the convention president's chair was a rising sun or a setting sun. He concluded that the sun was rising, rising on the future of the godly republic. Not only Christians who believe, as I do, that the Son has risen, but Americans of all faiths and of no faith, would be justified in hoping that Franklin was right.

Postscript

THE FAITH-BASED GLOBAL FUTURE

As is noted in the introduction, in June 1998 *Newsweek* magazine did a cover story focused on a black Pentecostal minister in Boston with ties to Philadelphia's Pastor Benjamin "Pops" Smith. In preparing for that story, the magazine's editors had consulted rather extensively with me. In the several years just before and ever since, my focus, as in this book, has been on the godly republic's founding, fortunes, and future, most especially the federal government's posture vis-à-vis church-state issues and community-serving faith-based organizations.

In March 2007, as this book was heading into editing, *Newsweek* kindly invited me in again. This time, however, they were interested in black Pentecostals and other Pentecostals *abroad*. Naturally, the discussion touched upon the United States, Iraq, and religion's role in geopolitics. One *Newsweek* editor posed a big and important question that I had thought about much but previously discussed not at all: What should America's international posture be vis-à-vis faith-based organizations abroad?

I prefaced my brief answer to his question by saying that I felt a bit like Karl Marx, who theorized about the laboring classes and global communism from the British Museum without knowing many actual proletarians. Unless you count New Jersey, I do not travel abroad (I made an exception in 1998 when the Vatican called). Well before I went to the White House in 2001, I knew many major religious leaders with international reach. I still do, but they are all based in the United States.

Still, after the *Newsweek* meeting, I researched what the well-traveled foreign policy and international relations experts had to say on the subject, and I did not feel so inadequate or inexpert after all. I wrote my thoughts down for an essay in *The Weekly Standard*, published in May 2007. This postscript is adapted from that essay, with a few data points added from my research files. If you read chapter 7's concluding section, you already have my basic answer. This postscript repeats a bit that is in that section, but also fleshes out a broader argument about how America and other democracies should greet the faith-based global future.

Start with the fact that Marx was wrong as hell. Today religion lives where communism died or never took hold. States have not withered, and neither have faiths. America is hardly alone in being a nation where religion matters as much or more today as it did a century ago. Such facts still surprise some scholars (self-confident secularism being the opiate of the intellectuals), but few now deny them.

In December 2006, speaking before journalists assembled by the Pew Forum on Religion and Public Life, Peter Berger admitted as much. Berger, an emeritus professor at Boston University, is a rightly esteemed sociologist of religion. "We live in an age of overwhelming religious globalization," he began. But, as late as a quarter-century ago, neither he nor most other academics saw this age coming. Most analysts, he explained, had the same stale orthodoxy about religion's inevitable demise. "The idea was very simple: the more modernity, the less religion. . . . I think it was wrong."

Except in Marx's old Europe, where it has proven half-right, the idea was all wrong. Anno Domini 2007 marks the European Union's fiftieth anniversary, and the following year, 2008 A.D., will be the fortieth since Pope Paul VI's encyclical *Humanae Vitae.* Europeans mocked the Pope's warnings about family planning cultures that promote abortion and produce few children. As a result, a fitting inscription for the European Union's gold watches would be "World's largest unfunded pension liability land mass."

Europe still has more Christians (over 500 million) than any other continent. In Rome and several other European cities, Catholicism, but not its practice, still permeates local culture while its architectural pageantry promotes foreign tourism. In the United Kingdom, estimates of how many self-described Christians are regular churchgoers range as low as 5 percent. In sum, post-1968 survey data on European belief and church attendance rates suggest that postindustrial modernity has indeed loosened if not broken Christianity's grip on the continent's diverse peoples.

Still, this decades-in-the-making European vacation from Christianity is not a permanent vacation from religion itself. From Scotland to France, Christianity's slide has been accompanied by more religion from other faith traditions including Islam. For example, in Britain today there are three times as many Muslim believers (over 1.6 million) as there are Methodist believers (about 500,000). The nation's growing Muslim population is devout, but the country's Methodist and other Christian communities are not. There is, however, as yet no hard demographic evidence to support the prediction that either England or all Europe is destined to become more Muslim than Christian. Nor, in particular, is it entirely clear that Europe's Catholics have fallen so far from the cradle that their children or grandchildren (if they start having some) will never return.

Most countries once ruled, in whole or in part, by Europeans have modernized to varying degrees, but without religion losing its hold on people. Christianity, in particular, is a growth religion in Africa, Asia, and Latin America. For example, one cannot begin to understand postcolonial Africa without knowing how profoundly religion matters—and which religions matter where and to whom. Nigeria is one small case in point. There are now about 20 million Anglicans in Nigeria, on the way to 30 to 35 million over the next generation. In 1900, Nigeria was one-third Muslim and had almost no Christians. By 1970, the country was about 45 percent Muslim and 45 percent Christian.

Anglicanism, of course, is not the global future, but Pentecostalism and other charismatic Christian religions might be. Throughout the twentieth century, various Pentecostal sects crept or swept through Latin America and Africa. In each continent all Pentecostals are now an estimated one-tenth to a fifth of the total population. In Asia, Pentecostals now number well over 150 million people, with concentrations in places like South Korea.

No matter what the host country or culture, Pentecostals tend to start fast but remain geographically concentrated in one city or region for a generation or two before spreading (sometimes slowly, sometimes like wildfire). Here in America, the century-old Pentecostal Church of God in Christ (COGIC), a predominantly African American denomination, now stretches from traditional storefront "Holy Ghost" or "blessing station" ministries in the South (still its regional home base) to a 26,000-member congregation in West Los Angeles, California where Hollywood celebrities crowd into cathedral pews next to the inner-city poor.

In 2005 and 2006, the cathedral's presiding pastor, COGIC Bishop Charles E. Blake, traveled extensively in Africa and met with top government leaders in Zambia and other nations. Through a new nonprofit organization called Save Africa's Children, he expanded the church's HIV/AIDS ministries in sub-Saharan Africa. Via satellite broadcasts, he and other U.S.-based Pentecostal pastors are heard by poor people in Africa and other places. When Blake goes to these countries, he is mobbed like a rock (or rock-of-ages) star.

Most international relations experts, however, do not know about Pentecostals in America or abroad. Many journalists who cover global affairs could not tell you who Bishop Blake is. A few might even have trouble identifying another California preacher who has partnered with Blake on several international initiatives, Rick Warren.

As discussed in chapter 3, at a Pew-sponsored journalists' junket in 2005 I was the opening act for Warren, author of *The Purpose-Driven Life: What on Earth Am I Here For?* My opening joke was that the conference organizers wanted the day's first two speakers to average 15 million in book sales (his 30 million and my next to none). Most laughed, but some were puzzled (apparently, they had not even read their conference background materials).

First published in 2002, and since reissued in many different languages, no nonfiction book ever has sold both in America and globally like Warren's prayer-and-meditation manual. Warren co-pastors a megachurch in California (called Saddleback, with over 80,000 members). The goateed, born-again baby-boomer boasts a Bible-believing pro-life, pro-family theology. True to stereotype, a few journalists at the gathering looked for Pat Robertson beneath Warren's Hawaiian-print shirt but could not find him. In fact, Warren has long since fallen out with many fellow white evangelical leaders. To them, his sins include cavorting with

Pentecostals and others they consider to be theologically incorrect, promoting "creation care" (environmental protection), and hobnobbing with pro-choice politicians, including Democrats, who share his global anti-poverty and public health agendas.

At the Pew gathering, the purpose-filled pastor got relatively few questions in the session and over meals about his international ministries and other globe-trotting adventures. His various training programs and "tool kits" have reached an estimated 400,000 ministers in over a hundred countries. His interfaith antipoverty and public health programs (most recently eradication of malaria) have purportedly reached millions. His biggest battles to date have been over how he has used his global bully pulpit. For instance, in November 2006 he saddled over to Syria and sounded off on human rights, but seemed dangerously naïve about that nation's terrorist ties. In February 2007, he was scheduled to preach in North Korea but postponed the trip. (Good call.)

Still by far the single biggest mega-church presence on the global scene is the Catholic Church. It claims a billion followers and growing. America's Catholics, roughly a quarter of the U.S. population, are just a twentieth of the Church's global flock. Pope Benedict XVI is considered "too strict" for many Catholics in America, not to mention Catholics in Europe. But he is generally viewed as a moderate by the conservative Catholic leaders and throngs in Africa. There are today two billion Christians worldwide, and Christianity in various orthodox forms, from Pentecostalism to Vatican-certified Catholicism, is the world's fastest-growing religion.

Take it from Penn State's superb global religions watcher, Philip Jenkins. In books published in 2002 and 2006, Jenkins established beyond any reasonable empirical or historical doubt that, for decades now, Catholicism and many other Christian sects have been growing rapidly in the southern hemisphere.[1] By or before 2050, Africa will supplant Europe as home to the most Christians. In 1900, Africa had an estimated 10 to 15 million Christians. In 1959 the Catholic Church had not yet appointed a single black African cardinal. By 2000, however, Africa had some 350 million Christians including well over 100 million Catholics. Some demographers would bet instead that Latin America will outdistance Africa and be first to succeed Europe as the continent with the most Christians. It has long had the heaviest country-by-country Catholic concentrations. Even as Pentecostals and other Christian sects have made converts, South America's Catholic seminaries have grown (up over 350 percent since 1972). The Vatican counts some 60,000 priests, 100,000 lay missionaries, and 130,000 nuns on the continent.

So, from Brazil to Belize, from Beirut to Boston, religion in over a hundred forms and in a thousand different ways has outlived modernity and post-modernity, too. And, whenever religious individuals, ideas, and institutions get newly mobilized into politics and public affairs, at home or abroad, look out, because they have the power to transform things, and fast. That simply goes double if they have well-positioned, well-resourced leaders to channel their power.

For example, just consider how the late Pope John Paul II changed both the Church and Latin America by throwing Catholicism's weight behind democracy movements there and on other continents. In 1987, the Pope confronted Chile's dictator, General Augusto Pinochet, with these words: "I am not the evangelizer of democracy; I am the evangelizer of the Gospel. To the Gospel message, of course, belong all the problems of human rights; and, if democracy means human rights, it also belongs to the message of the Church."

History teaches that democracy has not done well in countries dominated by Catholicism, Islam, or Confucianism. But, as I argued in Rome before the Pontifical Academy of Social Sciences in 1998, Catholicism changed after World War II. I invoked the political scientist Seymour Martin Lipset, who, writing that same year, agreed that the Church had changed in ways that improved democracy's global fortunes.

Similarly, writing in 1991, Harvard's Samuel P. Huntington explored democracy's worldwide march during the period 1974 to 1990, which he termed democracy's "third wave." Huntington identified thirty-three instances of democratization (versus just three of democratic reversal). Religion, he argued, was critical to this wave: "In many countries, Protestant and Catholic church leaders have been central in the struggles against repressive countries. . . . Catholicism was second only to economic development as a pervasive force making for democratization in the 1970s and 1980s."[2]

Correct, but after his excellent 1991 book on democratization, Huntington half-forgot how best to think about religion. In a series of controversial articles and books published in 1993 and thereafter, he speculated about the conditions under which the world might witness or avert a "clash of civilizations." He argued that ideology, economics, and nation-states would be far less central to future international conflicts than they had been in the past. He stressed that Western democracies did not have all the answers and scolded those who graded other "civilizations" by how kindred they were to American political norms.

But Huntington's conceptual framework was a sweeping, multi-variable mess that loosely related religion to ethnic, racial, regional, and other history-moving forces. His provocative prediction was not warranted by such empirical data as he mustered. When it came time to delineate "civilizations," he created his own categories: "Islamic" covered places from Albania to Azerbaijan; "Sinic" included China and Vietnam; "Japan" was its own "civilization." And so on.

I have heard ostensibly well-informed people describe the situation in Iraq, 2003–2007, in relation to Huntington's "clash" thesis. But it should be obvious that the contest between Sunnis and Shiites is an *intra*-religious conflict with centuries-old roots in Islamic history. It is not unlike the conflict (receded but not forgotten) in Northern Ireland between Catholics and Protestants, another intra-religious conflict with centuries-old roots in Christian history.

You know that you are skirting rather than seeing important realities when you are using identity concepts that are nobody's actual identity. You do not need to go globe-trotting to understand why. For example, New Orleans is home to Mary Queen of Vietnam Church. Its Catholic members are not Creoles or Cajuns. The church's "Post-Katrina Recovery News" website is in Vietnamese. Since the biblical-sized floods receded, its leaders have deepened ties to many English-speaking churches and community groups, Catholic and non-Catholic. To understand these leaders, their people, and their institution, to map their community relations, or to gauge their present or potential civic role, it would not help to categorize them either as "Sinic" expatriates or "Westerners" on the make.

Huntington's big-think Harvard colleague, Joseph S. Nye, has been less controversial and more cogent conceptually. Nye is famous for his 2004 work on so-called soft power, meaning how nations get what they want though attraction rather than coercion (multilateral ties, not military tussles; economic incentives, not muscle-bound sanctions).[3] America, he claims, has squandered opportunities to amass and use soft power. He does not deny that religion can pack a soft-power punch, but religion gets only seven passing mentions in his magnum opus.

Nye opens with Niccolò Machiavelli, who wrote that it is better for a ruler to be feared than to be loved. Nye challenges that dictum by claiming that soft power often succeeds where hard power fumbles or fails. Fair enough, but as Nye also knows, the medieval Italian for all seasons counseled that rulers need both hard-power swords and soft-power plowshares (or swords that rulers can opt to beat into plowshares as circumstances may dictate).

As Nye might have emphasized, history teaches that when religion is used as hard power it sooner or later destroys those who wield it. Christianity's hard power–wielding religions, including king-making Catholicism, had their days (even centuries) but resulted in ruins (and, in Catholicism's case, a junior role in North America). Protestant-inspired church-state separation doctrine is but a prudential prohibition against using religion as hard power at home, and a caution against using religion as hard power abroad. It is also an invitation for the state to be faith-friendly, promote religious pluralism, and avoid sectarian strife.

SPIRITUALPOLITIQUE

Thus, what I baptize as *spiritualpolitique* is a soft-power perspective on politics that emphasizes religion's domestic and international significance, accounts for religion's present and potential power to shape politics within and among nations, and understands religion not as some abstract force measured by its resiliency vis-à-vis "modernity" and not by its supporting role in "civilizations" that cooperate or clash but by staring at the particularities that render this or that actual religion as preached and practiced by present-day peoples so fascinating to ethnographers (who can spend lifetimes immersed in single sects) and so puzzling to faith-factoring social scientists (who seek, often in vain, to characterize and quantify religions or to track religion-related social and political trends).

Consider how this perspective might inform debates on what the United States should do in Iraq. Some have advocated increasing the U.S. presence in Iraq and staying there until violence is well under wraps. Others have devised or advocated various draw-down or get-out plans. Although it took a few years, almost all have acknowledged that the struggle behind most home-grown bombings that have killed innocent civilians in Iraq has specific religious roots.

But some on both sides in the debate over U.S. policy seem not yet to know that any conflict-ending compromise or resolution, no matter its military, economic, or other features, will not last unless it takes those particular religious differences very seriously. The conflict in Iraq is not a civil war. It is sectarian violence, complicated by the region's wider religious rifts and their intersections with state-supported terrorism networks.

Spiritualpolitique lesson one is that even in stable representative democracies, intra-national religious cleavages, whether long-buried or out in the open, always matter to who governs and to what ends. Thus, the religious cleavages in Iraq existed long before the U.S. occupation. Whatever the United States does, the violence will one day cease. But its sectarian sources will persist even if the country somehow, some day becomes a textbook, multiparty, stable parliamentary democracy. (If you doubt it, just study the Israeli Knesset in action.)

Spiritualpolitique lesson two is that constitutionalism, not democratization, matters most where religious differences run deepest or remain most intense. It was good to hold elections in Iraq. Majority rule via free and fair plebiscites is often among the first steps toward a more humane polity, whatever its official form and legal formalities. But majority rule can also mean the proverbial two wolves and a sheep deciding what is for supper. Constitutionalism, democracy or not, means that the government's powers are limited and any law-abiding civic minority's fundamental rights—starting with religious rights—are legally sacred.

In a functional constitutional system, the ruled can dismiss their rulers without bloodshed; there are limits (but almost never American-style checks and balances) on power-holders in addition to scheduled elections; and, last but not least, those who are in the out party or out parties (if there are organized parties—America itself really did not have any until Andrew Jackson's day) neither check under the hood nor try to win through bullets what they lost through ballots.

Nothing, however, complicates the march to constitutionalism like religious differences, especially when, as is almost always the case, those differences are fodder for what the founding fathers denounced as "foreign intrigues." Go back to chapter 1, consider what James Madison wrote in the Federalist Papers, and reflect on America's own history. When Madison discussed how political factions could tear a people apart, the very first source he mentioned was "a zeal for different opinions concerning religion."

The Constitution's ratification was threatened by Protestant true-believers who cursed the clause forbidding any religious tests for federal officeholding. They rejected, but Americans now happily live, Madison's vision of the religious future—a "multiplicity of sects" (Methodists, Muslims, Jews, Catholics, Quakers, and others) that each shape but do not dominate life in this large, commercial republic "under God."

As discussed in chapter 1, Madison and company cut a political deal known to us as the First Amendment's two religion clauses: "Congress shall make no law respecting an establishment of religion, or prohibiting the free exercise thereof . . . " This meant that, for the time being, each state could have a tax-funded and ceremonially favored religion if it wanted, but the national government would remain forever neutral on religion. In the early twentieth century, the Supreme Court erased the deal's last legal traces by holding that religious liberty is so "fundamental" that no religious establishments by the states are constitutionally permissible.

Until mid-century, not much changed. But then, as was discussed in chapters 2 and 3, in the early 1960s tradition-minded Protestants, largely self-exiled politically since the 1920s Scopes monkey trials, became convinced that the Court was going too far in ridding religion from the public square (the 1962 decision banning state-sponsored school prayer was the watershed moment). They entered the political fray. Thus began the evangelical mobilizations that revolutionized our two-party politics and shaped several recent presidential elections.

The single biggest program to result from born-again President George W. Bush's push, discussed in chapter 4, for faith-based initiatives has been international, not domestic: a $15 billion, five-year effort to address the global HIV/AIDS epidemic. In May 2005, Secretary of State Condoleezza Rice met with the aforementioned Bishop Blake and other church leaders to get the job done. In May 2007, President Bush proposed spending $30 billion more on the initiative.

Targeted mainly on fifteen countries, and zeroing in on Africa (where two-thirds of the over 3.5 million yearly deaths from the disease now occur), the soft-power program was championed inside the West Wing by Michael Gerson, the chief speechwriter who became the president's "compassion agenda" czar. Gerson is now a senior fellow at the Council on Foreign Relations. He and his Council colleague Walter Russell Mead are two foreign policy wonks who take religion seriously. And the Council's president, Richard N. Haass, has publicly opined that religion matters in world affairs today more than it has for centuries.

But Gerson, Mead, and Haass remain exceptions to the expert rule, and not only at the Council. In fact, to a remarkable degree, most foreign policy elites remain not only ignorant but reluctant when it comes to discussing religion. In November 2006, the Pew Charitable Trusts (parent to the Pew religion forum cited above) published in its magazine, *Trust*, a feature essay by a freelance writer named Sue Rardin. Entitled "Eyes Wide Shut," Rardin's article quoted numerous thought leaders and policy makers who expressed reservations about focusing on religion. She summarized their core concern as follows: "Addressing religious differences means entering discussions where moral values—our own as well as those of others—may not be governed by reason alone, but may be held more fiercely than if they were."[4]

There is only one word for American foreign policy elites, Democratic and Republican, left and right, who downplay or disregard religion to their peril, ours—and the world's—in deference to the dogma that being faith-free promotes objectivity: preposterous. Or, as Rardin editorialized well: "It is as imprudent to ignore the role of religion in foreign policy as it is to pretend that the elephant is in some other room, rather than right here."[5]

It is bad to doubt the overwhelming empirical evidence that religion matters to domestic politics as well as to how social services get delivered. But it is far worse to treat religion as a back-burner reality in global affairs when it is boiling over in so many places and (the good news) leveraging interfaith and public-private partnerships that are improving everyday life and healing old social and political wounds in so many nations.

The U.S. State Department needs to wake up and smell the incense. There is already an international legal framework for thinking out loud and acting in concert with other nations on religion's role in global affairs. Religious freedom is addressed in the 1948 United Nations Universal Declaration of Human Rights, Article 18. Its terms are echoed by several other UN declarations including a 1981 General Assembly–backed document calling for ending all state-sponsored religious discrimination.

This international legal framework is reinforced by several federal statutes that were passed with bipartisan support. For instance, a 1998 federal law, signed by President Bill Clinton, puts America firmly on the hook to support religious freedom abroad (the International Religious Freedom Act, or IRFA). Subject to that act, the State Department and other federal agencies are required to report any relevant information they have regarding "countries of particular concern." The 2006 list included Burma, China, Eritrea, Iran, North Korea, Saudi Arabia, Sudan, and Uzbekistan.

Not much, however, is actually done by Washington to act on these concerns, end religious persecution, or support nations that abide by both UN and U.S. standards governing respect for religious pluralism. Just how little can be glimpsed by comparing the federal government's faith-based funding at home versus abroad.

At home, domestic sacred places that serve civic purposes have been discriminated against in myriad ways by grant-making federal agencies. Things have gotten a bit better since the first relevant federal laws protecting their rights went on the books in 1996. The Bush administration boasts that over $2 billion a year in federal grants now goes to qualified, community-serving faith-based organizations. Even if that figure is accepted at face value (many experts dispute it), $2 billion is still a relative pittance: the federal government gives out hundreds of billions of dollars in such grants each year, and over a third of all organizations supplying certain social services in big cities are faith-based.

It is, however, a bishop's ransom compared to the $591 million that the United States Agency for International Development (USAID) granted faith-based organizations operating abroad in fiscal year 2005. In September 2006, Terri Hasdorff, director of the agency's faith-based and community initiatives center, testified before the House Subcommittee on Africa. She noted that "the vast majority of faith-based awards are made to a small number of groups."

I have no idea what the optimal funding figure would be, or precisely how much broader the faith-affiliated nongovernmental organization grantee roster should be. But with a $2.9 trillion total annual federal budget, with a crying need to demonstrate good will abroad and get critical lifesaving good works done, and with a heart to provide better public health and other services around the globe, the White House and the Congress might want USAID, the State Department, and other agencies to do a whole lot better. For 2008, the Bush administration requested about $21 billion for foreign assistance to particular countries. Diverse experts agree that this so-called bilateral aid has never been subjected to anything like a systematic empirical evaluation or performance review. I would suggest a test. For three years starting in fiscal year 2009, USAID should be authorized and funded to double its grants to assorted community-serving faith-based groups abroad, bringing the annual total to a bit over $1 billion. The agency should commission an independent study to assess whether religious groups seem to have any comparative advantages when it comes to cost-effectively achieving humanitarian assistance, economic development, public health, or other objectives.

Totalitarians, secular or religious, who know what they are about have always gone beyond merely banning this or that religion or establishing a state religion (Chairman Mao Tse-tung's little red bible and cult come quickly to mind) to killing religious leaders, gulag-ticketing or terrorizing religious followers, and destroying (physically in many cases) religion's last traces (books, buildings). Religion, however, almost always proves resilient, often reasserting itself in its very prerevolutionary or dictator-forbidden forms.

Thus, today's democracy-loving, constitutionalism-forging leaders in America and other nations should acknowledge, respect, and where appropriate, boost religious good works both at home and abroad. Just as is true with respect to domestic faith-based initiatives, when it comes to *spiritualpolitique,* God will help those who help others.

The Williamsburg Charter

A NATIONAL CELEBRATION
AND REAFFIRMATION
OF THE FIRST AMENDMENT
RELIGIOUS LIBERTY CLAUSES

Williamsburg, Virginia
June 25, 1988

Congress shall make no law respecting an establishment of
religion, or prohibiting the free exercise thereof; or
abridging the freedom of speech, or of the press; or the
right of the people peaceably to assemble, and to petition
the Government for a redress of grievances.

First Amendment to Constitution of the United States

Keenly aware of the high national purpose of commemorating the bicentennial
of the United States Constitution, we who sign this Charter seek to celebrate the
Constitution's greatness, and to call for a bold reaffirmation and reappraisal of
its vision and guiding principles. In particular, we call for a fresh consideration
of religious liberty in our time, and of the place of the First Amendment
Religious Liberty clauses in our national life.

We gratefully acknowledge that the Constitution has been hailed as America's
"chief export" and "the most wonderful work ever struck off at a given time by
the brain and purpose of man." Today, two hundred years after its signing, the
Constitution is not only the world's oldest, still-effective written constitution, but
the admired pattern of ordered liberty for countless people in many lands.

In spite of its enduring and universal qualities, however, some provisions of the
Constitution are now the subject of widespread controversy in the United States.

One area of intense controversy concerns the First Amendment Religious Liberty clauses, whose mutually reinforcing provisions act as a double guarantee of religious liberty, one part barring the making of any law "respecting an establishment of religion" and the other barring any law "prohibiting the free exercise thereof."

The First Amendment Religious Liberty provisions epitomize the Constitution's visionary realism. They were, as James Madison said, the "true remedy" to the predicament of religious conflict they originally addressed, and they well express the responsibilities and limits of the state with respect to liberty and justice.

Our commemoration of the Constitution's bicentennial must therefore go beyond celebration to rededication. Unless this is done, an irreplaceable part of national life will be endangered, and a remarkable opportunity for the expansion of liberty will be lost.

For we judge that the present controversies over religion in public life pose both a danger and an opportunity. There is evident danger in the fact that certain forms of politically reassertive religion in parts of the world are, in principle, enemies of democratic freedom and a source of deep social antagonism. There is also evident opportunity in the growing philosophical and cultural awareness that all people live by commitments and ideals, that value-neutrality is impossible in the ordering of society, and that we are on the edge of a promising moment for a fresh assessment of pluralism and liberty. It is with an eye to both the promise and the peril that we publish this Charter and pledge ourselves to its principles.

We readily acknowledge our continuing differences. Signing this Charter implies no pretense that we believe the same things or that our differences over policy proposals, legal interpretations and philosophical groundings do not ultimately matter. The truth is not even that what unites us is deeper than what divides us, for differences over belief are the deepest and least easily negotiated of all.

The Charter sets forth a renewed national compact, in the sense of a solemn mutual agreement between parties, on how we view the place of religion in American life and how we should contend with each other's deepest differences in the public sphere. It is a call to a vision of public life that will allow conflict to lead to consensus, religious commitment to reinforce political civility. In this way, diversity is not a point of weakness but a source of strength.

I. A TIME FOR REAFFIRMATION

We believe, in the first place, that the nature of the Religious Liberty clauses must be understood before the problems surrounding them can be resolved. We therefore affirm both their cardinal assumptions and the reasons for their crucial national importance.

With regard to the assumptions of the First Amendment Religious Liberty clauses, we hold three to be chief:

1. The Inalienable Right

Nothing is more characteristic of humankind than the natural and inescapable drive toward meaning and belonging, toward making sense of life and finding community in the world. As fundamental and precious as life itself, this "will to meaning" finds expression in ultimate beliefs, whether theistic or non-theistic, transcendent or naturalistic, and these beliefs are most our own when a matter of conviction rather than coercion. They are most our own when, in the words of George Mason, the principal author of the Virginia Declaration of Rights, they are "directed only by reason and conviction, not by force or violence."

As James Madison expressed it in his *Memorial and Remonstrance*, "The Religion then of every man must be left to the conviction and conscience of every man; and it is the right of every man to exercise it as these may dictate. This right is in its nature an unalienable right."

Two hundred years later, despite dramatic changes in life and a marked increase of naturalistic philosophies in some parts of the world and in certain sectors of our society, this right to religious liberty based upon freedom of conscience remains fundamental and inalienable. While particular beliefs may be true or false, better or worse, the right to reach, hold, exercise them freely, or change them, is basic and non-negotiable.

Religious liberty finally depends on neither the favors of the state and its officials nor the vagaries of tyrants or majorities. Religious liberty in a democracy is a right that may not be submitted to vote and depends on the outcome of no election. A society is only as just and free as it is respectful of this right, especially toward the beliefs of its smallest minorities and least popular communities.

The right to freedom of conscience is premised not upon science, nor upon social utility, nor upon pride of species. Rather, it is premised upon the inviolable dignity of the human person. It is the foundation of, and is integrally related to, all other rights and freedoms secured by the Constitution. This basic civil liberty is clearly acknowledged in the Declaration of Independence and is ineradicable from the long tradition of rights and liberties from which the Revolution sprang.

2. The Ever Present Danger

No threat to freedom of conscience and religious liberty has historically been greater than the coercions of both Church and State. These two institutions—the one religious, the other political—have through the centuries succumbed to the temptation of coercion in their claims over minds and souls. When these institutions and their claims have been combined, it has too often resulted in terrible violations of human liberty and dignity. They are so combined when the sword and purse of the State are in the hands of the Church, or when the State usurps the mantle of the Church so as to coerce the conscience and compel belief. These and other such confusions of religion and state authority represent the misordering of religion and government which it is the purpose of the Religious Liberty provisions to prevent.

Authorities and orthodoxies have changed, kingdoms and empires have come and gone, yet as John Milton once warned, "new Presbyter is but old priest writ large." Similarly, the modern persecutor of religion is but ancient tyrant with more refined instruments of control. Moreover, many of the greatest crimes against conscience of this century have been committed, not by religious authorities, but by ideologues virulently opposed to traditional religion.

Yet whether ancient or modern, issuing from religion or ideology, the result is the same: religious and ideological orthodoxies, when politically established, lead only too naturally toward what Roger Williams called a "spiritual rape" that coerces the conscience and produces "rivers of civil blood" that stain the record of human history.

Less dramatic but also lethal to freedom and the chief menace to religious liberty today is the expanding power of government control over personal behavior and the institutions of society, when the government acts not so much in deliberate hostility to, but in reckless disregard of, communal belief and personal conscience.

Thanks principally to the wisdom of the First Amendment, the American experience is different. But even in America where state-established orthodoxies are unlawful and the state is constitutionally limited, religious liberty can never be taken for granted. It is a rare achievement that requires constant protection.

3. The Most Nearly Perfect Solution

Knowing well that "nothing human can be perfect" (James Madison) and that the Constitution was not "a faultless work" (Gouverneur Morris), the Framers nevertheless saw the First Amendment as a "true remedy" and the most nearly perfect solution yet devised for properly ordering the relationship of religion and the state in a free society.

There have been occasions when the protections of the First Amendment have been overridden or imperfectly applied. Nonetheless, the First Amendment is a momentous decision for religious liberty, the most important political decision for religious liberty and public justice in the history of humankind. Limitation upon religious liberty is allowable only where the State has borne a heavy burden of proof that the limitation is justified—not by any ordinary public interest, but by a supreme public necessity—and that no less restrictive alternative to limitation exists.

The Religious Liberty clauses are a brilliant construct in which both No Establishment and Free Exercise serve the ends of religious liberty and freedom of con-science. No longer can sword, purse and sacred mantle be equated. Now, the gov-ernment is barred from using religion's mantle to become a confessional State, and from allowing religion to use the government's sword and purse to become a coercing Church. In this new order, the freedom of the government from reli-gious control and the freedom of religion from government control are a double guarantee of the protection of rights. No faith is preferred or prohibited, for where there is no state-definable orthodoxy, there can be no state-punishable heresy.

With regard to the reasons why the First Amendment Religious Liberty clauses are important for the nation today, we hold five to be pre-eminent:

1. The First Amendment Religious Liberty provisions have both a logical and historical priority in the Bill of Rights. They have logical priority because the security of all rights rests upon the recognition that they are neither given by the state, nor can they be taken away by the state. Such rights are inherent in the inviolability of the human person. History demonstrates that unless these rights are protected our society's slow, painful progress toward freedom would not have been possible.

2. The First Amendment Religious Liberty provisions lie close to the heart of the distinctiveness of the American experiment. The uniqueness of the Amer-ican way of disestablishment and its consequences have often been more obvious to foreign observers such as Alexis de Tocqueville and Lord James Bryce, who wrote that "of all the differences between the Old world and the New, this is per-haps the most salient." In particular, the Religious Liberty clauses are vital to har-nessing otherwise centrifugal forces such as personal liberty and social diversity, thus sustaining republican vitality while making possible a necessary measure of national concord.

3. The First Amendment Religious Liberty provisions are the democratic world's most salient alternative to the totalitarian repression of human rights and provide a corrective to unbridled nationalism and religious warfare around the world.

4. The First Amendment Religious Liberty provisions provide the United States' most distinctive answer to one of the world's most pressing questions in the late-twentieth century. They address the problem: How do we live with each other's deepest differences? How do religious convictions and political free-dom complement rather than threaten each other on a small planet in a pluralis-tic age? In a world in which bigotry, fanaticism, terrorism and the state control of religion are all too common responses to these questions, sustaining the justice and liberty of the American arrangement is an urgent moral task.

5. The First Amendment Religious Liberty provisions give American society a unique position in relation to both the First and Third worlds. Highly mod-ernized like the rest of the First World, yet not so secularized, this society—largely because of religious freedom—remains, like most of the Third World, deeply religious. This fact, which is critical for possibilities of better human understanding, has not been sufficiently appreciated in American self-understanding, or drawn upon in American diplomacy and communication throughout the world.

In sum, as much if not more than any other single provision in the entire Constitution, the Religious Liberty provisions hold the key to American distinctiveness and American destiny. Far from being settled by the interpretations of judges and historians, the last word on the First Amendment likely rests in a chapter yet to be written, documenting the unfolding drama of America. If religious liberty is neglected, all civil liberties will suffer. If it is guarded and sustained, the American experiment will be the more secure.

II. A TIME FOR REAPPRAISAL

Much of the current controversy about religion and politics neither reflects the highest wisdom of the First Amendment nor serves the best interests of the disputants or the nation. We therefore call for a critical reappraisal of the course and consequences of such controversy. Four widespread errors have exacerbated the controversy needlessly.

1. The Issue Is Not Only What We Debate, but How

The debate about religion in public life is too often misconstrued as a clash of ideologies alone, pitting "secularists" against the "sectarians" or vice versa. Though competing and even contrary worldviews are involved, the controversy is not solely ideological. It also flows from a breakdown in understanding of how personal and communal beliefs should be related to public life.

The American republic depends upon the answers to two questions. By what ultimate truths ought we to live? And how should these be related to public life? The first question is personal, but has a public dimension because of the connection between beliefs and public virtue. The American answer to the first question is that the government is excluded from giving an answer. The second question, however, is thoroughly public in character, and a public answer is appropriate and necessary to the well-being of this society.

This second question was central to the idea of the First Amendment. The Religious Liberty provisions are not "articles of faith" concerned with the substance of particular doctrines or of policy issues. They are "articles of peace" concerned with the constitutional constraints and the shared prior understanding within which the American people can engage their differences in a civil manner and thus provide for both religious liberty and stable public government.

Conflicts over the relationship between deeply held beliefs and public policy will remain a continuing feature of democratic life. They do not discredit the First Amendment, but confirm its wisdom and point to the need to distinguish the Religious Liberty clauses from the particular controversies they address. The clauses can never be divorced from the controversies they address, but should always be held distinct. In the public discussion, an open commitment to the constraints and standards of the clauses should precede and accompany debate over the controversies.

2. The Issue Is Not Sectarian, but National

The role of religion in American public life is too often devalued or dismissed in public debate, as though the American people's historically vital religious traditions were at best a purely private matter and at worst essentially sectarian and divisive.

Such a position betrays a failure of civil respect for the convictions of others. It also underestimates the degree to which the Framers relied on the American people's religious convictions to be what Tocqueville described as "the first of their political institutions." In America, this crucial public role has been played by diverse beliefs, not so much despite disestablishment as because of disestablishment.

The Founders knew well that the republic they established represented an audacious gamble against long historical odds. This form of government depends upon ultimate beliefs, for otherwise we have no right to the rights by which it thrives, yet rejects any official formulation of them. The republic will therefore always remain an "undecided experiment" that stands or falls by the dynamism of its non-established faiths.

3. The Issue Is Larger than the Disputants

Recent controversies over religion and public life have too often become a form of warfare in which individuals, motives and reputations have been impugned. The intensity of the debate is commensurate with the importance of the issues debated, but to those engaged in this warfare we present two arguments for reappraisal and restraint.

The lesser argument is one of expediency and is based on the ironic fact that each side has become the best argument for the other. One side's excesses have become the other side's arguments; one side's extremists the other side's recruiters. The danger is that, as the ideological warfare becomes self-perpetuating, more serious issues and broader national interests will be forgotten and the bitterness deepened.

The more important argument is one of principle and is based on the fact that the several sides have pursued their objectives in ways which contradict their own best ideals. Too often, for example, religious believers have been uncharitable, liberals have been illiberal, conservatives have been insensitive to tradition, champions of tolerance have been intolerant, defenders of free speech have been censorious, and citizens of a republic based on democratic accommodation have succumbed to a habit of relentless confrontation.

4. The Issue Is Understandably Threatening

The First Amendment's meaning is too often debated in ways that ignore the genuine grievances or justifiable fears of opposing points of view. This happens when the logic of opposing arguments favors either an unwarranted intrusion of religion into public life or an unwarranted exclusion of religion from it. History plainly shows that with religious control over government, political freedom dies; with political control over religion, religious freedom dies.

The First Amendment has contributed to avoiding both these perils, but this happy experience is no cause for complacency. Though the United States has escaped the worst excesses experienced elsewhere in the world, the republic has shown two distinct tendencies of its own, one in the past and one today.

In earlier times, though lasting well into the twentieth century, there was a *de facto* semi-establishment of one religion in the United States: a generalized Protestantism given dominant status in national institutions, especially in the public schools. This development was largely approved by Protestants, but widely opposed by non-Protestants, including Catholics and Jews.

In more recent times, and partly in reaction, constitutional jurisprudence has tended, in the view of many, to move toward the *de facto* semi-establishment of a wholly secular understanding of the origin, nature and destiny of humankind and of the American nation. During this period, the exclusion of teaching about the role of religion in society, based partly upon a misunderstanding of First Amendment decisions, has ironically resulted in giving a dominant status to such wholly secular understandings in many national institutions. Many secularists appear as unconcerned over the consequences of this development as were Protestants unconcerned about their *de facto* establishment earlier.

Such *de facto* establishments, though seldom extreme, usually benign and often unwitting, are the source of grievances and fears among the several parties in current controversies. Together with the encroachments of the expanding modern state, such *de facto* establishments, as much as any official establishment, are likely to remain a threat to freedom and justice for all.

Justifiable fears are raised by those who advocate theocracy or the coercive power of law to establish a "Christian America." While this advocacy is and should be legally protected, such proposals contradict freedom of conscience and the genius of the Religious Liberty provisions.

At the same time there are others who raise justifiable fears of an unwarranted exclusion of religion from public life. The assertion of moral judgments as though they were morally neutral, and interpretations of the "wall of separation" that would exclude religious expression and argument from public life, also contradict freedom of conscience and the genius of the provisions.

Civility obliges citizens in a pluralistic society to take great care in using words and casting issues. The communications media have a primary role, and thus a special responsibility, in shaping public opinion and debate. Words such as public, secular and religious should be free from discriminatory bias. "Secular purpose," for example, should not mean "non-religious purpose" but "general public purpose." Otherwise, the impression is gained that "public is equivalent to secular; religion is equivalent to private." Such equations are neither accurate nor just. Similarly, it is false to equate "public" and "governmental." In a society that sets store by the necessary limits on government, there are many spheres of life that are public but non-governmental.

Two important conclusions follow from a reappraisal of the present controversies over religion in public life. First, the process of adjustment and readjustment to the constraints and standards of the Religious Liberty provisions is an ongoing requirement of American democracy. The Constitution is not a self-interpreting, self-executing document; and the prescriptions of the Religious Liberty provisions cannot by themselves resolve the myriad confusions and ambiguities surrounding the right ordering of the relationship between religion and government in a free society. The Framers clearly understood that the Religious Liberty provisions provide the legal construct for what must be an ongoing process of adjustment and mutual give-and-take in a democracy.

We are keenly aware that, especially over state-supported education, we as a people must continue to wrestle with the complex connections between religion and the transmission of moral values in a pluralistic society. Thus, we cannot have, and should not seek, a definitive, once for all solution to the questions that will continue to surround the Religious Liberty provisions.

Second, the need for such a readjustment today can best be addressed by remembering that the two clauses are essentially one provision for preserving religious liberty. Both parts, No Establishment and Free Exercise, are to be comprehensively understood as being in the service of religious liberty as a positive good. At the heart of the Establishment clause is the prohibition of state sponsorship of religion and at the heart of Free Exercise clause is the prohibition of state interference with religious liberty.

No sponsorship means that the state must leave to the free citizenry the public expression of ultimate beliefs, religious or otherwise, providing only that no expression is excluded from, and none governmentally favored, in the continuing democratic discourse.

No interference means the assurance of voluntary religious expression free from governmental intervention. This includes placing religious expression on an equal footing with all other forms of expression in genuinely public forums.

No sponsorship and no interference together mean fair opportunity. That is to say, all faiths are free to enter vigorously into public life and to exercise such influence as their followers and ideas engender. Such democratic exercise of influence is in the best tradition of American voluntarism and is not an unwarranted "imposition" or "establishment."

III. A TIME FOR RECONSTITUTION

We believe, finally, that the time is ripe for a genuine expansion of democratic liberty, and that this goal may be attained through a new engagement of citizens in a debate that is reordered in accord with constitutional first principles and considerations of the common good. This amounts to no less than the reconstitution of a free republican people in our day. Careful consideration of three precepts would advance this possibility:

1. The Criteria Must Be Multiple

Reconstitution requires the recognition that the great dangers in interpreting the Constitution today are either to release interpretation from any demanding criteria or to narrow the criteria excessively. The first relaxes the necessary restraining force of the Constitution, while the second overlooks the insights that have arisen from the Constitution in two centuries of national experience.

Religious liberty is the only freedom in the First Amendment to be given two provisions. Together the clauses form a strong bulwark against suppression of religious liberty, yet they emerge from a series of dynamic tensions which cannot ultimately be relaxed. The Religious Liberty provisions grow out of an understanding not only of rights and a due recognition of faiths but of realism and a due recognition of factions. They themselves reflect both faith and skepticism. They raise questions of equality and liberty, majority rule and minority rights, individual convictions and communal tradition.

The Religious Liberty provisions must be understood both in terms of the Framers' intentions and history's sometimes surprising results. Interpreting and applying them today requires not only historical research but moral and political reflection.

The intention of the Framers is therefore a necessary but insufficient criterion for interpreting and applying the Constitution. But applied by itself, without any consideration of immutable principles of justice, the intention can easily be wielded as a weapon for governmental or sectarian causes, some quoting Jefferson and brandishing No Establishment and others citing Madison and brandishing Free Exercise. Rather, we must take the purpose and text of the Constitution seriously, sustain the principles behind the words and add an appreciation of the many-sided genius of the First Amendment and its complex development over time.

2. The Consensus Must Be Dynamic

Reconstitution requires a shared understanding of the relationship between the Constitution and the society it is to serve. The Framers understood that the Constitution is more than parchment and ink. The principles embodied in the document must be affirmed in practice by a free people since these principles reflect everything that constitutes the essential forms and substance of their society—the institutions, customs and ideals as well as the laws. Civic vitality and the effectiveness of law can be undermined when they overlook this broader cultural context of the Constitution.

Notable, in this connection is the striking absence today of any national consensus about religious liberty as a positive good. Yet religious liberty is indisputably what the Framers intended and what the First Amendment has preserved. Far from being a matter of exemption, exception or even toleration, religious liberty is an inalienable right. Far from being a sub-category of free speech or a constitutional redundancy, religious liberty is distinct and foundational. Far from being simply an individual right, religious liberty is a positive social good. Far from denigrating religion as a social or political "problem," the separation of Church and State is both the saving of religion from the temptation of political power and an achievement inspired in large part by religion itself. Far from weakening religion, disestablishment has, as an historical fact, enabled it to flourish.

In light of the First Amendment, the government should stand in relation to the churches, synagogues and other communities of faith as the guarantor of freedom. In light of the First Amendment, the churches, synagogues and other communities of faith stand in relation to the government as generators of faith, and therefore contribute to the spiritual and moral foundations of democracy. Thus, the government acts as a safeguard, but not the source, of freedom for faiths, whereas the churches and synagogues act as a source, but not the safeguard, of faiths for freedom.

The Religious Liberty provisions work for each other and for the federal idea as a whole. Neither established nor excluded, neither preferred nor proscribed, each faith (whether transcendent or naturalistic) is brought into a relationship with the government so that each is separated from the state in terms of its institutions, but democratically related to the state in terms of individuals and its ideas.

The result is neither a naked public square where all religion is excluded, nor a sacred public square with any religion established or semi-established. The result, rather, is a civil public square in which citizens of all religious faiths, or none, engage one another in the continuing democratic discourse.

3. The Compact Must Be Mutual

Reconstitution of a free republican people requires the recognition that religious liberty is a universal right joined to a universal duty to respect that right.

In the turns and twists of history, victims of religious discrimination have often later become perpetrators. In the famous image of Roger Williams, those at the helm of the Ship of State forget they were once under the hatches. They have, he said, "One weight for themselves when they are under the hatches, and another for others when they come to the helm." They show themselves, said James Madison, "as ready to set up an establishment which is to take them in as they were to pull down that which shut them out." Thus, benignly or otherwise, Protestants have treated Catholics as they were once treated, and secularists have done likewise with both.

Such inconsistencies are the natural seedbed for the growth of a *de facto* establishment. Against such inconsistencies we affirm that a right for one is a right for another and a responsibility for all. A right for a Protestant is a right for an Orthodox is a right for a Catholic is a right for a Jew is a right for a Humanist is a right for a Mormon is a right for a Muslim is a right for a Buddhist—and for the followers of any other faith within the wide bounds of the republic.

That rights are universal and responsibilities mutual is both the premise and the promise of democratic pluralism. The First Amendment, in this sense, is the epitome of public justice and serves as the Golden Rule for civic life. Rights are best guarded and responsibilities best exercised when each person and group guards for all others those rights they wish guarded for themselves. Whereas the wearer of the English crown is officially the Defender of the Faith, all who uphold the American Constitution are defenders of the rights of all faiths.

From this axiom, that rights are universal and responsibilities mutual, derives guidelines for conducting public debates involving religion in a manner that is democratic and civil. These guidelines are not, and must not be, mandated by law. But they are, we believe, necessary to reconstitute and revitalize the American understanding of the role of religion in a free society.

First, those who claim the right to dissent should assume the responsibility to debate: Commitment to democratic pluralism assumes the coexistence within one political community of groups whose ultimate faith commitments may be incompatible, yet whose common commitment to social unity and diversity does justice to both the requirements of individual conscience and the wider community. A general consent to the obligations of citizenship is therefore inherent in the American experiment, both as a founding principle ("We the people") and as a matter of daily practice.

There must always be room for those who do not wish to participate in the public ordering of our common life, who desire to pursue their own religious witness separately as conscience dictates. But at the same time, for those who do wish to participate, it should be understood that those claiming the right to dissent should assume the responsibility to debate. As this responsibility is exercised, the characteristic American formula of individual liberty complemented by respect for the opinions of others permits differences to be asserted, yet a broad, active community of understanding to be sustained.

Second, those who claim the right to criticize should assume the responsibility to comprehend: One of the ironies of democratic life is that freedom of conscience is jeopardized by false tolerance as well as by outright intolerance. Genuine tolerance considers contrary views fairly and judges them on merit. Debased tolerance so refrains from making any judgment that it refuses to listen at all. Genuine tolerance honestly weighs honest differences and promotes both impartiality and pluralism. Debased tolerance results in indifference to the differences that vitalize a pluralistic democracy.

Central to the difference between genuine and debased tolerance is the recognition that peace and truth must be held in tension. Pluralism must not be confused with, and is in fact endangered by, philosophical and ethical indifference. Commitment to strong, clear philosophical and ethical ideas need not imply either intolerance or opposition to democratic pluralism. On the contrary, democratic pluralism requires an agreement to be locked in public argument over disagreements of consequence within the bonds of civility.

The right to argue for any public policy is a fundamental right for every citizen; respecting that right is a fundamental responsibility for all other citizens. When any view is expressed, all must uphold as constitutionally protected its advocate's right to express it. But others are free to challenge that view as politically pernicious, philosophically false, ethically evil, theologically idolatrous, or simply absurd, as the case may be seen to be.

Unless this tension between peace and truth is respected, civility cannot be sustained. In that event, tolerance degenerates into either apathetic relativism or a dogmatism as uncritical of itself as it is uncomprehending of others. The result is a general corruption of principled public debate.

Third, those who claim the right to influence should accept the responsibility not to inflame: Too often in recent disputes over religion and public affairs, some have insisted that any evidence of religious influence on public policy represents an establishment of religion and is therefore precluded as an improper "imposition." Such exclusion of religion from public life is historically unwarranted, philosophically inconsistent and profoundly undemocratic. The Framers' intention is indisputably ignored when public policy debates can appeal to the theses of Adam Smith and Karl Marx, or Charles Darwin and Sigmund Freud but not to the Western religious tradition in general and the Hebrew and Christian Scriptures in particular. Many of the most dynamic social movements in American history, including that of civil rights, were legitimately inspired and shaped by religious motivation.

Freedom of conscience and the right to influence public policy on the basis of religiously informed ideas are inseverably linked. In short, a key to democratic renewal is the fullest possible participation in the most open possible debate.

Religious liberty and democratic civility are also threatened, however, from another quarter. Overreacting to an improper veto on religion in public life, many have used religious language and images not for the legitimate influencing of policies but to inflame politics. Politics is indeed an extension of ethics and therefore engages religious principles; but some err by refusing to recognize that there is a distinction, though not a separation, between religion and politics. As a result, they bring to politics a misplaced absoluteness that idolizes politics, "Satanizes" their enemies and politicizes their own faith.

Even the most morally informed policy positions involve prudential judgments as well as pure principle. Therefore, to make an absolute equation of principles and policies inflates politics and does violence to reason, civil life and faith itself. Politics has recently been inflamed by a number of confusions: the confusion of personal religious affiliation with qualification or disqualification for public office; the confusion of claims to divine guidance with claims to divine endorsement; and the confusion of government neutrality among faiths with government indifference or hostility to religion.

Fourth, those who claim the right to participate should accept the responsibility to persuade: Central to the American experience is the power of political persuasion. Growing partly from principle and partly from the pressures of democratic pluralism, commitment to persuasion is the corollary of the belief that conscience is inviolable, coercion of conscience is evil, and the public interest is best served by consent hard won from vigorous debate. Those who believe themselves privy to the will of history brook no argument and need never tarry for consent. But to those who subscribe to the idea of government by the consent of the governed, compelled beliefs are a violation of first principles. The natural logic of the Religious Liberty provisions is to foster a political culture of persuasion which admits the challenge of opinions from all sources.

Arguments for public policy should be more than private convictions shouted out loud. For persuasion to be principled, private convictions should be translated into publicly accessible claims. Such public claims should be made publicly accessible for two reasons: first, because they must engage those who do not share the same private convictions, and second, because they should be directed toward the common good.

RENEWAL OF FIRST PRINCIPLES

We who live in the third century of the American republic can learn well from the past as we look to the future. Our Founders were both idealists and realists. Their confidence in human abilities was tempered by their skepticism about human nature. Aware of what was new in their times, they also knew the need for renewal in times after theirs. "No free government, or the blessings of liberty," wrote George Mason in 1776, "can be preserved to any people, but by a firm adherence to justice, moderation, temperance, frugality, and virtue, and by frequent recurrence to fundamental principles."

True to the ideals and realism of that vision, we who sign this Charter, people of many and various beliefs, pledge ourselves to the enduring precepts of the First Amendment as the cornerstone of the American experiment in liberty under law.

We address ourselves to our fellow citizens, daring to hope that the strongest desire of the greatest number is for the common good. We are firmly persuaded that the principles asserted here require a fresh consideration, and that the renewal of religious liberty is crucial to sustain a free people that would remain free. We therefore commit ourselves to speak, write and act according to this vision and these principles. We urge our fellow citizens to do the same.

To agree on such guiding principles and to achieve such a compact will not be easy. Whereas a law is a command directed to us, a compact is a promise that must proceed freely from us. To achieve it demands a measure of the vision, sacrifice and perseverance shown by our Founders. Their task was to defy the past, seeing and securing religious liberty against the terrible precedents of history. Ours is to challenge the future, sustaining vigilance and broadening protections against every new menace, including that of our own complacency. Knowing the unquenchable desire for freedom, they lit a beacon. It is for us who know its blessings to keep it burning brightly.

Notes

1. President Gerald R. Ford, public remarks on Proclamation 4311 granting a full and complete presidential pardon to President Richard M. Nixon, September 8, 1974, Ford Library and Museum website (www.ford.utexas.edu/library/speeches).

2. Jon Meacham, *American Gospel: God, the Founding Fathers, and the Making of a Nation* (Random House, 2006).

3. Ibid., p. 144.

4. Philip Hamburger, *Separation of Church and State* (Harvard University Press, 2002), chaps. 8–14.

5. Meacham, *American Gospel*, p. 233.

6. Ibid., pp. 234–235.

7. Ibid., p. 234.

8. Ibid., pp. 234–235.

9. Ibid., p. 235.

10. Ibid.

11. Ibid., pp. 235–236.

12. Ibid., pp. 22–27.

13. Ibid., p. 22.

14. Ibid., p. 8.

15. Peter Henriques, *Realistic Visionary: A Portrait of George Washington* (University of Virginia Press, 2006), is one recent example.

16. Peter A. Lillback's *George Washington's Sacred Fire* (Providence Forum, 2006) is one recent example.

17.   An amount equal to the entire after-tax advance on the book went in 2006 to the newest and neediest of them, La Salle Academy, one of the independent Catholic Miguel Schools of Philadelphia that serve low-income children without regard to religion.

1.   THE FOUNDERS' FAITHFUL CONSENSUS

1.   National Association of Evangelicals, *NAE Insight,* Washington, D.C., July–August 2002, p. 1.

2.   Ibid.

3.   Barack Obama, *The Audacity of Hope: Thoughts on Reclaiming the American Dream* (Crown, 2006), pp. 208–209.

4.   Ibid., pp. 209–215.

5.   Garrett Ward Sheldon, *The Political Philosophy of James Madison* (The Johns Hopkins University Press, 2001), p. 15.

6.   Jeffrey H. Morrison, *John Witherspoon and the Founding of the American Republic* (University of Notre Dame Press, 2005), p. 31.

7.   Ibid.

8.   Ibid.

9.   Ibid., p. 33.

10.   Dumas Malone, *Jefferson and the Rights of Man* (Little, Brown, 1951), p. 110.

11.   Ibid., p. 111

12.   Ibid.

13.   Joseph Loconte, "Faith and Founding: The Influence of Religion on the Politics of James Madison," *Journal of Church and State* (Autumn 2003), p. 714.

14.   Malone, *Jefferson,* p. 103.

15.   Loconte, "Faith and Founding," p. 714.

16.   Ibid.

17.   Ibid.

18.   Ibid.

19.   *The Federalist Papers,* ed. Clinton Rossiter (New American Library–Mentor Books, 1961), No. 55, p. 346; No. 51, p. 322; No. 37, p. 321; No. 10, pp. 78–80.

20.   James Bryce, as quoted in Morrison, *John Witherspoon,* pp. 154–155, n106.

21.   Sheldon, *Political Philosophy of James Madison,* p. 21.

22.   Rossiter, *Federalist Papers,* No. 10, p. 78.

23.   Ibid., No. 37, pp. 230–231.

24.   Ibid., p. 229.

25.   Sheldon, *Political Philosophy of James Madison,* p. xii.

26.   Ibid., p. xiii.

27.   All quotations from Madison's Nos. 10 and 51 that follow in this section

and the next are from Rossiter, *Federalist Papers*, No. 10, pp. 77–84; No. 51, pp. 320–325.

28. Sheldon, *Political Philosophy of James Madison,* p. 15.
29. Ibid.
30. Morrison, *John Witherspoon,* p. 112.
31. Malone, *Jefferson,* p. 170.
32. Ibid., p. 179.
33. Ibid., p. 178.
34. Ibid., pp. 172–173, 178.
35. Ibid.
36. Ibid., p. 178.
37. Rossiter, *Federalist Papers,* pp. 244, 246.
38. Ibid., pp. 286–287.
39. Ibid., pp 292–293.
40. Ibid., pp. 295, 298.
41. *The Federalist Papers,* ed. Isaac Kramnick (Penguin Books, 1987), p. 58.
42. As cited in ibid., p. 58.
43. Benjamin Franklin, "Observations Concerning the Increase of Mankind, Peopling of Countries, Etc.," written in Pennsylvania, 1751, reprinted in Larzer Ziff, ed., *Benjamin Franklin: Autobiography and Selected Writings* (Holt, Rinehart, and Winston, 1959), pp. 210, 211.
44. Kramnick, *Federalist Papers,* p. 66.
45. Herbert J. Storing, *What the Anti-Federalists Were For* (University of Chicago Press, 1981).
46. Kramnick, *Federalist Papers,* p. 59.
47. Ibid.
48. Ibid.
49. Ibid.
50. Rossiter, *Federalist Papers,* No. 51, p. 322.
51. Ibid., p. 510.
52. Ibid., pp. 512–513.
53. Ibid., pp. 513–514 (capitalization in the original).
54. Edward S. Corwin, *The Constitution and What It Means Today,* revised by Harold W. Chase and Craig R. Ducat (Princeton University Press, 1978), p. 285.
55. James Bryce, *The American Commonwealth* (Macmillan, 1914), p. 229.
56. Corwin, *Constitution,* p. 285.
57. Rossiter, *Federalist Papers,* No. 78, p. 465.
58. Ibid., No. 20, p. 138.

2.   THE COURT'S NEUTRALITY DOCTRINE

1. Editorial, "The Rally Next Door: Justice Sunday Was a Hard Right Case for Alito—Where's the Other Side?" *Philadelphia Daily News,* January 10, 2006, p. 13.

2. John J. DiIulio, Jr., "It Takes an Intellectual . . . to Misconstrue the Constitution," *The Weekly Standard,* January 16, 2006, pp. 35–39.

3. Philip Hamburger, *Separation of Church and State* (Harvard University Press, 2002), pp. 183–184.

4. Ibid., p. 481.

5. Ibid., p. 297.

6. Ibid.

7. Ibid., p. 298.

8. Ibid., p. 324.

9. Ibid., p. 325.

10. Ibid.

11. Ibid., pp. 455, 463.

12. Ibid., p. 463.

13. Ibid., p. 455.

14. Ibid., pp. 422–434, 454–478.

15. Ibid., p. 455.

16. Ibid.

17. Ibid., p. 461.

18. Ibid.

19. Ibid., pp. 461–462.

20. Ibid.

21. Ibid., pp. 218–219.

22. For an overview, see John J. DiIulio, Jr., "The American Catholic Voter," *Commonweal,* March 24, 2006, pp. 10–12.

23. The idea to codify and distribute the information came from inside the Clinton White House, courtesy several presidential domestic policy advisors led by the noted political scientist William Galston.

24. Charles C. Haynes et al., *The First Amendment in Schools* (First Amendment Center, 2003), p. 42.

25. Ronald B. Flowers, *That Godless Court? Supreme Court Decisions on Church-State Relationships* (Westminster/John Knox Press, 1994), p. 91.

26. Ibid.

27. Gary J. Simpson, "School Vouchers and the Constitution—Permissible, Impermissible, or Required?" *Cornell Journal of Law and Public Policy* (Summer 2002), p. 566

28. Ibid., p. 571.

29. Ibid., p. 575. Professor Simpson's analysis, though I disagree with it in the end, is outstanding.

30. Hamburger, *Separation*, p. 486.

31. Ibid., pp. 486–487.

32. U.S. Civil Rights Act of 1964, Title VII, Section 702, amended in 1972; *Corporation of the Presiding Bishop v. Amos* (1987).

33. Steven H. Shiffrin, "The Pluralistic Foundations of the Religion Clauses," *Cornell Law Review* (November 2004), p. 63.

34. Steven H. Shiffrin, "Liberalism and the Establishment Clause," *Chicago-Kent Law Review* (2003), p. 727.

35. My independent exploration here verifies virtually everything that has been reported on the matter by the Rockefeller Institute's Roundtable for Religion, on which I have served as an advisor; for example, see Mark Ragan and David J. Wright, "Scanning the Policy Environment for Faith-Based Social Services in the United States: What Has Changed Since 2002?" State University of New York at Albany, December 2005, pp. 35–40.

3.   THE PEOPLE'S CHARITABLE CHOICE

1. The January 19, 2005 statement was made before the National Ten-Point Leadership Foundation in Boston. The December 17, 2001 statement was made at New York City's Abyssinian Baptist Church.

2. For a summary of executive orders associated with the OFBCI, see Anne Farris et al., *The Expanding Administrative Presidency: George W. Bush and the Faith-Based Initiative* (Religion Roundtable, Rockefeller Institute, State University of New York at Albany, August 2004).

3. Amy Black et al., *Of Little Faith: The Politics of George W. Bush's Faith-Based Initiative* (Georgetown University Press, 2004).

4. For example, see George H. Gallup and Timothy Jones, *The Next American Spirituality* (Cook, 2000), chap. 1 and app. 1, 2.

5. George H. Gallup International Institute and the Center for Research on Religion and Urban Civil Society, *The Religious State of the Union* (2003).

6. Baylor Institute for Studies of Religion, *American Piety in the 21st Century* (Baylor University, 2006), p. 11.

7. Ibid., p. 12.

8. National Conference on Citizenship and Saguaro Seminar, *America's Civic Health Index: Broken Engagement* (2006), p. 17.

9. Baylor Institute, *American Piety*, p. 15.

10. For a brief overview, see John J. DiIulio, Jr., "The Catholic Voter," *Commonweal*, March 24, 2006, pp. 10–12.

11.   For an interesting journalistic perspective, see David Rieff, "Nuevo Catholics," *New York Times,* December 24, 2006.

12.   I am thinking here in particular of certain reactions that followed from my role as a leadoff speaker for Reverend Warren at a gathering of top national journalists: "The Faith Angle," a conference sponsored by the Pew Forum on Religion and Public Life and held at Key West, Florida, May 22, 2005.

13.   For example, see three Pew Forum on Religion and Public Life reports: *Faith-Based Funding Backed, But Church-State Doubts Abound* (April 10, 2001), *Lift Every Voice: A Report on Religion in American Public Life* (2002), and *Many Americans Uneasy with Mix of Religion and Politics* (August 24, 2006).

14.   Ibid. Also, Pew Forum on Religion and Public Life, *Americans Struggle with Religion's Role at Home and Abroad* (2002).

15.   For example, see Public Agenda Foundation, *For Goodness Sake: Why So Many Want Religion to Play a Greater Role in American Life* (2001).

16.   John J. DiIulio, Jr., "Mandate Mongering," *The Weekly Standard,* November 18, 2002; "Wooing Purple America," *The Weekly Standard,* November 15, 2004; "You Gotta Be Purple to Win," *The Weekly Standard,* November 20, 2006.

17.   DiIulio, "The Catholic Voter."

18.   Public Agenda Foundation, *For Goodness Sake,* p. 13.

19.   Ibid., table 5.

20.   Alan Wolfe, "The Opening of the Evangelical Mind," *The Atlantic Monthly,* October 2000, p. 56.

21.   Public Agenda Foundation, *For Goodness Sake,* table 7.

22.   Francis Collins, *The Language of God: A Scientist Presents Evidence for Belief* (Free Press, 2006).

23.   For example, see John McAdams, "Testing the Theory of the New Class," *Sociological Quarterly,* 1987, pp. 23–49.

24.   Morris P. Fiorina, *Culture War? The Myth of a Polarized America* (Pearson Longman, 2005), p. 102.

25.   Ibid., pp. 98, 103.

26.   For example, see Pew Research Center, *Trends 2005* (2005), chap. 2

27.   Ibid., p. 29.

28.   Ibid.

29.   James Q. Wilson, "Religion and Politics in America Today" (Robert A. Fox Leadership Program, Fox Forum, University of Pennsylvania, Philadelphia, November 2005).

30.   Laura R. Olson and John C. Green, " 'Gapology' and the Presidential Vote," *PS: Political Science,* July 2006, p. 444.

31.   Laura C. Olson and John C. Green, "The Religion Gap," *PS: Political Science,* July 2006, p. 457

32.   Jeffrey Bell, *Populism and Elitism: Politics in the Age of Equality* (Regnery Publishing, 1992).

33. For example, see Donald E. Stokes and John J. DiIulio, Jr., "The Setting: Valence Politics in Modern Presidential Elections," in Michael Nelson, ed., *The 1992 Elections* (Congressional Quarterly Press, 1993), chap. 1.

34. DiIulio, "You Gotta Be Purple to Win."

35. Fiorina, *Culture Wars*, p. 3.

36. Frank J. Thompson and John J. DiIulio, Jr., eds., *Medicaid and Devolution: The View from the States* (Brookings Institution Press, 1998).

37. Davis Osborn and Ted Gaebler, *Reinventing Government: How the Entrepreneurial Spirit Is Transforming the Public Sector* (Plume, 1993).

38. For an overview, see John J. DiIulio, Jr., "Government by Proxy: A Faithful Overview," *Harvard Law Review*, March 2003, pp. 1272–1284. Parts of this section are adapted largely from this article. The classic treatment is Donald F. Kettl, *Government by Proxy: (Mis?)Managing Federal Programs* (Congressional Quarterly Press, 1988). Also see John J. DiIulio, Jr. et al., *Improving Government Performance: An Owner's Manual* (Brookings Institution Press, 1993); John J. DiIulio, Jr. and Donald F. Kettl, *Fine Print: The Contract with America and the Administrative Realities of American Federalism* (Center for Public Management, Brookings Institution, March 1995); and James W. Fesler and Donald F. Kettl, *The Politics of the Administrative Process* (Chatham House, 1996), chap. 11.

39. Kettl, *Government by Proxy*.

40. Martha Derthick, *Keeping the Compound Republic: Essays on American Federalism* (Brookings Institution Press, 2001), p. 63.

41. Chris Edwards and John Samples, eds., *The Republican Congress 10 Years Later: Smaller Government or Business as Usual?* (Cato Institute, 2005).

42. Peter Frumkin, "After Partnership: Rethinking Public-Nonprofit Relations," in Mary Jo Bane et al., eds., *Who Will Provide? The Changing Role of Religion in American Social Welfare* (Westview, 2000), p. 199.

43. For example, see Stephen V. Monsma, *When Sacred and Secular Mix: Religious Nonprofit Organizations and Public Money* (Rowman and Littlefield, 1996).

44. Andrew Walsh, ed., *Can Charitable Choice Work? Covering Religion's Impact on Urban Affairs and Social Services* (Pew Program on Religion and the News Media, 2001), p. 2.

45. Alvia Y. Branch, *Faith and Action: Implementation of the National Faith-Based Initiative for High-Risk Youth* (Public/Private Ventures, 2002).

46. *Unlevel Playing Field*, White House Office of Faith-Based and Community Initiatives, August 2001, p. 13 (available via www.whitehouse.gov at the OFBCI link).

47. Stephen V. Monsma et al., *Working Faith: How Religious Organizations Provide Welfare to Work Services* (Center for Research on Religion and Urban Civil Society and Manhattan Institute, 2002), p. 14.

48. David Kuo, Testimony, U.S. House Subcommittee on Criminal Justice,

Drug Policy, and Human Resources, June 21, 2005; David Kuo, *Tempting Faith: An Inside Story of Political Seduction* (Free Press, 2006).

49. Alan Cooperman, "Grants to Religious Groups Fall, Study Says," *Washington Post*, February 15, 2006; Michael Fletcher, "Few Black Churches Get Funds," *Washington Post*, September 19, 2006.

50. Joe Klein, *Politics Lost: How American Democracy Was Trivialized by People Who Think You're Stupid* (Doubleday, 2006), p. 140.

51. John J. DiIulio, Jr., "Equal Protection Run Amok," *The Weekly Standard*, December 25, 2000 , pp. 25–26. Several conservative writers for *Commentary* and other outlets later echoed the concerns that I had expressed; see E. J. Dionne and William J. Kristol, eds., *Bush v. Gore* (Brookings Institution Press, 2001).

4. THE PRESIDENT'S BIPARTISAN PRAYER

1. I had heard as much from several White House staff who were very much in a first-person position to know. To date, however, the only published account is David Kuo, *Tempting Faith: An Inside Story of Political Seduction* (Free Press, 2006), chap. 14.

2. John J. DiIulio, Jr., "The Challenge for Faith-Based Initiatives," *Philadelphia Inquirer*, April 27, 2006.

3. The CNS has since resumed the name Corporation for National and Community Service, or CNCS.

4. John J. DiIulio, Jr., "The Political Theory of Compassionate Conservatism," *The Weekly Standard*, August 23, 1999, and "What Is Compassionate Conservatism?" *The Weekly Standard*, August 7, 2000. Also see John J. DiIulio, Jr., "The Bush Presidency: A View From Within," in Fred I. Greenstein, ed., *The George W. Bush Presidency: An Early Assessment* (Johns Hopkins University Press, 2003), chap. 10.

5. For several months, copies of most Bush campaign draft domestic and social policy campaign position papers or talking points were sent to me for forthright comment. I was particularly critical of various early proposals concerning the proposed "Office of Faith-Based Action" and its ombudsman-style director. Also, I assisted to varying degrees with speeches—lots on the campaign-launching July 22, 1999 "Duty of Hope" speech, a bit on various social policy and government reform topics, and, following a long hiatus, a few phrases in the 2000 inaugural address. I also was consulted during the belated transition process, including a visit in which I cautioned that new Executive Office of the President (EOP) operations are normally quite small, often poorly planned, and rarely get real civic results.

6. John M. Bridgeland , Stephen Goldsmith, and Leslie Lenkowsky, "Service

and the Bush Administration's Civic Agenda," in E. J. Dionne, Jr. et al., eds., *United We Serve: National Service and the Future of Citizenship* (Brookings Institution Press, 2003), p. 56.

7.   John J. DiIulio, Jr., "Know Us by Our Works," *Wall Street Journal*, February 14, 2001.

8.   For example, see Frank Bruni and Laurie Goodstein, "New Bush Office Seeks Closer Ties to Church Groups," *New York Times*, January 29, 2001.

9.   Amy E. Black et al., *Of Little Faith: The Politics of George W. Bush's Faith-Based Initiative* (Georgetown University Press, 2004).

10.   American Jewish Committee and the Feinstein Center for American Jewish History at Temple University, *In Good Faith: Government Funding of Faith-Based Social Services* (2001), reprinted in E. J. Dionne and Ming Hsu Chen, eds., *Sacred Places, Civic Purposes: Should Government Help Faith-Based Charity?* (Brookings Institution Press, 2001), pp. 311–312.

11.   Requests for federal waivers are hardly uncommon and emanate from diverse quarters (for instance, professional associations representing nurses who want relief from state laws that their members believe to be disadvantageous professionally). In this case, without consulting me, White House senior advisor Karl Rove, having received an inquiry from a Salvation Army representative who he knew from previous Republican party–related work, properly passed the inquiry on to Don Eberly, then the deputy director of the OFBCI. Eberly rightly handed it over to the OFBCI's legal counsel, Don Willett, who, in turn, sent the matter over to the Office of Management and Budget (OMB) for a standard "policy circular" review. A month before the story broke, the OMB had concluded that the request was inconsistent with existing policies and routinely filed away its finding. The matter never even reached me or, to my knowledge, any other White House senior staff members.

12.   For two public statements, see John J. DiIulio, Jr., "The Best of Times for Faith," *Washington Times*, December 2, 2001, and "Bush Keeps the Faith," *The Weekly Standard*, February 18, 2002.

13.   For a typical report, see "Bush Is Said to Scale Back His Religion-Based Initiative," *New York Times*, October 14, 2001.

14.   For example, see Anjetta McQueen, "Bush Touts New 'Religious Charities' Plan," *Congressional Quarterly Weekly*, February 9, 2002, pp. 401–402.

15.   Elizabeth Bumiller, "Accord Reached on Charity Aid Bill after Bush Gives in on Hiring," *New York Times*, February 8, 2002, p. 19.

16.   President Bush, as quoted in Anne Farris et al., *The Expanding Administrative Presidency: George W. Bush and the Faith-Based Initiative* (Religion Roundtable, Rockefeller Institute, State University of New York at Albany, August 2004), p.16.

17.   Farris, *The Expanding Administrative Presidency*, p. 6.

18.   Alison Zinser and Daniel Warsh, "Faith-Based Initiatives: Five Years Later, Where Are We?" *Sound Politicks* (University of Pennsylvania), Fall 2006, p. 17.

19.   For a sample, see John J. DiIulio, Jr. et al., *Improving Government Performance: An Owner's Manual* (Brookings Institution Press, 1993); John J. DiIulio, Jr., ed., *Deregulating the Public Service: Can Government Be Improved?* (Brookings Institution Press, 1994). For an early effort specifically directed at bringing performance-based practices to parole and other criminal justice agencies, see John J. DiIulio, Jr., et al., *Performance Measures for the Criminal Justice System* (U.S. Bureau of Justice Statistics, October 1993).

20.   During my time in the White House and thereafter, I came to know and admire the organization and its leaders. It is, in my view, on a par with such rightly well-respected national evangelical Christian service organizations as Prison Fellowship Ministries. In fact, in my capacity as pro bono chief consultant on the documentary *God and the Inner City*, first aired by the Public Broadcasting Service, I selected Teen Challenge to be among the three faith-based programs that were sympathetically profiled. The other two were a black Pentecostal-led youth outreach ministry in Boston and the Amachi program for mentoring children with incarcerated parents as it has unfolded in Philadelphia.

21.   Center for Alcohol and Substance Abuse, *So Help Me God: Substance Abuse, Religion, and Spirituality* (November 2001). The two foundations that sponsored the report were the Bodman Foundation and the John Templeton Foundation. No new data or studies published since this assessment would require any changes in it, but subsequent research with which I have been somewhat involved would underline it with respect to multiyear data regarding who enters and who completes the program.

22.   For example, see John J. DiIulio, Jr., "The New Civil Rights Struggle," *Wall Street Journal*, June 20, 2002.

23.   John J. DiIulio, Jr., "Homeland Insecurity," *The Weekly Standard*, April 22, 2002; "Mandate Mongering," *The Weekly Standard*, November 18, 2002; "The Future of Compassion," *Philadelphia Inquirer*, December 1, 2002; and "Why I Apologized to the Bush White House," *Philadelphia Daily News*, December 9, 2002.

24.   For one journalistic overview, see Carl Cannon, "Stepchildren of Justice," *The National Journal*, February 18, 2006.

25.   John J. DiIulio, Jr., "Faithful Consensus," in E. J. Dionne et al., eds., *One Electorate Under God?* (Brookings Institution Press, 2004), part 2.

5.   THE NATION'S SPIRITUAL CAPITAL

1.   Robert D. Putnam, "Bowling Alone: America's Declining Social Capital," *Journal of Democracy*, January 1995, pp. 65–78.

2. C. Everett Ladd, "The Data Just Don't Show Erosion of America's 'Social Capital,'" *The Public Perspective,* June/July 1996, pp. 5–22.

3. As of this writing, Putnam is working on a new book about religion in America. I was glad to put his research team in touch with some of the community-serving ministers that I first mentioned to him back in the mid-1990s. Whatever the book argues, with Putnam behind it, the work will be well worth reading and studying.

4. Robert D. Putnam et al., *Better Together: Report of the Saguaro Seminar* (John F. Kennedy School of Government, Harvard University, 2001), p. 65.

5. National Conference on Citizenship and Saguaro Seminar, *America's Civic Health Index: Broken Engagement* (Center for Civic Enterprises, 2006), p. 16.

6. Putnam, *Better Together,* p. 23.

7. For an overview, see Jerry Footlick, *A Model School: How Philadelphia's Gesu School Is Remaking Inner-City Education* (Gesu School, 2002).

8. The picture was captioned "Putting in a Goode Word," *Philadelphia Daily News,* March 10, 2006, p. 10.

9. Ibid.

10. Joseph P. Tierney, "The Catholic Puzzle Revisited," Program for Research on Religion and Urban Civil Society, University of Pennsylvania, April 2006.

11. Mary Jo Bane, "The Catholic Puzzle," in Mary Jo Bane et al., eds., *Taking Religion Seriously* (Harvard University Press, 2005).

12. George Weigel, "The Problem with Religious Philanthropy: Catholic Giving," *Philanthropy,* May/June 2005, p. 28.

13. For an overview, see Ronald J. Sider and Diane Knippers, eds., *Toward an Evangelical Public Policy: Political Strategies for the Health of the Nation* (Baker Books, 2005).

14. Catherine Wilson, "A Different Kind of Mandate: Latino Faith-Based Organizations and the Communitarian Impulse" (Ph.D. diss., Department of Political Science, University of Pennsylvania, 2003).

15. For a sample, see the following: Ram A. Cnaan and Carl Milofsky, "Small Religious Nonprofits: A Neglected Topic," *Nonprofit and Voluntary Sector Quarterly,* 1997; Ram A. Cnaan et al., *The Newer Deal: Social Work and Religion in Partnership* (Columbia University Press, 1999); Ram A. Cnaan and Stephanie C. Boddie, "Philadelphia Census of Congregations and Their Involvement in Social Service Delivery," *Social Service Review,* 2001, pp. 559–580; Ram A. Cnaan et al., *The Invisible Caring Hand: American Congregations and the Provision of Welfare,* foreword by John J. DiIulio, Jr. (New York University Press, 2002); Ram A. Cnaan et al., "Bowling Alone But Serving Together: The Congregational Norm of Community Involvement," in Corwin Smidt, ed., *Religion as Social Capital* (Baylor University Press, 2003), pp. 19–31.

16.   Ram A Cnaan, *The Other Philadelphia Story: How Local Congregations Support Quality of Life in Urban America* (Penn Press, 2006); also see Cnaan and Stephanie C. Boddie, *Black Church Outreach: Comparing How Black and Other Congregations Serve Their Needy Neighbors* (Center for Research on Religion and Urban Civil Society, University of Pennsylvania, 2001).

17.   Cnaan, "Bowling Alone But Serving Together."

18.   See especially Cnaan, *The Newer Deal.*

19.   Cnaan and Boddie, *Black Church Outreach*, pp. 13–16.

20.   Hara Wright-Smith, *Standing Our Ground: Community and Commuter Congregations Serving an Inner City* (Program for Research on Religion and Urban Civil Society, University of Pennsylvania, 2006).

21.   Stephanie Clintonia Boddie, "One More River to Cross: African-American Congregations at the Dawn of a New Millennium" (Ph.D. diss., School of Social Work, University of Pennsylvania, 2002), p. vii. Also see Jill Witmer Sinha, "African-American Youth and Communities of Faith: Capitalizing on Compassion, At Risk for Greatness" (Ph.D. diss., School of Social Work, University of Pennsylvania, 2004).

22.   For an overview, see John J. DiIulio, Jr., "Black Churches and the Inner-City Poor," in Christopher Foreman, ed., *The African-American Predicament* (Brookings Institution Press, 2001), chap. 10.

23.   Robert Joseph Taylor et al., *Religion in the Lives of African Americans: Social, Psychological, and Health Perspectives* (Sage Publications, 2004), p. 21.

24.   Ibid., p. 61.

25.   Ibid.

26.   James C. Cavendish, "Church-Based Community Activism: A Comparison of Black and White Catholic Congregations," *Journal of the Scientific Study of Religion*, 2001, pp. 371–384.

27.   For an overview, see Byron R. Johnson et al., "The 'Invisible Institution' and Black Youth Crime: The Church as an Agency of Local Social Control," *Journal of Youth and Adolescence*, 2000, pp. 479–498; and David B. Larson et al., "Escaping from the Crime of Inner Cities: Church Attendance and Religious Salience among Disadvantaged Youth," *Justice Quarterly*, June 2000, pp. 377–391.

28.   Nisha Danielle-Stephanie Botchwey, "Taxonomy of Religious and Secular Nonprofit Organizations: Knowledge Development and Policy Recommendations for Neighborhood Revitalization" (Ph.D. diss., Department of City and Regional Planning, University of Pennsylvania, 2003), p. 173.

29.   Mark Chavez, "Religious Congregations and Welfare Reform: Who Will Take Advantage of 'Charitable Choice'?" *American Sociological Review*, 1999, pp. 836–846.

30.   Cnaan and Boddie, *Black Church Outreach*, p. 19.

31. Jill Witmer Sinha, *Cookman United Methodist Church and Transitional Journey: A Case Study in Charitable Choice* (Center for Public Justice, August 2000).

32. Without taking us far from our main topic, suffice it to say that those welfare-to-work requirements remained in effect through 2006. The initial five-year authorization in the 1996 welfare reform law, known as Temporary Assistance to Needy Families, or TANF, expired in 2002 but was kept in effect via a dozen congressional resolutions that temporarily extended them. Finally, a TANF reauthorization that included all key welfare-to-work provisions and also charitable choice provisions, little modified from their 1996 casts, was approved by Congress in late 2005 and signed into law by President Bush in February 2006.

33. Stephen V. Monsma, *Putting Faith in Partnerships: Welfare-to-Work in Four Cities*, foreword by John J. DiIulio, Jr. (University of Michigan Press, 2004). All welfare-to-work program data referenced in this section are from my foreword to this book.

34. Back in 2002, I gave my dozen-plus binders containing clips to two outstanding fellow political scientists in the Philadelphia region, Jo Renee Formicola of Rutgers University and Mary Seegers of Seton Hall, who specialize in research on religion and American politics.

35. John Wilson, "DiIulio Keeps Explaining, But Is Anyone Listening?" *Christianity Today*, April 1, 2001.

36. John J. DiIulio, Jr., "Broken Bottles: Liquor, Crime, and Disorder," *The Brookings Review*, 1999.

37. For an overview, see Jeff Levin and Harold G. Koenig, eds., *Faith, Medicine, and Science: A Festschrift in Honor of Dr. David B. Larson* (Haworth Pastoral Press, 2005), including my own personal remembrance, pp. 32-33.

38. For an overview, see Byron R. Johnson, *Objective Hope: Assessing the Effectiveness of Faith-Based Organizations—A Review of the Literature* (Center for Research on Religion and Urban Civil Society, Manhattan Institute and University of Pennsylvania, 2001).

39. In addition to the aforementioned studies by Cnaan and others, Public/Private Ventures, a research intermediary organization initiated by the Ford Foundation over two decades ago and since supported by numerous foundations including the Pew Charitable Trusts, has produced among the best studies of this type, all available at ppv.org.

40. Joseph P. Tierney and Jean Baldwin Grossman, *Making a Difference: An Impact Study of Big Brothers Big Sisters* (Public/Private Ventures, 1995; reissued September 2000).

41. Jean Baldwin Grossman and Joseph P. Tierney, "The Fallibility of Comparison Groups," *Evaluation Review*, 1993.

42. John J. DiIulio, Jr., "The Three Faith Factors," *The Public Interest*, 2002. In

the foreword to Johnson, *Objective Hope*, I used "intentional" religion for what I since have termed "programmatic" religion.

43. Anne Morrison Piehl, *Faith-Based Prisoner Reentry* (National Academy of Sciences, Committee on Law and Justice, report, July 2006), pp. 17–18.

6. THE REPUBLIC'S FAITH-BASED FUTURE

1. Opinion and Order of Judge Robert W. Pratt, *Americans United for Separation of Church and State et al. v. Prison Fellowship Ministries et al.*, U.S. District Court, Southern District of Iowa, June 2, 2006; Robert P. George and Gerard V. Bradley, "Barring Faith: A Federal Judge Strikes Down Prison Ministries," *The Weekly Standard*, July 17, 2006.

2. Pratt, Opinion and Order, p. 3.

3. For example, see ibid., pp. 17, 88.

4. Ibid., pp. 62–64.

5. Ibid., p. 117.

6. Ibid., pp. 82–83.

7. Ibid., p. 102.

8. Ibid., pp. 5, 90.

9. Byron Johnson, *The InnerChange Freedom Initiative: A Preliminary Evaluation of a Faith-Based Prison Program* (Center for Research on Religion and Urban Civil Society and Manhattan Institute, 2003).

10. Ibid., p. 23.

11. Diana B. Henriques and Andrew Lehren, "Religion for a Captive Audience, Paid for by Taxes," *New York Times*, December 10, 2006.

12. John J. DiIulio, Jr., "The *New York Times* versus Religion," *The Weekly Standard*, October 23, 2006.

13. The summary of Catholic social teaching that follows in this section is adapted from passages in John J. DiIulio, Jr., "The Moral Compass of True Conservatism," in *The Fractious Nation?* ed. Jonathan Reider (University of California Press, 2003).

14. Michael Harrington, *The Other America: Poverty in the United States* (Macmillan, 1962).

15. All biblical quotes are from the New American Bible (Catholic Bible Press, Thomas Nelson Publishers, 1987).

7. THE FAITH-BASED FUTURE'S BLESSINGS

1. Much of this "civic value stocks" discussion is reprised from passages of John J. DiIulio, Jr., "Not By Faith Alone: Religion, Crime, and Substance Abuse,"

in E. J. Dionne and Kayla Drogsz, eds., *Sacred Places, Civic Purposes: Should Government Help Faith-Based Charities?* (Brookings Institution Press, 2002), chap. 6.

2. Erik Eckholm, "Plight Deepens for Black Men, Studies Warn," *New York Times*, March 20, 2006.

3. "Study Finds Black Men 'Disconnected' from Society," National Public Radio, *All Things Considered*, Michael Martin interview with Harry Holzer, broadcast March 20, 2006; Paul Bonner, "Reversing Downward Trend for Black Men," *Durham, N.C. Herald-Sun*, March 23, 2006; Clarence Page, "Plight of Disconnected Black Youths Worsens," *Baltimore Sun*, March 24, 2006; Larry Copeland, "Blacks Losing Ground Financially," *USA Today*, March 26, 2006; Voice of America News, "Crisis Deepens among Young African American Males," Federal Information and News Dispatch Service, March 28, 2006; Mary Mitchell, "We Can't Let Dire Reports Snuff Hopes for Black Youth," *Chicago Sun-Times*, April 25, 2006; Leslie Talmadge, "Forum Takes on Hidden Racism," *Boston Globe*, May 21, 2006; Jabari Asim, "Salvation, One Boy at a Time," *Washington Post*, June 3, 2006. It is also worth noting here that in March 2005, Reuters and other news organizations ran stories about the deepening plight of black males in the United States.

4. Bruce Western and Becky Pettit, "Incarceration and Racial Inequality in Men's Employment," *Industrial and Labor Relations Review*, October 2000.

5. John M. Bridgeland, John J. DiIulio, Jr., and Karen Burke Morison, *The Silent Epidemic: Perspectives of High School Dropouts* (Civic Enterprises, March 2006); "Dropout Nation," *Time*, April 10, 2006; "Oprah's Special Report: America's Schools in Crisis," April 11–12, 2006.

6. James B. Conant, *Slums and Suburbs: A Commentary on Schools in Metropolitan Areas* (McGraw Hill, 1961).

7. John J. DiIulio, Jr., "Catholic Social Teaching, Racial Reconciliation, and Criminal Justice," *Journal of Catholic Social Thought*, Winter 2006.

8. Stephen Thernstrom and Abigail Thernstrom, *America in Black and White: One Nation, Indivisible* (Simon and Schuster, 1997).

9. Hugh Price as quoted in Steven A. Holmes and Richard Morin, "Poll Reveals a Contradictory Portrait with Promise and Doubt," *Washington Post*, June 4, 2006.

10. Ibid.

11. Daniel Patrick Moynihan, *The Negro Family: The Case for National Action* (U.S. Department of Labor, March 1965), p. 29.

12. Ibid., pp. 34–35.

13. Ibid., p. 43.

14. Ibid., p. 45.

15. Ibid., pp. 29, 30, 45.

16. Ibid., p. 32.

17. Ibid., p. 14.

18. Ibid., p. 38.

19. Ibid.

20. Ibid., p. 39.

21. Ibid., p. 45.

22. Ibid., p. 47.

23. Ibid., p. 26.

24. William Julius Wilson, *The Truly Disadvantaged: The Inner City, the Underclass, and Public Policy* (University of Chicago Press, 1987).

25. James Alan Fox, *Trends in Juvenile Violence* (U.S. Bureau of Justice Statistics, U.S. Department of Justice, March 1996); Howard N. Snyder et al., *Juvenile Offenders and Victims: 1996 Update on Violence* (Office of Juvenile Justice Delinquency Prevention, U.S. Department of Justice, February 1996).

26. Joseph P. Tierney et al., *Murder Is No Mystery: An Analysis of Philadelphia Homicide, 1996–1999* (Public/Private Ventures, Spring 2001).

27. Ibid.

28. Robert G. Wood, "Marriage Rates and Marriageable Men: A Test of the Wilson Hypothesis," *The Journal of Human Resources*, Winter 1995.

29. Robert A. Semple, "Minimum Income in Ghetto Urged," *New York Times*, December 14, 1966.

30. Ibid.

31. John J. DiIulio, Jr., "I Was There," *Commentary*, October 1996, and "Liberalism's Last Stand?" *The Public Interest*, Winter 1996.

32. For a slightly more positive summary with minimal partisan or ideological spin, see Ron Haskins, "Welfare Reform: The Biggest Accomplishment of the Revolution," in Chris Edwards and John Samples, eds., *The Republican Revolution 10 Years Later: Smaller Government or Business as Usual?* (Cato Institute, 2005), chap. 9.

33. Ibid.

34. Charis E. Kubrin et al., "Deindustrialization, Disadvantage and Suicide among Young Black Males," *Social Forces*, March 2006.

35. John J. DiIulio, Jr., "My School Choice: Literacy First," *The Weekly Standard*, October 19, 1998.

36. Robert M. Franklin and Stephanie C. Boddie, *Healthy Marriages in Low-Income Communities: Expanding the Dialogue with Faith Leaders* (Annie E. Casey Foundation, 2004), p. 37.

37. Kenneth D. Johnson, ed., *God's Gifts: A Christian Vision of Marriage and the Black Family* (Seymour Institute for Advanced Christian Studies, 2005).

38. Linda Jucovy, *Just Out: Early Lessons from the Ready4Work Prisoner Reentry Initiative* (Public/Private Ventures, February 2006); Chelsea Farley and Sandra Hackman, *Ready4Work: Interim Outcomes Are In* (Public/Private Ventures, September 2006).

39. Farley and Hackman, *Ready4Work*, p. 3.

40. Robert M. Franklin, "Cosby's Call and Our Response: What the Church and Community Should Do," Emory University, undated manuscript, p. 11.

41. Ibid., p. 3.

42. Jerry Weinberger, *Benjamin Franklin Unmasked: On the Unity of His Moral, Religious, and Political Thought* (University Press of Kansas, 2005).

43. Walter Isaacson, *Benjamin Franklin: An American Life* (Simon and Schuster, 2003), p. 468.

44. Ibid., p. 87.

45. Ibid., pp. 87–88.

46. Ibid., p. 468.

47. Benjamin Franklin's Letter to Reverend Ezra Stiles, March 9, 1790, in *Benjamin Franklin: Autobiography and Selected Writings* (Holt, Rinehart and Winston, 1959), p. 274.

48. Jay Tolson, "European, Not Christian: An Aggressive Secularism Sweeps the Continent," *U.S. News & World Report*, May 30, 2005.

49. Sue Rardin, "Eyes Wide Shut," *Trust* (Pew Charitable Trusts, November 2006), p. 13.

POSTSCRIPT

1. Philip Jenkins, *The Next Christendom: The Rise of Global Christianity* (Oxford University Press, 2002), and *The New Faces of Christianity: Believing the Bible in the Global South* (Oxford University Press, 2006).

2. Samuel P. Huntington, *The Third Wave: Democratization in the Late Twentieth Century* (University of Oklahoma Press, 1991), p. 85.

3. Joseph S. Nye, *Soft Power: The Means to Success in World Politics* (Public Affairs, 2004).

4. Sue Rardin, "Eyes Wide Shut," *Trust*, November 2006.

5. Ibid.

Index

Text: Palatino
Display: Bauer Bodoni
Compositor: Binghamton Valley Composition
Indexer: Marcia Carlson Indexing Service
Printer and binder: Maple-Vail Book Manufacturing Group

THE AARON WILDAVSKY FORUM FOR PUBLIC POLICY

Edited by Lee Friedman

This series is to sustain the intellectual excitement that Aaron Wildavsky created for scholars of public policy everywhere. The ideas in each volume are initially presented and discussed at a public lecture and forum held at the University of California.

AARON WILDAVSKY, 1930–1993

"Your prolific pen has brought real politics to the study of budgeting, to the analysis of myriad public policies, and to the discovery of the values underlying the political cultures by which peoples live. You have improved every institution with which you have been associated, notably Berkeley's Graduate School of Public Policy, which as Founding Dean you quickened with your restless innovative energy. Advocate of freedom, mentor to policy analysts everywhere."

(Yale University, May 1993, from text granting the honorary degree of Doctor of Social Science)